A Place for Play

A Place for Play

a companion volume to the Michigan Television film
Where Do the Children Play?

Edited by Elizabeth Goodenough
With a foreword by Richard Louv

ISBN: 978-0-615-20282-2

Designed by Jody Fisher, Ann Arbor, Michigan

Front cover photograph by Mark Powell

Back cover art by Yesica, Cherlene, Valeria, Lorena, Maria, and Erika, Harms Elementary School

"Loving Life: Wild Zones and the Edible Schoolyard" © David Hawkins

Grateful acknowledgment is made to the following journals and publishers
for permission to reprint previously published material:

Places: A Quarterly Journal of Environmental Design: Excerpts from "Shared Outdoor Spaces and Community Life"
by Clare Cooper Marcus, vol. 15, no. 2 (2003).

Thames & Hudson for "It's Human Nature to Play" from *The Playbook,* by Alex MacLean (2006).

THE NATIONAL INSTITUTE FOR
PLAY

Wind

by Caitlyn Fisher, age 9

Wind, wind in the trees
How it blows past the branches
Wind in the air, in the sky everywhere

Contents

IV Playgrounds Matter

V Child-Centered Cities

About the Players

Elizabeth Goodenough

ACKNOWLEDGMENTS

On the long pilgrimage toward the achievement of a documentary film, there must be many believers. Five years ago the offices of University of Michigan Interim President Joseph White and Senior Vice Provost Lester Monts provided seed funding for this project. When Michigan Television later agreed to take on the production of the film developed originally in collaboration with Christopher Cook and Katherine Weider, Jay Nelson and Jennifer Howard of Michigan Public Media worked to further define outreach and film components. Grants from the Ruth Mott Foundation launched Flint outreach, the study guide, and development of the film *Where Do the Children Play?* Further grants from The W. K. Kellogg Foundation and Blue Cross/Blue Shield of Michigan enabled us to arrive at our destination: to begin making a film.

Along the way Sheila Wilder, Melanie Karner,

Craig Regester, Ann Brennan, and Charlie Bright of the Residential College at the University of Michigan supported fundraising and outreach efforts, while RC students provided inspiration, initiative, and industry in development of this volume. Malika Middlebrooks who helped with the study guide and Ayn Reineke, Nithya Joseph, and Alex Gorsuch photographed by David Lamb on page x represent the finest artistic talent that Residential College students bring to projects such as this one. Subjects for the film were selected from among school children they met through their fieldwork in the course called The Poetry of Everyday Life, which Fred Peters of the Literature Program enabled me to teach.

I want to thank Julie Ellison of the University of Michigan for her early model of this course and Matt Perry and Rosemarie Hester for their intelligence and flair in devising models of collaboration for my college students and their fourth and fifth graders at Ann Arbor Academy and Summers-Knoll School. Robert Grese of the Matthaei Botanical Garden welcomed us to his beautiful outdoor facilities for class meetings and a university premiere of the film December 5, 2007.

Laurence Goldstein, editor of the *Michigan Quarterly Review*, provided such faith in the Secret Spaces of Childhood and the double issue of *MQR* that he devoted to this subject that others came to see the cause as worthy. The book *Secret Spaces of Childhood* published by the University of Michigan provided the bedrock for this project thanks to Phil Pocoda, LeAnn Fields, and Mary Bisbee-Beek.

Working with gifted fundraisers and generous funders was made possible by Susan Howbert from the Council of Michigan Foundations who proved to be an angel of wisdom with her advice, tenacity, and counsel. Leslie Lee and the Herrington-Fitch Family Foundation provided funding as well as hospitality and inspiration in the earth-centered retreat of Pine Hollow for pilgrims along the way: Betsy Upton Stover, Nancy Colina, Carol Paine McGovern, and Susan Glass. All of these individuals and family foundations cherish the ideal of outdoor play and universal access to natural spaces for all children.

From these special relationships came grants from the Colina Foundation, the DeRoy Testamentary Foundation, and the R. E. Olds Foundation to support *A Place for Play*. Sally and Ian Bund provided funding as well as the best that friendship offers: ongoing enthusiasm, gatherings of support, vital conversations. Lana Pollack of the Michigan Environmental Council understood the difficulties and supported the importance of academic and community partnerships.

Rob Collier of the Council of Michigan Foundations featured the project at the 35th annual conference, and Lisa Wozniak of the Michigan League of Conservation Voters hosted the Ann Arbor debut of the film at Leslie Science Center.

Cindy Burkhour of Access to Recreation and Katrina Klaphake of Rudolph Steiner School in Ann Arbor made critical connections to expand the future of the project. Since November 2007, Joan Almon and Ed Miller of the Alliance for Childhood have been instrumental in extending the outreach of the project nationally. Their intensive campaign over six months has been supported by a grant from the Foundation for Global Community made possible by Avery Cleary, Founder of Hooked on Nature, whose discernment and generous spirit are a model to me. For distributing the study guide and supporting this anthology, I am grateful to Annie Martin of Wayne State University Press Landscapes of Childhood series. Miguel Satut of the W. K. Kellogg Foundation enabled Roundtable, Inc. to launch a national engagement campaign under the enlightened leadership of Martha Fowlkes and Robert Lavelle. To Margi Dewar and the U–M Ginsberg Center, I am grateful for the establishment of a center for the ongoing work of "Where Do the Children Play?"

The Office of Senior Vice Provost Lester Monts funded the color photography collected here. Stuart Brown of the National Institute for Play helped mentor this film project from its inception. For editorial help along the way, I am indebted to Ellen Quigley, Robert Ellsberg, Ellen McCarthy, and Rachael Cohen. Friends like Peggy Ellsberg, Rebecca McGowan, Sandy Wicner, Judith Vida, Margaret Butler, my mother Margaret van Dusen, and above all my husband Gil Leaf helped me know I was not walking alone. I want to thank Jan Cohen and Jody Fisher who gave unstintingly of their time. Without the help of these individuals I could have done nothing.

For tens of thousands of years, for all of human history and prehistory, human children went outside and spent much of their lives in nature either working or playing. And within the space of two or three decades in western society, we're seeing the virtual end of that.

RICHARD LOUV
AUTHOR, *LAST CHILD IN THE WOODS*
CHAIRMAN, CHILDREN & NATURE NETWORK

FOREWORD

Some of us remember a time when grandmothers would lean over, look into our eyes with a mixture of sternness and humor, and say: "The word 'bored' isn't in my vocabulary."

In fact, the word wasn't in anybody's vocabulary until the nineteenth century, according to Patricia Meyer Spacks, a professor of English at the University of Virginia, and author of *Boredom: The Literary History of a State of Mind*. In medieval times, according to Spacks, if someone displayed the symptoms we now identify as boredom, that person was thought to be committing something called "acedia," a "dangerous form of spiritual alienation—a devaluing of the world and its creator." Acedia—or accidie—was considered a sin. That's taking the matter a bit too far. But boredom is the opposite of play, and that's just no fun.

"Now go outside and play!" our grandmother, or mother or father, might have said, in another time. As I wrote in *Last Child in the Woods: Saving*

Our Children from Nature-Deficit Disorder, kids today are more likely to spend the bulk of their childhoods indoors, under protective house arrest. As one suburban fifth-grader put it: "I like to play indoors better 'cause that's where all the electrical outlets are."

Welcome to the not-so-great state of Acedia, where all the children are above average, until tested. The shift away from traditional, spontaneous, free-range play has accelerated over the past three decades, with huge declines in spontaneous outdoor activities such as bike riding and swimming, according to studies by the National Sporting Goods Association, a trade group, and American Sports Data, a research firm. Bike riding is down 31 percent since 1995.

The truth is, what this country needs is a Leave No Child Inside movement. And it's happening. The hard work of individuals and organizations, working in this field for decades, is beginning to pay off. Over the past two years, state and regional campaigns have formed in cities across the United States and Canada. At the same time, a host of related initiatives—among them the simple-living, walkable-cities, nature-education, and land-trust movements, as well as public health concerns about child obesity—have begun to find common cause, and collective strength. In several states, legislators and governors are approving legislation to encourage nature time for children.

So, *Where Do the Children Play?*—the study guide, this collection, and the accompanying film—comes at an opportune time. *A Place for Play* complements and enhances the Michigan Television 2007 documentary film. Research findings detailed here explain the science behind why we should care about how children spend their time.

A rich selection of suggestions, tips, personal experiences, and programs by nonscientists provide answers for the how—how we can get children outside and otherwise engaged in a health-promoting way of life.

The two books and the documentary offer the stories of individuals and organizations working to protect childhood. Some of the groups represented in this treasury include Alliance for Childhood, Natural Learning Initiative, Detroit Connections, Child's Right to Play, and Growing Up in Cities. Also included are Adventure Playgrounds, National Institute for Play, and Sustainable Cities. Wild Zones, the Outdoor Classroom Project, and CUNY Children and Environments Center are playing an extraordinary role. And we hear from children, too, who've contributed poetry and drawings.

At its best, boredom forces creativity. Unfortunately, many kids today pack the malls, pour into the video archives, and line up for the scariest, goriest summer movies they can find. Yet, they still complain, "I'm borrrred." Like a sugared drink on a hot day, such entertainment leaves kids thirsting for more—for faster, bigger, more violent stimuli. Today's commonplace answer to boredom—insidious overstimulation, of one note, one beat, continuous—blunts the senses and saps joy from childhood, and later from adulthood. Here is an antidote. Thank you, Elizabeth Goodenough, for bringing this anthology to life, and to Chris Cook, for a powerful documentary. Now, let's go outside and play.

Richard Louv
Chairman, Children & Nature Network
May 13, 2007

Elizabeth Goodenough

INTRODUCTION

There is always one moment in childhood when the door opens and lets the future in.

GRAHAM GREENE, *THE POWER AND THE GLORY* (1940)

Our dog, a Welsh corgi named Clara, led me into Bird Hills Park behind our house. There I found trillium by day and stars by night. Crystallized limbs clinking with ice, deer crashing through brush, chasing squirrels, wet earth smells, the sound of my own breath, tracks of rabbit, raccoon, and fox, crows gathering in treetops, warning cries of birds announced my arrival. Ducking under vines, brushing rough bark, following trails of mud, dust, and frozen snow, I sat on boulders at twilight. Why did it take three years of residence here and a corgi on a leash to pull me into the largest park in Ann Arbor? Move-in fatigue? Inertia? Frantic busyness? Resisting the unknown? Had I succumbed to the conditioning of being inside, where the electronics are located? As a child I had ventured blocks away and trespassed freely into nearby yards. I made snow angels and mud pies, skipped through sprinklers, found a fallen bird's nest, climbed trees and stockade fences, all on property I did not own.

If you have spent time driving around suburbs and cities in Canada and the United States, you probably are alert to the fact that children no longer play outside much. When you drive through streets devoid of children, your first assumption may be that they are at school or in parks competing in team sports. Gradually, it dawns on you that as more green space is paved over, as inner cities are further neglected, as fear of strangers intensifies, suburban children are relegated to worlds without sidewalks or main streets connecting them to a wider community of neighbors. Children who live in inner cities—especially those who are poor—face even harsher challenges. At this point you ask, where do the children play?

As I write these words, my childhood suburban paradise of pine woods faces subdivision. Building dams with twigs, hosing water into sand, climbing through brambles, we once created cities on earth and lookouts in trees. Yet the woods out back, like early teachers who shape the people we become, often disappear without a news report or even a phone call.

In fact, the nature of childhood has changed dramatically in just one generation. Not surprisingly, children's time in sedentary activities—playing video games, surfing the web, viewing DVDs, instant messaging—has increased enormously. Children stay inside more, often alone, and usually inactive. Schools have cut back on gym, and many reduce or eliminate outdoor recess periods. A growing number of schools are being built without playgrounds. The overwhelming majority of children are now driven to school rather than walking, bicycling, or even taking a bus. In the last twenty years, the average range of independent mobility for North American twelve year-olds has shriveled from one mile to 550 yards. Children have less privacy, yet paradoxically, have more unrestricted access to adult media. As vicarious pursuits and synthetic playgrounds take over, does minimal engagement with plants and animals threaten nature itself?

A new report from the American Academy of Pediatrics says that what children really need for healthy development is time for more old-fashioned play. Deprivation affects mental and physical health as well as cognitive and social capacities. Experts are only now coming to understand the implications of these changes for health and development. When the UNICEF Innocenti Research Centre released its latest report card on the well-being of children in 21 wealthy nations in 2007, the United States and United Kingdom were rated at the bottom of the list overall, and the United States came in last or next to last on three of six criteria: health and safety, behaviors and risks, and family and peer relationships.

Reports and statistics such as these suggest that childhood itself is increasingly under fire as a worldwide demographic, cultural invention, and social institution. Grim as the figures are, they only hint at the reality of growing up in a society disrupted by violence, driven by competition, and divorced from nature. As Brian Sutton-Smith, a play specialist, has put it, the opposite of play isn't work. It's depression. How can our communities restore this life-enhancing experience that prevents the decline of mental health and offers happiness and healing memories?

In 2007, a one-hour documentary for public television called *Where Do the Children Play?* grew from a collaboration between Christopher Cook's award-winning documentary *The Sprawling of America* (2001) and my book *Secret Spaces of Childhood* (University of Michigan Press, 2003). *Where Do the Children Play?* examines how restrictive patterns of sprawl, congestion, and endless suburban development across America are affecting children's mental and physical health and development. It focuses on the suburban, rural, and urban continuum in relation to obesity and children's informal learning about the natural world. According to Roger Hart of the Children's Environments Research Group, who has studied children over three decades, the film "goes well beyond these two important issues to deal more broadly with how children's free time has changed. It challenges communities of all kinds to address the policy issues that need to be faced in relation to children's outdoor activities and their health and well-being."

As a companion volume to *Where Do the Children Play?* this anthology extends the implications of the film. Framed by film interviews with experts, *A Place for Play* picks up where the documentary leaves off, exploring the benefits of play, universal access to natural resources, and the challenges of child-centered design initiatives. It offers practical advice, research-based summaries, and meditations for parents and teachers, and concludes with an aerial portfolio of playscapes around the world. Describing model programs such as Growing Up In Cities as well as homegrown, urban, and schoolyard experiments, the authors examine the ongoing influence of outdoor adventures and experiential learning for the young. Such initiatives offer ways to assess a community's outdoor play and recreational assets as well as the local barriers to play, especially for the most vulnerable children.

The purpose of this anthology is to encourage children and adults, together and alone, to recapture energy, joy, and possibility in outdoor play, storytelling, and the arts. If some of what follows conveys nostalgia, it also offers belief in the power of participatory learning to renew the future. *A Place for Play* sheds light on the inspiration that recreation draws from its physical context. It explains why freedom and contact with living things have always been at the heart of emotional memory. Text and image inform our understanding of how we are interconnected. Research, practices, and vignettes show that the space of play and place for play are interdependent categories that pattern experience and shape the people we become. The observations and antics we bring to our first environments are transferred to every landscape of endeavor that follows. This process of self-discovery deserves to be treated with as much care and respect by educators and families as the cultivation of literacy and the mastery of mathematical skills.

Recognizing the recent demise of spontaneous outdoor activity, Richard Louv heralds the need for a Leave No Child Inside movement in his foreword to this volume. Using our vanished frontier as a marker of Americans' relationship to nature, his *Last Child in the Woods: Saving Our Children from Nature-Deficit Disorder* sets the stage for understanding how children themselves have become our last frontier. Their bodies, minds, and spirits are now contested ground in our changing global order. Choices made by planning and school boards, parks and corporations, families and legislators today will determine how the next generation envisions the future and reshapes the earth.

As the writers in Part I of this book demonstrate, play uncovers the hidden history of places. Ecologically rich environments ensure that play takes many forms. Just as theories of creation begin with space, Jack Zipes reminds us that where play takes place, children have a mechanism for unfolding that is far beyond what we can imagine. Children invent alternative contexts for conversation, visualization, movement, and interaction with real objects. They find release and involvement, stimulation and peace. Although play may arise anywhere, even in a cement cell, children are beckoned to the natural world, as Bob Hughes suggests, as they savor sensations of being alive.

Exposure to natural settings has been associated with enhanced cognitive function and diminished stress, as Nancy Wells summarizes in Part II. Brain studies demonstrate that play is a vehicle for increasing neural structures, and a means by which all children practice the skills they will need in later life. Other writers in this section demonstrate how, in Stuart Brown's words, nature and play are fundamental partners. Asking whether children need nature or have sufficient leisure, they outline research and practices for reconnecting children with green spaces nearby. If children don't play in their own neighborhoods, what attachment to these places will develop later on? All the essays provide evidence that the settings in which children find themselves enabled or deprived of play matter to their ethical development, spiritual attunement, and emotional survival.

During school, unstructured, open-ended play is essential to the health of the young. Writers in Part III report that play enhances social skills, teaches conflict resolution, increases fitness, improves learning, and reduces stress by connecting youth with natural environments. Mark Powell shows how closely nature and nation are connected in "the hidden curriculum" of fort culture. Although playgrounds themselves often become the most contentious of sites for school administrators, his photographs and those of Wendy Banning make me wonder why community organizing does not aim at making schoolyards the most beautiful and alive places in the neighborhood.

Communities, teachers, and families need to organize a resistance movement against the rigid all-day confinement of children in schools. Elizabeth Jones and Eric Nelson and Rosemarie Hester offer practical suggestions and key reforms in and out of school. They argue for fresh elemental environments away from television, computers, violent video games, and microchip-embedded toys. The unique stories of Part III prove that natural worlds do not need to be big, wide, open spaces. They can be very small areas. Even tiny outdoor terrains offer loose parts. From "acorns, sticks, rocks, seed pods and shells," for example, can evolve new "critters" like those Ann Savageau makes by hand with children. Even a lima bean folded in a wet paper towel will sprout a pale root to be touched and perhaps never forgotten.

Teachers at colleges and elementary schools can take action on specific issues obstructing free play, co-create democratic spaces with children, assess long-term results, and network for freedom to be outdoors. Janie Paul, a painter and University of Michigan professor of art, maintains a relationship between her studio practice and inner-city school children in Detroit. In a place without much access to nature, filled with pressures of poverty and social injustice, Paul and her college students work to co-create spaces sensitive to the environment. Such practices and programs advance democracy and renew civic mission as well as "burnish the image of research universities." But the topsy-turvy of what actually happens shows what teachers need to learn so they too can play.

When playworker Penny Wilson came to the Midwest from London, sponsored by the Alliance for Childhood, she was interviewed for the documentary film *Where Do the Children Play?* As part of this project's outreach in Flint, funded by the Ruth Mott Foundation, she met with students at Hamady Elementary for the morning, giving them free rein to create ideal places in their classroom. Boys and girls constructed mansions and skyscrapers with sheets, masking tape, tables, clothespins, and chairs, creating narratives in three dimensions. Cabresha Nard, 11, popped in and out as she and her friends built a plastic archway. "Somebody had this crazy idea of putting all our mansions together into one mansion, so that's what we did," Cabresha said.

Sometimes educators and parents are told that children will be spoiled if they get "too much" of what they want. But in this scenario of shared mansions, no one was locked out, dominated, or defeated. Collaboration meant Cabresha's "we" could be connected in abundance.

Playscapes such as these provide a microscopic peek at the culture of their designers. In contrast to those eager to produce office parks and condominiums, David Hawkins and writers in Part IV reflect on ways to retrieve land for natural use among generations. Although we have gradually distanced children from living things, these essays argue that park departments, arboreta, youth gardens, and planting programs such as Gary Rieveschl's present themselves at this crucial moment to reverse the trend. One of the most important issues considered in Part IV is how wild zones, adventure playgrounds, and playworkers might overcome exclusion and isolation so that children of all abilities have access to play and natural resources. Zoning that permits sprawl, prohibits sidewalks, and isolates housing from recreational areas forces adults to drive children to parks and playgrounds. If the local playground is accessible by ramp and curb cut, the equipment often is not. Yet Penny Wilson shows how inclusive play can enhance the liveliness and fun of everybody.

In *The Death and Life of Great American Cities* (1961), Jane Jacobs notes that "social capital" in urban areas accrues when planners promote informal contact among neighbors. Street crime lessens and children are happier and better cared for. Levels of trust are raised when walk-to-school programs succeed. Part V establishes a basis for understanding the ecologically challenging aspects of contemporary design in the "concrete jungle" of actual cities. Its contributors emphasize the political choices that we face as individuals, as a society, and as a species dwelling together in a vulnerable world.

Working from the refreshing perspective that adults themselves must enter sensuous and beloved locales to transform them, Part V looks backward to play forward. William Crain, for example, battles with the NYC Parks Department to keep real grass in the parks and playgrounds. Suzanne Lennard focuses on how downtowns can offer comfortable walking distances and spaces close to home where kids can play. Applying a biocentric view to the realm of urban planning, such pioneers in the emerging field of design psychology as Clare Cooper Marcus explain why environmental autobiography contributes to how adults envision spaces for children. Concluding with the macrocosmic vantage point epitomized by the aerial photography of Alex MacLean, Part V reviews and critiques philosophies of design that dominate public discourse on urban planning.

The National Institute for Play, the Children & Nature Network, the League of Conservation Voters, the Alliance for Childhood, Hooked on

Nature, and many other groups are already partnering with a diverse array of individuals and agencies to engage communities in conversation about the relationship that children and nature must have to thrive and be sustained. Such coalitions can work together to mobilize the community to reduce one or more specific local barriers to play and natural resources. Together, we can work with national and regional organizations to enhance the efforts of child-serving and environmental organizations and educational institutions in communities nationwide. Besides financial support, conservancy education requires public will, vision, and practical intelligence. But in the long run, this experiment may cost less than to remediate the social problems endemic to growing up without a neighborhood or animal friends.

Nancy Willard

TREE HOUSE

Start with a tree,
an old willow with its feet in the water,
and one low branch to let you in
and a higher branch to let you
upstairs,
and a lookout branch to show you
how far you've come,
(the lake before you,
the woods at your back),

and now you are close
to those who live in these rooms
without walls, without doors:
one nuthatch typing its way up the bark,
two mourning doves calling the sun out of darkness,
three blackbirds folding their wings tipped with sunset,
twelve crows threading the air and stitching
a cape that whirls them away
through the empty sky,

and don't forget the blue heron
stalking the shallows for bluegills,
and don't forget the otter backpaddling past you,
and the turtles perched on the log like shoes
lined up each night in a large family,

and don't forget the owl
who has watched over you
since you were born.

Be the housekeeper of trees,
who have nothing to keep
except silence.

Nancy Willard's most recent books include a collection of poems, *In the Salt Marsh* (Knopf), a book for children, *The Flying Bed* (Scholastic), and a book of essays on writing, *The Left-Handed Story: Writing and the Writer's Life* (University of Michigan Press).

I. PLAY TAKES PLACE

Winnicott, a child psychologist, said that playing is the way that our internal worlds find their way out into the external world through playing and through interacting with other people in playful situations.

So the first playful interaction is when the mother sticks her tongue out and the baby copies It, and it becomes a game. And he sees that as the first interaction through play that goes on, and on, and on. And through this playful translation of the world and ourselves, we learn to live creatively, which is a burning creativity, a desire for life, and a love of new things and learning experiences that give us a fresh perspective on the world.

Originally, playing allowed us to learn the basic survival skills. I do a lot of playwork training with people from all over the world. And I start by asking adults to remember their playing as a child, and you

> **Play is a set of behaviors that is freely chosen, personally directed, and intrinsically motivated.**

get the most wonderful rich conversations coming out. I get the same stories from Bangladesh, from Jamaica, from Chicago, from Denmark—the same types of playing are coming out and that's not a coincidence. Playing is about hiding, and running, and digging, and fire, and danger, and dressing up, and pretend, and hanging out with your mates.

Gordon Sturrock said, "Don't try to define play. It's like trying to define love." But playworkers do have a phrase to help us identify play: play is a set of behaviors that is freely chosen, personally directed, and intrinsically motivated. We use that phrase as a touchstone for whether we're providing a rich play environment for children.

Penny Wilson, Playworker, London, Play Association Tower Hamlets (PATH). Quoted from film interview, *Where Do the Children Play?* (2007)

Jack Zipes

AT THE DROP OF A HAT NO WHERE

Jack Zipes is Professor of German and Comparative Literature at the University of Minnesota. Aside from publishing several books on fairy tales, he is the founder and director of Neighborhood Bridges, a storytelling program in the Minneapolis public school system. He has described this program in his book, *Speaking Out: Storytelling and Creative Drama for Children* (2005).

Watch a child anywhere. There is no place she won't play, and no-place is that utopian sphere where we are all free to play and experiment so that we can be in touch with ourselves and our environment at the same time. No-places are those spots and spaces that are designated briefly by children (and adults) as spaces of play, what the Germans call *Spielräume*—where we imaginatively play with possibilities and envision what we can do with our dreams and potential. But no-places are disappearing; they have become constricted. When I was a child, we used to take over the streets to play stick ball, touch football, and many other games. Woe to the cars that dared to come by! There were vacant lots or parks that we would occupy and organize ourselves to play cops and robbers or house. We went off to play by ourselves, sometimes in dump heaps. But play increasingly has become regulated and regimented. Spaces are guarded, protected, limited, owned, and controlled. If there is play, adults determine the rules. Children are supervised and surveyed through a camera's eye. More and more, our experiences of life are being controlled and policed by what Michel Foucault called the "panoptic eye."

Nevertheless, a child still will play anywhere, create a space, where there is no place, and no-place becomes his space even if it is only for a moment—a moment in which he gleans something important and learns about his potential, projects his visions, tests himself.

He will ride his bike and pretend to be a race-car driver on a speedway or perhaps a cowboy riding a horse to warn people in a town of an imminent attack. He will play basketball by himself on an outdoor court and win a championship game in the last second. She will burst into a run and skip over cans or obstacles to win the 100-meter hurdles in the Olympics. She suddenly will tell her friends in the playground a dream about magnificent clothes and a dance she attended, and they all will start acting it out, using her dream as a prompt. A little girl in her backyard begins to play house, talking to herself, her dog and imaginary people. A brother and sister, bored at the beach, will build a city and create sand figures that talk and enter into conflicts. The sand is their place of struggle because sand had been no-place, no one's space, and they occupy it briefly to designate it and themselves.

As long as children are curious, they will create their own spaces to play, or appropriate spaces, because the world is their laboratory in which it is necessary to experiment to find one's place. Unfortunately, most people never find their proper place, a place they appropriate and can call their own and feel that it is their own. It is not because they don't search for it. It is because they are crippled at a young age. Their imaginations and curiosities are tamed and disciplined. Their arms and legs are tied. They are whipped into shape by their families and schools. They are filled with lies and false illusions that promise a new world that is a world of consumerism that consumes them. Their minds are numbed and washed so that they will sanitize themselves and adapt to the conditions around them without much protest. They are afraid to deviate and to be called deviates. They are given less and less space to play and come into their own.

For a long time, we have been moving toward a "brave new world," to perfect the human mind and body, perhaps to become flawless and immortal. We are being driven to excel and be number one in every endeavor and to profit from every situation. Parents invest in their children and plan their lives even before they are born. They are left little room in which to play even in infancy. And yet…

Children are naturally subversive because they are naturally curious, and if we as adults can learn to grasp how we use power to manipulate children and to respect the curiosity of children, they will grow through play, anywhere, at the drop of a hat, and they will flourish in any place or no-place. And perhaps we will, too.

Schools, even the best of them, are penal and painful institutions. I know this is a gross exaggeration. But they are fundamentally based on the principles and the practice of discipline, whether corporeal or mental. Schools always have been made tolerable by the illegal play of children, whether it be in the halls, classrooms, bathrooms, locker rooms, or playgrounds. In general, however, it is taboo to play against or with the restrictions of the school. Play must be assigned. It must have an assigned place.

What would happen, however, if school furthered play no matter where and enabled children to take over space and transform it the way they desired? What would happen if children collaborated with adults, teachers, and artists, to form a children's public sphere in which each child had a right to explore and imagine a world different from that in which she was living? Actually, we know what would happen, for many experiments in progressive education have been tried, based on play, dating back in America to the beginning of the twentieth century. Pedagogical methods based on play have been explored successfully by Montessori and Reggio Emilia schools throughout the world. Unfortunately, these experiments have not taken root or been supported in the majority of the schools worldwide, and we have not grasped how significant play is to the development of children. In fact, it is more important than ever before, at a time when functional literacy, rote learning, and examinations rule the schools, that play be fostered within all institutions of learning.

It is not easy, but it is well worth the effort. For the last eight years, I have collaborated with teaching artists, teachers, administrators, and children to develop a storytelling and creative drama program in the elementary schools of Minneapolis and St. Paul called Neighborhood Bridges. The basic philosophical purpose of the program is to animate children so that they will become narrators of their own lives, players conscious of the choices that they make and will have to make. To do this, we, the teaching artists, enter a classroom and transform it with the assistance of the teacher and the children into a Spielraum for two hours. The five phases to our play involve improvised storytelling and writing, shared stories and the invention of stories, theater games, the acting out of stories, and the creation of new stories. What is crucial in this program is the transformation of the classroom space into a no-place. To be specific, we gradually move all the chairs and desks to the side so that the classroom becomes an area in which we can experiment in any way we desire. Although our program has a structure, it is a flexible one that gradually enables children to take control of the materials and games that we provide. For me, the most interesting part of the two hours occurs when the children, organized into three groups, are asked to perform skits based on the stories that they have heard and have created. They are asked to go to three different places within the transformed classroom to discuss their stories and decide how they want to make them into plays, to divide the roles among themselves, and to use found objects within the space of the classroom if they need them for their plays.

Generally speaking, all hell breaks loose, but what appears to be chaos is actually an explosion of their imaginations that leads to new insights. For ten minutes, the children move about, chatter, gesticulate, argue, rehearse or don't rehearse, while the adults observe their actions. Only if there is a major conflict, or only if they are asked for help, will the teachers or teaching artists participate. From the outset, their role is that of animators who introduce games and stories, and coaches who try to bring about cooperation, critical thinking, and imaginative play. In a children's public sphere, adults are necessary as mediators and facilitators, but their goal is to make themselves disposable. They are to be replaced by children who create their own place in which to play and learn more about their lives.

It is fascinating to observe the ten-minute rehearsal time that the children have to produce their skits, works in progress. Quite often the groups, after they discuss their stories to recall the plots and to divide roles, fall apart. Some of the children will rehearse; others will look for objects to use. Two or three will imagine themselves in a scene that they keep changing. Sometimes children from one group will merge with the children in another group. There is no clear division of space as they bounce about talking loudly, singing, and uttering strange sounds. Their stories and skits keep changing. They have no scripts, and often one of the children will serve as the narrator/director to provide some semblance of order to their performance.

At one point, the rehearsal space becomes a theater space. Two groups will sit on the floor and form the audience. One group will perform in front of them, learning theatrical skills and how to articulate what they have conceived. Their entire skit is based on improvisation, and agreements made in rehearsal are often broken and changed during the performance so that something unimaginable is imagined. The unexpected is the norm of the play.

The children are asked to reflect upon their plays and the play in general at the end of two hours through a writing game. This reflection is prompted by their experiences, and the writing is not an imposition. Rather, it is a request through prompting to write about what they have been experiencing. When asked, children will act, write, draw, and sing at the drop of a hat. Their minds are full, not drained. They have been sparked and keep the sparks alive. They become uninhibited and creative even if they are shy, once they know that no-place is their space.

ENTERING THE WORLD OF PLAY

Joan Almon is Coordinator of the U.S. Alliance for Childhood, an advocacy organization seeking to restore creative play and other healthy essentials to children's lives. She lectures and writes frequently on play and early childhood.

I began to work with young children when I was in my twenties. I was untrained and inexperienced, but I was convinced of two things: that there was a spark of spirit in every child that needed to be kept alive and that there was a way for a classroom full of young children to play deeply with each other without sinking into chaos.

It took me some years to realize how closely related these two realities are—the spirit of the child and her capacity to play. Gradually I began to experience the hum that fills a room when children are engaged in deep-rooted play. At such moments, the thought would arise in me, "This is as close to heaven as you are likely to get in this lifetime." The children seemed to have tapped into the same wellsprings of creativity that abounded when the world was young and in the process of being created.

Years later, I met Fred Donaldson, a unique individual who travels the world playing with children, adults, and animals, both wild and domestic.[1] He speaks of play as being the activity where we forget we are different. We meld together. He experiences such play as love. I understand what he means.

It is hard to describe such deep forms of play. To enter the play arena is like opening a door into an internal space that we otherwise rarely enter. In this space, reality is different. Competition ceases to exist, as do thoughts of doing harm to another. This is a space of profound safety and goodwill where we grow and create. Deep play expands our horizons and our potential and capacity. It is an enormous gift that, sadly, is overlooked and undervalued. Like Esau in the Bible, we are willing to trade our birthright of deep play for the equivalent of a bowl of porridge—for the newest toy or gimmick on the market or the latest software or academic program for precociously teaching young children what they so easily can learn a bit later. We fail to understand the power of play and consistently sell it short.

Play as a Healing Force

In the 1970s and 1980s when I did most of my teaching, nearly all children could play well, although some needed a bit of help. Today, I hear reports from teachers all over the country that children have forgotten how to play.[2] They know how to play with computers but not with other children. They know how to play with high-tech toys but not how to create worlds with little more than sticks and stones and healthy make-believe forces. They know all sorts of facts but lack their own imagination. This is not true of all children, of course, but of enough to be a growing concern, for the absence of play in childhood is a huge loss for children. It not only hampers their normal development and learning, but it also deprives them of their chief means for healing themselves when something has gone wrong.

I think of Sammy who came into my mixed-age kindergarten when he was about four years old. His use of language was well developed, but his voice was that of a very young child, almost a baby. His play was also unusual. Every day he took seven or eight wooden stumps and built a small circular house for himself. He would climb inside and cover the house with a cloth. The house had no doors and no windows.

According to his mother, Sammy had begun to regress six months earlier, when his baby sister began to attract much more attention than he did. He developed baby speech and insisted on drinking from a bottle again.

When I looked into his play house, I saw that he was curled up in a tight little circle. He had made a womb for himself. I was concerned, but at the same time had a sense that he knew what he needed and that our task was to protect him so he could have this play experience. My assistant and I made sure no one disturbed his play. For about two months he played in the same way during play time. The rest of the morning he participated in our activities, and seemed quite fine, although his baby language continued.

Then, one day, he left a little opening in his house, not a very big one, but it proved important. A couple of days later, he made a bigger opening, and then he went out looking for a friend. He chose a lovely boy named Bill and brought him into his house. They played in it for a few days, but the house was rather cramped. Then it began to grow with more stumps, cloths, and other building materials. Over a few weeks, it grew big enough for other children to come inside and play. Gradually, Sammy's voice came back to normal. He had worked something through with that remarkable wisdom children have that guides their play and directs them toward self-healing.

Another child, Shannon, seemed high strung and fearful and always spoke with a thin, high-pitched voice that could easily get on my nerves. One day she approached me with a doll. She wanted me to wrap it in cloth, but the cloth she had brought me was about six feet long. I was about to send her back for a smaller cloth, but thought, "Perhaps she needs this." I took her doll and began to wrap it slowly, thinking that if she became restless I would speed up a bit.

She watched with infinite patience and when the doll was fully swaddled she took it into her arms. After that, she was much more relaxed and her voice, too, came into a normal range. It was as if she felt bare in the world and needed to be wrapped in a warm and protective sheath.

How do children know what they need and act it out in play? A tremendous wisdom is at work when children play; a kind of genius guides them to play out the very scenes they most need for their growth and development. I saw it over and over, in small ways and in large. It is a tragedy that so many of today's children have forgotten how to play and cannot access this genius and wisdom within themselves. I know that many people rave about how brilliant today's children are—at a young age they can write and read and use a computer and other high-tech machines, but so often they cannot relate strongly with other human beings or enter the deeper spaces of play. To me, they seem impoverished in the areas that matter most.

Restoring Play to Childhood

In this volume, Sandra Hofferth of the University of Maryland shares her research on the declines in imaginative play and outdoor play. She points out that children are spending growing amounts of time on computers, and decreasing amounts of time in non-computer play—and they spend almost no time in outdoor play.

The lack of outdoor play was made visible to

me on a beautiful Sunday in Chicago, when I was driving a British friend all over the city looking at Frank Lloyd Wright homes. It was the first warm day of spring. We covered miles of ground visiting poor neighborhoods, middle-class and wealthy areas. That whole glorious day, we saw only two groups of children outside playing. Both were in low-income neighborhoods, and both groups were playing in dangerous spaces. The more-affluent neighborhoods looked like ghost towns. Beautiful yards and safe streets beckoned to children but no children were to be seen. Where were they? Most likely inside in front of screens.

Electronic entertainment has changed children's lives radically over the last sixty years. But it is not the only hindrance to play. Another is that play has been eliminated from nearly all kindergartens in the United States and it is now being removed from a growing number of preschools in favor of academic instruction. This early focus on academic instruction robs children of time to play, but it also awakens them to a set of concerns and learning standards that do not coexist well with open-ended creative play. Deep, make-believe play requires a mood of freedom and self-direction. Continually being called out of those spaces to be instructed in letters and numbers weakens the child's capacity to enter into play. Soon, the children forget where the doorway is, or if they remember and try to reenter, they often are scolded for misbehavior,

or even drugged to fit into a system that is sadly skewed against them.

After age six or seven children discover new doorways into chambers of learning. They *want* to be instructed in reading, writing, and arithmetic and they learn it with gusto and relative ease, especially if they played well and learned the lessons of early childhood. Eliminating play in favor of academic instruction is such a loss, and so little is gained.

Fortunately, when a child has forgotten how to play, he or she can be brought back to it. Such children need to see that adults value play, and they need some help in re-entering the space of play. They also need healthy nourishment for their imaginations in the form of story telling, including fairy tales and nature tales. Involving children with puppetry, the arts, physical movement, and real work, such as cooking, cleaning, woodworking, and gardening are great aids in restoring children's play. The relationship between hands-on work and imaginative play is one of the unexplored treasures of early childhood. Yet children have been brought back to creative play by first having them do real work.

I think of Andy, who seemed to have lost his ability to play. He mainly wandered around the kindergarten and lashed out at other children or knocked down their play areas. He was very bright and highly stimulated intellectually, but he did not know how to relate to other children or how to use his hands for purposeful activity.

Every day I invited him to help me with some basic work. At first he always said, "I don't know how," an expression I almost never heard in the kindergarten. Most young children pick up activities quickly by imitating adults and feel tremendous confidence that they can do what we do. Andy was different. Although he had no disabilities, he needed enormous help to get his fingers to sew or dry dishes or use a hammer. He simply didn't know how and wasn't able to imitate my doing it, as other children could. With help, he gradually was able to do such tasks, and his ability to play also began to grow. Within six weeks, he was very popular with the other children, for he invented wonderful play scenarios and integrated six or seven children into them without being too bossy. He became a great player.

Within the Alliance for Childhood, we asked ourselves how can we bring children back into play.[3] While some of us were experienced in doing this in preschool and kindergarten settings, we felt we needed help in bringing older children back to play. We turned to Penny Wilson, an experienced playworker from London's adventure playgrounds for help. Her work in the United States during the past two years already is having a profound impact.[4]

At the invitation of Joe Modrich, head of the parks department in Franklin Park, Illinois, near O'Hare Airport, Penny began training the park staff in the art of playwork, which is a profession in the United Kingdom and in Europe. Playworkers know how to encourage children to play without dominating their play. After Penny's first visit to Franklin Park, many of the staff were able to integrate play into their programs. The children learning figure skating were able to choreograph their own programs, the ice hockey team became more playful, and the summer camp became less "rules-based" and more spontaneous with play. Children loved it and the parents appreciated their children's enthusiasm.

One of my favorite stories was from the head of the after-school program. She described how parents came after work looking tired and stressed and generally picked up their children quickly and hurried home. Once creative play became a regular part of her program, she found that the parents would watch the children play through a large window and she could see them visibly relax. In our stressful times, play is needed at all ages.

Playwork is beginning to catch on in the United States in parks, children's museums, and other venues. In a few years, we hope there will be enough interest to warrant full trainings for playworkers.

Restoring Play in Preschools and Kindergartens

For thirty years, creative play has been driven slowly out of kindergartens and now it is vanishing from preschools as well. In most kindergartens, open-ended, child-initiated play has been replaced with adult-initiated group instruction. Yet a recent international study found that children showed much greater gains in cognitive ability and in language development at age seven if their preschools encouraged child-initiated learning rather than instruction by a teacher.[5]

In California and other states, a growing number of kindergartens are resorting to scripted teaching for instructing children in literacy and numeracy.[6] Scripted lessons can be given for two or more hours each day, and teachers are expected to follow the script exactly. Inspectors enter the room to check on them and they are marked down if they are not following the scripted text. Some programs even tell the teachers which questions to expect for each lesson and how to answer them. Nothing is left to the spontaneous or creative interaction between child and teacher. This approach is now gaining ground in preschools.

From a developmental perspective, a tragic disconnect exists between such methods and the inherent ways that children learn through play and imitation. One educator recently said to me, "People don't believe in child development anymore."

The disconnect between children's development and current practices is so great that the Alliance for Childhood issued a "Call to Action on the Education of Young Children."[7] It is signed by over 150 leading educators and health professionals. The Call to Action states:

We are deeply concerned that current trends in early education, fueled by political pressure, are leading to an emphasis on unproven methods of academic instruction and unreliable standardized testing that can undermine learning and damage young children's healthy development.

For thirty years, we have watched a steady rise in academic pressure on young children and a steady decline in children's health and well-being. I think the two are closely related. Changing the patterns of early education in this country will not be easy, nor will restoring play throughout childhood, but I am encouraged by renewed interest in play and by the report of the American Academy of Pediatrics encouraging parents to let their children play.[8]

The pathway toward meaningful change is usually uphill and rocky, often with steep abysses on either side. But growing numbers of parents, educators, health professionals, and policy makers recognize the problem and want to restore play to childhood. If we work together creatively, we should be able to find our way up that rocky path and reopen the doors to play.

Notes

1. Author of *Playing By Heart: The Vision and Practice of Belonging* (self-published, 1993), Fred

works with "original play," an approach based on touch and rumble-tumble play. This form of play human beings and animals have in common. See http://www.originalplay.com.

2. In 2004, the Alliance for Childhood worked with Olga Jarrett at Georgia State University on an informal study of experienced kindergarten teachers. They described how educational policies had changed over ten years with the net result that no time was left in kindergarten for child-initiated play. Several teachers added, "If I give the children time to play, they don't know what to do. They have no ideas of their own." The Alliance hears such comments frequently.

3. The Alliance for Childhood is a partnership of educators, health professionals, and others who work to improve the health and well-being of all children. www.allianceforchildhood.org.

4. Playwork is an established profession in the UK and other European countries. Playworkers work in adventure playgrounds and other settings where they provide oversight while allowing children to initiate and direct their own play. See http://www.playscotland.org/whatisplay_whatplaywork.html.

5. See High/Scope's recent international study on gains from preschools that emphasize child-initiated activities rather than teacher-directed learning: http://www.highscope.org/Content.asp?ContentID=257.

6. Scripted programs, such as McGraw Hill's Open Court, are used widely beginning in preschool and kindergarten. In Los Angeles, for instance, long hours are devoted each day to a teacher reading from a script to teach literacy and mathematics in kindergartens. For further information on scripted teaching, see http:// www.nea.org/neatoday/0502/coverstory.html?mode=print#coverstory.

7. See "A Call to Action on the Education of Young Children" at http://www.allianceforchildhood.org/pdf_files/call_action?education.pdf.

8. See http://www.aap.org/pressroom/play-public.htm.

The heart of puppetry is breathing life into anything that does not breathe on its own—an eraser and a large paperclip become an old man with a crutch; a mug with reading glasses taped over its nose (I mean handle) becomes a professor; a rolled up old sock perched on one or two fingers becomes a head, the hand and the other fingers its body and arms.

ANN MESRITZ GRONVOLD
PUPPETEER AND STORYTELLER

Margery B. Franklin

WORDS IN PLAY

Children's Use of Language in Pretend

Margery B. Franklin, Ph.D., is Professor Emeritus at Sarah Lawrence College, where she taught psychology from 1965 to 2002. From 2002 to 2007, she was director of the Child Development Institute at Sarah Lawrence. A Fellow of the American Psychological Association, Dr. Franklin has co-edited four volumes and published articles on children's play, aesthetic development, and developmental theory.

Watching children play outdoors, we see that they engage in a range of activities, from free physical activity such as running and climbing to games in which they take on roles such as explorer, firefighter, or schoolteacher and improvise story lines. If props are available, children playing outdoors also may engage in miniature-world play, using small objects such as human figures and trucks to enact scenarios, usually within a bounded space such as a sandbox. Pretend play is a symbolizing medium comprised of several interacting components: *person*, *actions*, *objects*, *space*, and *language*. My discussion here, and the examples, focus on sociodramatic play.[1] In such play, *person* refers to the bodily self, as present in the scene. The child takes on an identity other than her own and uses her body to represent the other—mother, baby, superhero, train conductor. Many of the *actions* that appear in sociodramatic play, such as pretending to mow the grass, more or less replicate gestures of everyday life. Other actions, such as flapping one's arms in pretend flight, are very rough approximations of the real action. *Objects* can be used in their original function—a pail as a pail—or radically transformed in the context of play—a scrap of cloth becomes a magical cape. *Space* is another important component of the play medium. In some instances, the actual physical space of the playground or classroom serves as a support for play but is not imaginatively transformed. In other cases, transformations of space are central to the play process—a corner of the playground becomes a forest, a path becomes a river. Sometimes a child's actions or handling of objects provides sufficient clues to establish consensual meaning, particularly if the children have often played together. In our culture, flapping your arms in a rhythmic way while running around *means* flying. However, actions alone may not be sufficient to communicate intended meanings.[2] Observing children at play, we notice that a good deal of talk often is going on, and we remark that many pretend play sequences would be impossible or seriously curtailed without the children's use of speech. Let us look at several ways in which children use *language* in play by considering observations of kindergarten children at play in a playground that has grass, trees, and paths, as well as playground equipment. It is important to keep in mind that on playgrounds, as in the classroom, the environmental context

influences the children's choice of scenario. The following sequence is more likely to have taken place in a playground with trees and grass than on a plain cement ground. However, providing appropriate materials—such as large blocks, pails, and shovels—fills a cement space with possibilities, as children who have grown up in an urban environment will attest.[3]

Nancy: Let's pretend we're explorers, and going to look for buried treasure.

Sarah: Okay, but I want to be first, I want to be first.

Nancy: You can be first but I have the map. *[goes to teacher]*

[Sarah waits for Nancy to return; Nancy returns with paper and pencil, draws some lines on the paper and stuffs it in her pocket.]

Nancy: Now we need hammers. *[She picks up two sticks and hands one to Sarah.]*

Sarah: This is a hammer?

Nancy: Yes. *[demonstrates hammering motion with stick]* Let's go.

Sarah: Where are we going?

Nancy: Into the jungle. *[Nancy leads the way toward the trees; Sarah follows. They kneel down and scratch in the earth.]*

Nancy: *[picking up a stone]* I found it! I found it!

Sarah: Yes, yes! Me too! *[picking up another]*

[*Both children stand up and walk back to the center of the playground. The game seems to have ended.*]

This example reveals several distinct uses of language in the context of play. While children sometimes spontaneously launch into pretending, on other occasions they invite each other to play by saying "Let's pretend" and then specifying what the game is to be, as Nancy does in the opening statement above. We refer to this use of language as *establishing and specifying the play sphere*.[4]

Language is also used to *establish identities for objects, persons, and spaces*. In the example above, a piece of paper becomes a "map" because it is so designated. A more dramatic example of transformation is provided by designating the sticks as "hammers," a designation that is questioned by one of the players but subsequently accepted when the naming is supplemented by a hammering action. The children's identity as explorers is established by Nancy and accepted by Sarah. Such identities can be set by assigning roles to oneself or others, as in this case. Here, the children consolidate their identities by speaking in the voice of their characters: "I found it! I found it!" We also see language used to transform a corner of the playground into "the jungle."

Establishing identities for objects, persons, and spaces is central to the play process. *Narrative construction* is equally important. In all but the most rudimentary pretend play, we recognize a plot line that unfolds as improvisation.[5]

[*Three five-year-old girls come together on the playground. One suggests that they play "pilgrim." The others agree. They kneel on the ground at the edge of the playground, under a tree. They arrange sticks in a small pile, and then sit down.*]

Elisa: This is our fire, so we can cook.

Melissa: I'm going to the well to get water. [*picks up pail and walks a short distance from "fire" and returns*] Here's water for us.

Elisa: Now it's time for dinner. Here's the stew. [*picks up another small pail and makes gesture of dishing up food—stops*] We need plates.

Cindy: [*picking up three leaves from the ground*] Here. They're small but it's all we have. We're poor pilgrims.

Elisa: [*continuing with dishing out stew*] Okay. Hey, we need more logs for the fire. [*gets up to retrieve more sticks which she lays carefully on top of the others*]

Melissa: [*making eating motions*] Mmmm …this stew is delicious!

Cindy: [*standing up*] Hey! The Indians are coming! Let's get out of here.

Elisa: Maybe they're friendly Indians. Let's see.

Cindy: I'm getting out of here. [*runs to center of playground*]

Melissa: I'm staying.

Elisa: Me too. But let's play something else.

Here, the children have agreed to play "pilgrim" without designating specific roles such as "mother." They launch and sustain the narrative by speaking in the voices of their characters. The narrative evolves as the children take turns identifying objects ("This is our fire"), articulating mini-episodes that make up the story ("Now it's time for dinner"), and expressing feelings ("This stew is delicious!"). In this scene, the play runs smoothly. The only disagreement concerns the threat of the Indians, with the difference of viewpoint readily resolved. The narrative is constructed *within* the frame of play, as the children speak in the voices of their imagined characters. In the first example, by contrast, most of the narrative line is carried by statements that set the context but are not within in it. Only when Nancy says "Into the jungle" in response to Sarah's question, "Where are we going?" is it clear that the children's verbalizations are within the play frame—although Sarah's prior question is open to interpretation on this score.

To this point, I have identified three general ways in which language is used in pretend play: to *establish and specify the play sphere*, to *establish identities for objects, persons, and space*, and to *construct the narratives of play*. Looking closely at two examples, I also have suggested that each of these functions can be realized through speech that is *within* the frame of play (sometimes referred to as "text") or through speech that establishes meanings in a manner akin to stage directions (sometimes referred to as "context-establishing speech"). In addition to the uses of language in play that I have mentioned, we must note the crucial role of *negotiation* in establishing and maintaining play, whether this is pretend play or of another genre. In pretend play, arguments and agreements occur around what to play, who takes which role, appropriate actions for different characters, and the construction of the narrative sequence.

Increasing attention is being given to the design of outdoor play spaces for children. I suggest that more of this attention should be focused on how to design outdoor play spaces that are conducive to children's imaginative play. School playgrounds in urban environments tend to be large barren spaces, appropriate for dodge-ball and other athletic and physical activities but not at all conducive to imaginative play. The schoolyards of some urban schools, particularly the progressive schools that explicitly encourage and value imaginative play, are more likely to have equipment that encourages such play. In suburban or rural areas, parts of the natural environment often exist within a school play space, although that space may be shared with swing sets, jungle gyms, slides, and so forth. While pretend play can take place around jungle gyms and other such equipment, the natural environment of trees, grass, twigs, and pebbles provides an ideal setting for all kinds of pretend. Adding a small shed, moveable large blocks, pails, shovels, paintbrushes, and perhaps small figures and vehicles increases possibilities for pretend play. Teachers have an important role in establishing an environment that facilitates play, helping hesitant children get their play started, providing resources (such as additional props), and settling disputes. But, optimally, they stay in the background while children construct their worlds of imagination.

Notes

1. Observations of play were done in the Early Childhood Center at Sarah Lawrence College.

2. I was interested to see that Marcel Marceau, the eminent mime, used written signs on stage to establish the context in which his gestural enactments were to be interpreted.

3. For description and analysis of children's outdoor play in various settings, see R. C. Moore, *Childhood's Domain: Play and Place in Child Development* (Berkeley: MIG Publications, 1990).

4. For a more extended discussion of the uses of language in pretend, see M. B. Franklin, "Play as the Creation of Imaginary Situations: The Role of Language," in *Toward a Holistic Developmental Psychology,* ed. S. Wapner and B. Kaplan (Hillsdale, N.J.: Lawrence Erlbaum Associates, 1983).

5. On the improvisatory nature of play, see K. Sawyer, *Pretend Play as Improvisation: Conversation in the Preschool Classroom* (Mahwah, N.J.: Lawrence Erlbaum Associates, 1997). For discussion of narrative construction in reality-oriented and fantasy-oriented play, see S. Engel, "The Narrative Worlds of What Is and What If," *Cognitive Development* 20 (2005): 214–25.

Child-initiated play will be the goal of the playworkers at New York's Burling Slip playground. Playworkers will not be directing play, games, and arts and crafts, as a recreation worker might. Playworkers are necessary on the Burling Slip playground to effectively manage the diverse set of "loose parts," sand, and water that are fundamental to manipulative, interactive, and cooperative play. The playground is conceived as a complement to the traditional public playground with its emphasis on gross-motor play—climbing, swinging, sliding, and running. At Burling Slip children will engage in a wide repertoire of play activities, from exploring, sensing, and manipulating new materials, to using them for building, transporting, and creating new "worlds" with other children. Imaginative play is enhanced within such a diverse, manipulatable environment. The playworkers will be the creative managers of the environment, engaged in an ongoing redesign of the playground every day. They will set the "stage" with a changing array of play "props" for children to initiate new and ever-changing performances with these materials.

ROGER A. HART, DIRECTOR
CHILDREN'S ENVIRONMENTS RESEARCH GROUP, CUNY

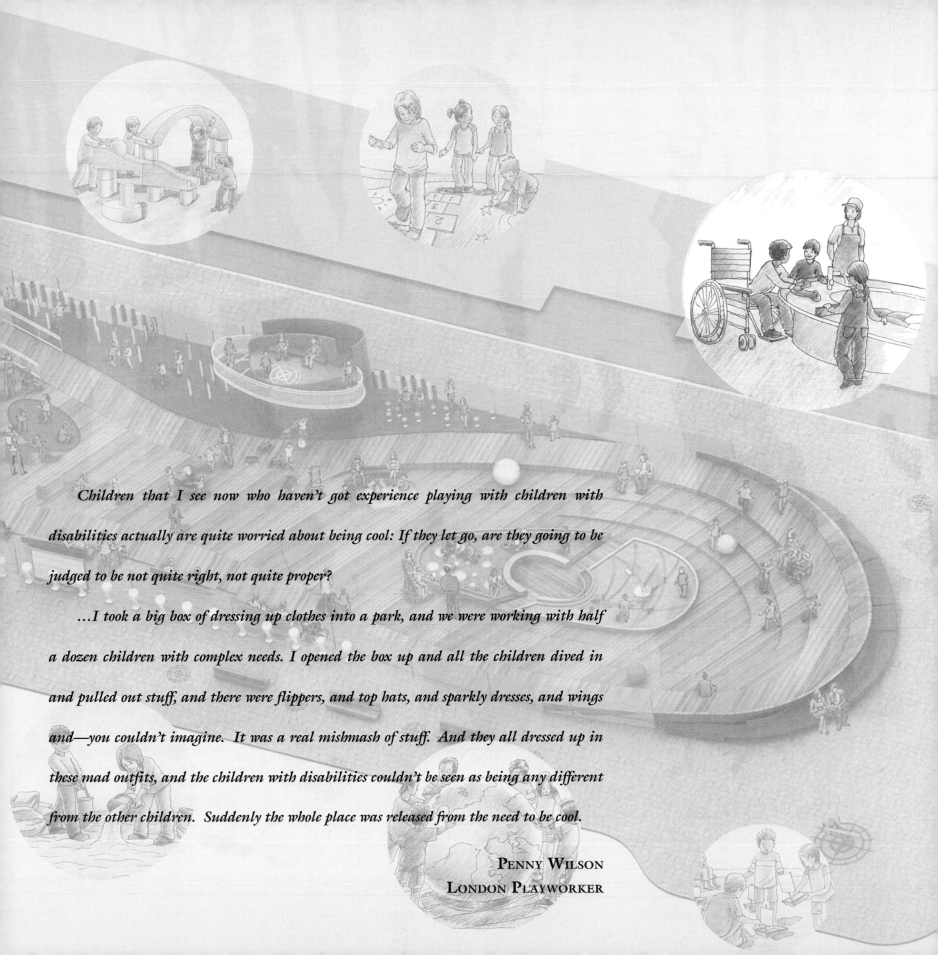

Children that I see now who haven't got experience playing with children with disabilities actually are quite worried about being cool: If they let go, are they going to be judged to be not quite right, not quite proper?

...I took a big box of dressing up clothes into a park, and we were working with half a dozen children with complex needs. I opened the box up and all the children dived in and pulled out stuff, and there were flippers, and top hats, and sparkly dresses, and wings and—you couldn't imagine. It was a real mishmash of stuff. And they all dressed up in these mad outfits, and the children with disabilities couldn't be seen as being any different from the other children. Suddenly the whole place was released from the need to be cool.

PENNY WILSON
LONDON PLAYWORKER

Bob Hughes

FOUR PLAYWORK MEDITATIONS

Bob Hughes has been a playworker since 1970. He is a prolific author and has lectured all over the world. He is currently the co-ordinator of PlayEducation, a playwork research and training agency based in the United Kingdom.

Because "playworker" is not a profession in the United States, this term requires some elaboration, especially because it may be assumed to be equivalent to "recreation leader." The concept of playwork is borrowed from Europe, where it is a well-accepted profession. More than one type of playworker can be found in Europe, but generally the emphasis has been for playworkers to enable children to engage in "free play," rather than directed play.

Roger A. Hart

- "Anyone want to a cup of tea?" The five-year-old was putting the water-filled kettle on the cooker, and turned to address her children—two Barbie dolls, an alligator, one of her brother's Action Men, a rather worn teddy, and a Giant Cabbage Patch doll. "Come on now," she said, "wash your hands and sit at the table." She re-arranged the dolls, seating them around a small plastic table containing tiny teacups and plates. "There you are," she said and then went through the motions of cutting slices of cake from the pretend food her mother had brought from the Early Learning Centre, and placing them on the plates. "Eat nicely," she said to the alligator in a rather prim voice, "or you won't get any sweeties. Jessica," she said, referring to one of the Barbies, "come and help me do the washing up, will you?" Again that attempted adult voice. She propped the chosen Barbie near the draining board, telling it about her day and what they needed to buy when they went shopping. As she did this, a playworker came up to her and, putting her arm around her, said, "Your mum's here." The child ran out of the playhouse and up to the gate where her mother was waiting. "Come on honey," said her mother in a rather prim voice, "time for bed."

- He sits patiently beside a bucket full of water, assembling twigs into a tiny tepee filled with scraps of paper. He is only seven and the concentration of the operation creates furrows in his brow. Eventually he is finished. The little pyramid of wood is ready. He has been given six red matches and he strikes the first one on a stone. It goes out. "How did that happen?" He strikes another, shielding

the flame from the wind this time. He takes the lit match in his cupped hands rather too quickly toward the twigs and the match goes out again. "Oh no!" He repeats the operation, this time gently taking the flame to the paper and twigs. The paper catches fire and ignites the twigs and suddenly there is a small red and blue flame and the sweet smell of wood smoke. He cheers. "Hurray!" And then piles more wood onto the fledgling fire. Unaware that, just like him, the fire is also a living, breathing thing, he gives it too much fuel and insufficient air. The flame dies as the last of the paper and twigs are smothered. "Shit," he says, under his breath.

- Her heart was pounding. Had she overdone it? Looking down into her friends upturned faces, through the leaves and branches, she realized that it was a long way down. And then the soft wind blew through the branches once again. The rustle of the leaves and the creaking sway of the branches evoked long-forgotten, far away, perhaps ancient memories, while the sun dappled the bark. Her fear evaporated and she began to climb upward again, toward where the sun broke through the arboreal barrier. She had seen squirrels this high, and different birds, but for her this was a first. As the branches grew higher, they were thinner too, and swayed more in the gentle breeze, making her feel like she was on the tall mast of a galleon at sea. The sun warmed her face and the blue sky grew larger as she broke free of the cover of leaves and her head protruded through the top of the canopy. Wow, she said, wow. She could see the town in the distance and the motorway, but here it was just the wind, the leaves, and the creaking branches. Now how do I get down?

- I am the great artist, he said to himself. Here I have my paints, my brushes, paper, glitter, material, glue, and my water. He was in the "art" room, the space on the playground dedicated to painting and making. He looked around. His friends, another boy of the same age and a girl a year or so older, were making models—he, a car, made out of clay, and she, a fire, made from sticks, paint, and colored paper. This will be my subject for today, he thought. I shall produce a cool picture of my two friends with their fire and car. During previous sessions, he had created wonderful masterpieces. "The bride with the cut throat," was one of his favourites, although he also liked the spinning wheel. He giggled, remembering the paper on the potter's wheel spinning madly as he pored paint onto the paper, which had then sprayed over them all. It was a deep, throaty giggle. He drew two black wheels for his friend's car, and then the chassis in red, with his friend in darker red. He drew the fire in red too, and the friend building it, but this time she had sprouting black hair. He signed it with a flourish. Excellent.

Each of the above episodes was observed in a playspace operated by playworkers, adults trained to understand the phenomenon of play and to know when and why any intervention might be justified from the child's viewpoint. Although what the children were thinking at the time is obviously speculation, the playworkers saw this kind of challenge being undertaken by children on an hourly basis.

The playworker's main function is to ensure that children have the necessary props and environments to play with, which will ensure that they will be able to access diverse and unadulterated experiences. This will help them to develop the flexibility that will increase their potential to adapt to change, as well as experiencing excitement and fun.

It is not the playworker's function to intervene in the children's play to facilitate socialization or domestication to satisfy a transitional social model. Playworkers believe that the benefits of play are timeless and that episodes such as those above just as easily could have happened ten thousand years ago or could happen in ten thousand years' time. That is, if we allow children to continue to play. If we don't, then it won't matter, we won't be here as a species anyway.

II. RESEARCHING FUN

If you follow group play, preschool boys and girls age three to five are diving, hitting, chasing, screaming, interacting with each other, which sounds and looks like mayhem, except that they keep smiling at each other. That kind of open rough and tumble play helps preschool kids determine whether they're fast or slow, whether they're extroverted or introverted, whether they can take their lumps easier than someone else.

A generation or two ago, parents were pretty much hands off. There was not the perception that it was dangerous to be out in the streets in a city. In a rural setting, you generally didn't have an automobile to take you to football or volleyball, so that kids were left largely on their own after school to make up whatever kind of play they wanted to.

In suburban America, the parents and the culture organize the child's time, which really doesn't leave a lot of free choice. They may be rich experiences for the child, but they're often driven by adult need rather than spontaneously erupting from within the child.

We don't know fully what the effects of that will be later on adult behavior. There is evidence that imaginativeness and a sense of freedom with your own internal story telling, your own narrative, your own fantasies, is lessened in those children who are organized continuously to go to gymnastics, to go to ballet, to go to Little League, and never entirely free—based on the seasons or the ecology of where you live—to figure out who you are and what to do and to use play as the medium.

> Play in preschool... sounds and looks like mayhem, except that they keep smiling at each other.

Stuart Brown, Founder/President, National Institute for Play. Quoted from film interview, *Where Do the Children Play?* (2007)

Sandra L. Hofferth

AMERICAN CHILDREN'S OUTDOOR AND INDOOR LEISURE TIME

Sandra L. Hofferth is a professor of family science at the University of Maryland, College Park, and Director, Maryland Population Research Center. Her research interests lie in the health consequences of family time allocation and activity for children. She is co-investigator on a project exploring the intergenerational consequences of paternal involvement.

Are children less active and spending more time indoors than in the past? We suspect that this is the case. Television, computing, and video games, all relatively new activities, are indoor activities and require little physical exertion. As they increase, time spent outside is likely to decrease unless a way is found to integrate computers and out-of-door activities for children. In this essay, I report on the most recent data that examine how much time children actually spend in a variety of different types of activities.

Although we don't have comparable numbers from the distant past, we do have a comparison between 1997 and 2003, the most recent years for which comprehensive data are available. The data come from two Child Development Supplements to the Michigan Panel Study of Income Dynamics, a 30-year longitudinal survey of a representative sample of U.S. men, women,

41

children, and their families. Families with children under age thirteen in 1997 were asked to provide information on their children in 1997 and again in fall 2002 to spring 2003. As part of each study and assisted by parents, children filled out diaries of their activities over a 24-hour period for a weekday and a weekend day. Based on these diaries, estimates of children's weekly time in a variety of activities were calculated. When weights are used, as was done here, these data are representative of the U.S. population of children in the appropriate ages in these two years.

What Is the Good News?

First of all, between 1997 and 2003, six- to twelve-year-olds' time spent playing (primarily indoors) did not experience the decline that had occurred between 1981 and 2003. (Included in "play" are pretend play and dress-up play; playing games such as card games, board games, social games, and puzzles; playing with toys; electronic video and computer games; and other unspecified play.)

In addition, the television viewing time of children ages six to eight did not increase between 1997 and 2003.

And the Bad News?

Children were not very physically active in 2003. The proportion of six- to eight-year-olds who spent time on outdoor activities was small,

only twelve percent in 2003, about the same as in 1997. (Included in "outdoor activities" are walking for pleasure, hiking, pleasure drives, horseback riding, fishing, hunting, camping, going to the beach, gardening, boating, snowmobiling, and motorcycling.) The proportion of nine- to twelve-year-olds spending time out of doors actually declined. Only 8 percent of nine- to twelve-year-olds spent time playing outside in 2003, half of the sixteen percent recorded in 1997. The time spent was also very small. Of those who spent any time out of doors, in 2003 the average weekly time spent by six- to twelve-year-olds was four hours and ten minutes. In addition, the proportion of children six to eight and nine to twelve who spent time playing sports, either informally or with a team, declined from 76 to 60 percent between 1997 and 2003. (Included in "sports" are team sports such as football, basketball, baseball, volleyball, hockey, soccer, and field hockey; individual sports such as tennis, squash, and racquetball, golf, swimming, skiing, ice or roller skating, sledding, bowling, ping pong or pinball, judo, weight lifting, jogging or running, bicycling, gymnastics; and other activities such as playing Frisbee or catch, exercises such as yoga, and lessons in any of the above.)

Does it Matter Where Children Live?

In warm-weather states compared to other states, children participate in more outdoor activities, indoor play is lower, and sports participation tends to be higher. But even in warm states, children were less active in 2003 compared with 1997, as indicated by a decline in time spent in sports.

So What Were They Doing, Instead?

Studying. Children spent more time studying in 2003 compared with 1997. Two-thirds of children studied on a given day or week in 2003 and study time was up about 25 percent.

Reading. Children spent more time reading books for pleasure. Almost half read in a given week in 2003, compared with two out of five in 1997. Spending more time reading for pleasure has been shown to be associated with higher scores on tests of verbal skills.

Sleeping. In addition, children spent almost two more hours sleeping in 2003 than in 1997.

School. Younger children six- to eight-year olds spent a bit more time in school; the latter's time is now comparable to that of nine- to twelve-year-olds, about 33 hours per week.

Playing with the computer. Children are spending more time on the computer. The proportion of children who used the computer increased between 1997 and 2003. The proportion that used the computer for studying was small and did not increase. Most of the time that children are using the computer, they are playing, not studying. Playing on the computer has increased both in terms of the proportion who play on the computer and the amount of time they spend. The proportion of children age six to eight playing with the computer rose from 11 to 24 percent and the proportion age nine to twelve rose from 20 to 28 percent. Non-computer play time actually declined for all children. As a result, computer play took a larger chunk out of children's total play time in 2003 than in 1997. If computer use had not increased, total play time would have declined.

Watching television or playing video games. The time spent watching television and playing video games rose for nine- to twelve-year-olds, though not for six- to eight-year-olds. In 2003, children age six to eight spent twelve and a half hours watching television and children nine to twelve spent almost fifteen hours a week watching television. Forty percent of the nine- to twelve-year-olds played video games and those who did so spent 6 hours per week playing video games.

Video games are a male activity. In 2003, 57 percent of boys and only 17 percent of girls played a video game during the week of the interview. Including everyone, boys played for three hours and 49 minutes compared with 47 minutes for girls. Just looking at those who played, boys played about seven hours per week, compared with four and a half hours for girls.

Other Sources

Panel Study of Income Dynamics, www.psidonline.isr.umich.edu.

Hofferth, Sandra L. 2008. "Home Media Influences on Children's Achievement and Behavior.," www.popcenter.umd.edu/people/hofferth_sandra/.

—2008. "Changes in Preadolescent and Adolescent Children's Time, 1997 to 2003."

www.popcenter.umd.edu/people/hofferth_sandra/.

Hofferth, Sandra L., and Jack Sandberg. 2001. "Changes in American Children's Time, 1981–1997." In *Children at the Millennium: Where Have We Come From, Where are We Going?* Advances in Life Course Research, vol. 6, ed. S. L. Hofferth and T. J. Owens, 193–229. Oxford, England: Elsevier.

Nancy M. Wells

DO KIDS NEED NATURE?

A Brief Review of the Research Evidence

Nancy M. Wells received her Ph.D. in psychology and architecture from the University of Michigan. She is an assistant professor in the Department of Design and Environmental Analysis and is on the graduate faculty in the Horticulture Department at Cornell University. As an environmental psychologist, her research focuses on influences of the built and natural environment on human health and well-being through the life course.

Introduction

Most adults recall the joy of childhood time spent outdoors. Whether you played in the backyard, explored the local wild lands, participated in periodic hiking and camping adventures, maintained a garden, or just became engrossed in a wooded window view from a classroom, you are likely to have fond childhood memories of nature and the outdoors. You also may have an intuitive sense that nature is good for us—in particular, that the natural environment is beneficial to children. But what do we know about children's connections to nature? What does the empirical research evidence indicate?

This chapter provides a brief overview of the research evidence concerning children's connection to the natural environment. This article is not an exhaustive review of the literature, but rather, provides a thumbnail sketch of the current empirical findings. We will consider both the research evidence regarding children's affinity for the natural environment and that suggesting a variety of beneficial effects from exposure to nature for children.

Favorite Places in Childhood

> Pharaoh...crouched in the weeds nearby, his legs tucked underneath him, and picked at the vegetation, which now reached his neck. He was lost in his thoughts....He didn't want to leave this place, the sweet smell of wildflowers and the diving sparrow. There was a certain tranquility here, a peacefulness that extended into the horizon like the straight, silvery rails. (Kotlowitz 1991, 7)

This quotation comes from Alex Kotlowitz's book *There Are No Children Here*. In his book, the journalist describes the struggles of two brothers, Pharaoh and Lafayette, growing up in a grim, crime-ridden public housing complex. The boys witness gang warfare and the deaths of friends, but for nine-year-old Pharaoh, a small area of vegetation, a patch of nature, offers a peaceful retreat that he cannot find elsewhere.

Pharaoh's experience illustrates a strong connection to nature that commonly is expressed among children. Several studies have documented that children prefer environments that are dominated by natural elements (Korpela 2002). In a British study, researchers asked 237 children who lived in either public or private housing what they liked most about where they lived. Many (75 and 45 percent, respectively) answered in terms of places to play outside (Department of Education 1973). A study conducted by Robin Moore (1986) showed that when urban children aged 9 to 12 were asked to create a map or a drawing of their "favorite places," 96 percent of the illustrations were of outdoor places. In fact, only four drawings mentioned interior spaces and just one drawing was devoted exclusively to building interiors. Subsequent research by Rachel Sebba (1991) with a sample of 174 children indicated that 46 percent reported an outdoor place when asked "what is your favorite place." Sebba's study also suggested that a gender difference may exist in preference for the outdoors—with boys more likely than girls to indicate such a preference. When adults were asked to describe the most significant or favorite place of their childhood, 97 percent indicated outdoor places (Sebba 1991).

Interestingly, while considerable evidence has been found that children value time spent in nature, some deviation from this trend has been measured. Korpela, Kyttä, and Hartig (2002) surveyed Finnish children aged 8 to 12 years about their favorite places and found, in contrast to prior research, that natural settings did not dominate. Moreover, the literature suggests that the preference for nature is less common as youth enter adolescence (Kaplan and Kaplan 2002). Korpela and colleagues report that an unpublished Finnish study found that seven to nine year-olds preferred natural places more than ten to twelve year-olds (Pihlström 1992, cited in Korpela Kyttä, and Hartig 2002). In her study of 91 Estonian children, Barbara Sommer (1990) reported that while overall 58 percent of the children preferred natural areas, the eleven to thirteen year-olds were more likely to prefer natural places than fifteen to seventeen year-olds. Adolescence may be a period in life that particularly merits further research with respect to relationships with the natural environment; however, the evidence is fairly consistent that younger children value nature.

Children's Social Well-Being

Aside from children's affinity for nature, considerable evidence suggests the beneficial effects of nature on children's social well-being. Qualitative research conducted by Sheridan Bartlett (1997, 1998) describes the experiences of young children who, for a variety of reasons, are unable to spend time outdoors. Bartlett describes one child as follows:

> Lee often throws tantrums in the doorway when his older brothers go outdoors…Windows are kept shut, and outside doors are locked…Lee is a frustrated child. What he most wants, active play outdoors with other children, is off limits, literally out of reach….In his attempts to escape…he experiences himself as wild, uncontrollable, and potentially dangerous; but also as thwarted and helpless….Lee has long since exhausted the limited possibilities in [the] two rooms, and his frustration alternates with listless withdrawal. (Bartlett 1997, 43–44)

From Bartlett's description of Lee's experience, it is easy to imagine that if a child is trapped constantly indoors, unable to spend time outside, it will take a significant toll. In a study of five year-old children in Zurich, Switzerland, Marc Hüttermoser (1995) found that those who could not play easily outdoors unsupervised, due to traffic conditions and parental constraints, had fewer playmates than children with easy outdoor access. The former group also exhibited poorer social, behavioral, and motor skills. Several research studies have been conducted within Chicago Public Housing complexes—places not unlike the homes of both Pharaoh and Lee. These studies, led by Frances Kuo, Andrea Faber Taylor, and William Sullivan at the University of Illinois in Champaign-Urbana, examine a variety of outcomes among residents of architecturally identical public housing buildings that differed only in the amount of trees and vegetation around the buildings. One group of buildings was surrounded by numerous trees; the other was relatively barren. Public housing residents are assigned essentially randomly to an apartment, thereby precluding the potential problem of "self-selection bias." In other words, we know that people in the buildings surrounded by trees are unlikely to vary significantly from those in the barren buildings (e.g., nature lovers versus non-nature lovers; or single parents versus married couples). This allows for greater confidence in interpreting the outcomes as being due to the differences in vegetation. One of the early studies by this research team documented that people used the green, treed spaces more than the barren outdoor spaces (Coley, Kuo, and Sullivan 1997). The authors conclude that natural landscaping promotes opportunities for social interaction as well as improving the supervision of children in poor urban neighborhoods. Subsequently, Andrea Faber Taylor and her colleagues (1998) reported that green, treed spaces facilitated more creative play among children and were more supportive of intergenerational interaction.

Together, these qualitative and quantitative studies suggest that by facilitating connections to both other children and adults, time spent outdoors in nature is critical to children's social development and well-being.

Children's Concentration and Cognitive Functioning

A related area of research focuses on how the natural environment affects children's cognitive functioning or concentration. Is it possible that access to or views of nature could enhance children's ability to focus their attention? The research evidence suggests that the answer is "Yes."

Several studies indicate that nature may bolster children's capacity to focus their attention or concentrate. In one of the few longitudinal studies focusing on the effects of nature on children, Wells (2000) found that children aged 7 to 12 years who relocated to homes with more nearby nature exhibited a greater improvement in cognitive functioning than those whose move was not associated with more access to nature. This study involved children whose families relocated as part of a self-help housing program. The fact that the families had little or no choice in where they moved helps to rule-out a "self-selection bias."

In another study, conducted in Sweden, children attending an "outdoors in all weather" daycare facility surrounded by orchards, pastures, and woodlands had a better ability to concentrate, as well as exhibiting better motor coordination, than children in an urban day care center surrounded by tall buildings (Grahn et al. 1997). Moreover, studies conducted by Andrea Faber Taylor, Frances Kuo, and their colleagues suggest that activities in green settings may help to decrease symptoms of children who struggle with Attention Deficit Disorder (ADD) (Faber Taylor et al., 2001).

The researchers report that following activities in green settings, children exhibited fewer and less severe symptoms of ADD. In a second study, Faber Taylor and colleagues (2002) found that a view of nature from the residence fosters self-discipline, concentration, and a greater capacity to delayed gratification among girls living in Chicago public housing. More recently, these researchers reported the results of a web-based survey of parents whose children had ADD or Attention Deficit/Hyperactivity Disorder (ADHD). Parents rated the after-effects of common after-school and weekend activities on their children's ADHD symptoms. Symptoms included difficulty focusing on unappealing tasks, difficulty completing tasks, difficulty listening or following directions, and difficulty resisting distraction. Results indicated that activities in green, outdoor settings reduced children's symptoms regardless of whether the activities occurred alone, in pairs, or in groups (Kuo and Faber Taylor 2004). Together, this collection of studies offers considerable evidence that the natural environment bolsters attention or concentration among children with and without ADD or ADHD.

If a connection exists between the natural environment and cognitive functioning, you might wonder what might explain such a relationship. A theory developed by Stephen Kaplan and Rachel Kaplan at the University of Michigan offers some insight (S. Kaplan, 1995; Kaplan and Kaplan 1983, 1989). The theory, known as "Attention Restoration Theory" (ART), builds on the work of early American psychologist William James. James (1890) posited that humans have two types of attention: "voluntary attention," which requires effort, and "involuntary attention," which is captured effortlessly.

According to ART, voluntary or "directed" attention, as it has been renamed, fatigues with use. This is a common experience of students during final exam week, accountants by April 15, and for many of us after an evening of checkbook-balancing. When directed attention is overused, neural inhibitory mechanisms that work to block out distraction when we focus our attention become fatigued. Ultimately, a state of "Directed Attention Fatigue" (DAF) may occur. DAF is characterized by difficulty concentrating and often, by irritability.

So, you might ask, where does nature come into this story? According to ART, characteristics of the natural environment are particularly well-suited to aid in recovery from DAF. You may have noticed yourself that feelings of cognitive weariness are eased by spending time pulling weeds in the garden, taking a walk in a nearby park, or going on an extended backpacking vacation.

Kaplan and Kaplan (1983) have specified

four characteristics of the natural environment that facilitate cognitive recovery. First, nature provides a sense of "being away." This sense may be provided by a wilderness backpacking trip or by a natural view from the window (Hartig et al., 1991; Tennessen and Cimprich 1995).

Second, the natural environment provides a sense of "fascination." The shimmer of aspen leaves, the flight of a robin, the gurgle of a flowing stream—simple aspects of nature engage involuntary attention and thereby allow directed attention to rest and recover.

Third, environments that provide "extent" are conducive to cognitive recovery because they allow a person to become immersed in a setting without necessitating a cognitive "shifting of gears." These are settings that have depth and consistency, giving a person a feeling that he or she can become immersed in the environment.

Last, a setting that is "compatible" with a person's inclinations will allow directed attention to rest and recover. These four characteristics commonly are found in the natural environment and thus, nature appears to be one of the best contexts for cognitive restoration—for adults as well as children.

Kids' Psychological Well-Being

Evidence has been found that exposure to nearby nature may enhance children's psychological well-being or mental health. Nancy Wells and Gary Evans at Cornell University studied a group of nearly 300 children living in a rural setting. They found that access to nearby nature buffered the impact of stressful life events such as being picked on at school, having a grandparent die, moving, being subject to peer pressure, and fighting with siblings (Wells and Evans 2003). This research relates to an area of study in child development focusing on environmental and social opportunities that foster the resilience of children.

Several possible explanations may account for the natural environment's capacity to enhance children's psychological well-being and "buffer" them from life stress. Perhaps, as Attention Restoration Theory would suggest, children with more exposure to nature have better cognitive resources; they are more able to think clearly about their problems, which allows them to manage life stress more effectively.

Alternatively, perhaps children who have more nature near their homes have more playmates or friends, as suggested by the studies indicating that nature draws people together and enhances social connections (Coley et al., 1997; Taylor et al., 1998; Hüttenmoser, 1995). This social support could allow them to cope more effectively with stress. It is particularly intriguing to consider the potential role of nature as a buffer or moderator of stress and adversity for a child like Pharaoh, who is growing up in inner-city public housing and coping with life-threatening stressors on a daily basis.

Environmentalism

In addition to the social, cognitive, and psychological benefits of nature for children, educators and environmentalists have wondered whether exposure to the natural environment during childhood might be associated with adult environmentalism. A growing body of literature suggests that childhood experiences with nature may be associated with environmentalism in later life. Early studies examining such linkage focused specifically on adults who were dedicated conservationists. The first study of its kind, conducted by Tanner (1980), asked adult environmentalists to identify childhood experiences that may have been influential on their career path. The respondents indicated that activities such as bird watching, hunting, fishing, and other activities in relatively pristine natural areas were particularly influential. Subsequent studies have provided support for Tanner's results among environmental educators or professionals in the United States (Corcoran 1999; Peterson and Hungerford 1981), the United Kingdom (Palmer 1993), El Salvador (Sward 1999), and in both the United States and Norway (Chawla 1999).

In a related body of literature, researchers have examined the extent to which childhood nature experiences predict individual's environmental knowledge or attitudes in adolescence or early adulthood. Unlike the early studies, these have focused on members of the general population rather than environmental professionals or activists. Alan Ewert of Indiana University, along with Greg Place of Chicago State University and Jim Sibthorp of the University of Utah (2005) examined predictors of ecocentric versus anthropocentric beliefs. They found that among undergraduates, childhood time spent in nature engaged in either appreciative or consumptive (e.g., hunting and fishing) endeavors, witnessing the destruction of natural areas, and exposure to nature through books and television were predictors of ecocentric later beliefs. Similarly, Bixler, Floyd and Hammitt (2002) report a positive association between children's play in wilderness environments and their subsequent adolescent interest in wildlands, environmental preferences, outdoor recreation, and occupations related to the outdoor environment. An interesting study was conducted by Raymond Chipeniuk (1995), who examined the relationship between childhood foraging for natural objects such as acorns, clover, catfish, and turtles, and adolescent knowledge of biodiversity. He found that the breadth of childhood foraging for natural things was associated positively with biodiversity knowledge later in life.

A recent study by Wells and Lekies (2006) examined connections between childhood nature activities and adult environmentalism. The researchers found that people who spent time engaged in "wild" nature activities such as hiking, camping, hunting, or fishing, as well as those who engaged in "domesticated" nature activities such as picking flowers, planting trees, or caring for plants, were more likely as adults to have positive environmental attitudes. These activities were also predictive of environmental behaviors such as recycling and voting based on environmental issues; however, "domesticated" nature experiences were less predictive in this regard. Similarly, Virginia Lohr and Carolyn Pearson-Mims (2005) report that children who picked vegetables, took care of plants, or reported having lived next to a garden or flower bed were more likely to have positive attitudes about trees in their adulthood. Elisabeth Kals and her colleagues (Kals et al., 1999) found a modest connection between children's time spent in nature between the ages of 7 and 12 and their adult "indignation about insufficient nature protection."

Together, these studies clearly suggest that childhood experiences in nature influence adult environmental knowledge, attitudes, or behaviors. It is noteworthy, however, that all of these studies rely on retrospective self-report, in that the research participants report their recollection of their own childhood activities. An obvious weakness of this research is that we cannot be completely certain whether childhood nature activities *lead to* adult environmental outcomes or rather, if environmental attitudes in adulthood color recollections about childhood

activity. In the future, researchers should strive to employ third-party objective reports of nature activities and/or collect data over a long period of time, objectively documenting individuals' nature activities and environmental attitudes from childhood to adulthood.

Childhood Physical Activity and Obesity

A final connection between the natural environment and children's well-being relates to physical health. The epidemics of childhood inactivity and obesity (Luepker 1999; Sturm 2005) are well-publicized in both the academic and popular press.

An estimated 22 million children under age 5 are now overweight worldwide (Deckelbaum and Williams, 2001). The number of overweight children in the United States has approximately doubled in the last two to three decades (Deckelbaum and Williams, 2001). Alarmingly, childhood obesity is a predictor of adult obesity as well as a wide range of poor health outcomes including cardiovascular disease, high LDL (low density lipoprotein) cholesterol, and Type 2 diabetes. While a variety of reasons have been suggested for the obesity trend, it is clear that both physical activity and diet play a role.

The growing tendency for children to spend their time indoors engaged in computer games, web-surfing, or watching television is a clear factor contributing to the obesity and inactivity problem. Children 3 to 12 years old spend, on average, 27 percent of their time (or 13.5 hours per week) watching television and just 1 percent (or one-half hour per week) outdoors engaged in unstructured activities (Hofferth and Sandberg 2001). Time spent outdoors has been found to be related positively and consistently to children's physical activity (Sallis, Prochaska and Taylor 2000). Studies document that outdoor play is associated with more physical activity and is more vigorous than indoor play (Baranowski et al. 1983; Henninger, 1980). In a recent study, Fjørtoft (2004) found that among children ages 5 to 7 years old, "functional" or physically active play such as jumping, running, climbing, and crawling were predominant during play in natural areas characterized by mixed vegetation and varied topography.

These studies suggest that in addition to the other benefits of the natural environment for children, time spent in nature also is likely to bolster levels of physical activity and reduce the likelihood of becoming overweight. In the context of rising rates of childhood obesity, with abundant temptations for children to be sedentary and to overeat, time outdoor in natural areas is critical strategy in the fight against the epidemic.

Conclusions and Implications

A growing body of evidence suggests that access to nature and time spent outdoors enhance the social, cognitive, psychological, and physical well-being of children. The research literature suggests that the preservation of natural areas is not a mere nicety—an optional amenity—but rather that it is critical to foster children who not only survive, but thrive. In addition to the beneficial effects related to health and well-being, childhood time spent outdoors also may promote a connection to the natural environment, thereby increasing the likelihood these children will grow up to embrace pro-environmental attitudes and engage in ecologically friendly behaviors. This idea suggests that one very promising benefit of having children play in nature is that they may be more likely to protect natural areas as adults and help to preserve nature for future generations. Without such a connection to nature, without a commitment to preserve, maintain, and prioritize natural areas, in a few decades we will ask "Where *will* the children play?"

References

Bartlett, S. N. 1997. "No Place to Play: Implications for the Interaction of Parents and Children." *Journal of Children and Poverty 3:* 37–48.

Coley, R. L., F. E. Kuo, and W. C. Sullivan. 1997. "Where Does Community Grow? The Social Context Created by Nature in Urban Public Housing." *Environment and Behavior* 29, no. 4: 468–94.

Deckelbaum, R. J., and C. L. Williams. 2001. "Childhood Obesity: The Health Issue." *Obesity Research* 9, no. 4: 239S–43S.

Department of the Environment. 1973. *Children at Play*. London: Her Majesty's Stationery Office.

Faber Taylor, A., A. Wiley, F. E. Kuo, and W. C. Sullivan. 1998. "Growing Up in the Inner city: Green Spaces as Places to Grow." *Environment and Behavior* 30, no. 1: 3–27.

Fjørtoft, I. 2004. "Landscape as Playscape: The Effects of Natural Environments on Children's Play and Motor Development." *Children Youth and Environments* 14, no. 2: 21–44.

Grahn, P., F. Måtrensson, B. Lindbald, P. Nilsson, and A. Ekman. 1997. Ute på dagis. (Outside for daycare). Stad & Land nr. 145. Alnarp: MOVIUM. Institutionen för landscapsplanering, Sveriges landbruksuniversitet.

Hartig, T., M. Mang, and G. W. Evans. 1991. "Restorative Effects of Natural Environment Experiences." *Environment and Behavior* 23: 3–26.

Hofferth, S. A. and T. J. Owens. 2001. "Changes in American Children's Time, 1981–1997." In *Children at the Millennium: Where Have We Come From, Where Are We Going?* ed. S. A. Hofferth and T. J. Owens. New York: Elsevier Science.

Hüttenmoser, M. 1995. "Children and Their Living Surroundings: Empirical Investigations into the Significance of Living Surroundings for the Everyday Life and Development of Children." *Children's Environments* 12: 403–13.

James, W. 1890. *The Principles of Psychology*. New York: Henry Holt.

Kaplan, R., and S. Kaplan. 1989. *The Experience of Nature: A Psychological Perspective*. New York: Cambridge University Press.

———. 2002. "Adolescents and the Natural Environment: A Time Out?" In *Children and Nature: Psychological, Sociocultural, and Evolutionary Investigations*, ed. P. H. Kahn and S. R. Kellert. Cambridge, Mass.: MIT Press.

Kaplan, S. 1995. "The Restorative Benefits of Nature: Toward an Integrative Framework." *Journal of Environmental Psychology* 15: 169–82.

Kaplan, S., and R. Kaplan. 1983. *Cognition and Environment: Functioning in an Uncertain World*. Ann Arbor, Mich.: Ulrich's.

Kirkby, M. 1989. "Nature as a Refuge in Children's Environments." *Children's Environments Quarterly* 6: 1–12.

Kotlowitz, A. 1991. *There Are No Children Here*. New York: Anchor Books.

Korpela, K. 2002. "Children's Environments." In *Handbook of environmental psychology*, ed. R. B. Bechtel and A. Churchman, 363–73. New York: John Wiley.

Korpela, K., M. Kyttä, and T. Hartig. 2002. "Restorative Experience, Self-Regulation, and Children's Place Preferences." *Journal of Environmental Psychology* 22: 387–98.

Kuo, F. E., M. Bacaicoa, and W. C. Sullivan. 1997. "Transforming Inner-City Landscapes: Trees, Sense of Safety and Preference." *Environment and Behavior* 30, no. 1: 28–59.

Kuo, F. E., and A. Faber Taylor. 2004. "A Potential Natural Treatment for Attention-Deficit/ Hyperactivity Disorder: Evidence from a National Study. *American Journal of Public Health* 94: 1580–86.

Luepker, R. V. 1999. "How Physically Active Are American Children and What Can We Do about It?" *International Journal of Obesity* 23, no. 2: S12–S17.

Moore, R., and D. Young. 1978. "Childhood Outdoors: Toward a Social Ecology of the Landscape." In *Human Behavior and Environment: Advances in Theory and Research*, vol. 3, *Behavior and Natural Environment*, ed. I. Altman and J. Wohlwill, 83–127). New York: Plenum Press.

Sallis, J. F., J. J. Prochaska, and W. C. Taylor. 2000. "A Review of Correlates of Physical Activity of Children and Adolescents." *Medicine and Science in Sports and Exercise* 32, no. 5: 963–75.

Sebba, R. 1991. "The Landscapes of Childhood: The Reflections of Childhood's Environment in Adult Memories and in Children's Attitudes." *Environment and Behavior* 23, no. 4: 395–422.

Sullivan, W. C., and F. E. Kuo. 1996. "Do Trees Strengthen Urban Communities, Reduce Domestic Violence?" *Technology Bulletin* #4. USDA Forest Service, Urban and Community Forestry Assistance Program.

Sturm, R. 2005. "Childhood Obesity—What We Can Learn from Existing Data on Societal Trends," Part 1. *Preventing Chronic Disease* [serial online] 2, no. 1: 1–9. http://www.cdc.gov/ped /issues/2005/ jan/04_0038.htm.

Tennessen, C. M., and B. Cimprich. 1995. "Views to Nature: Effects on Attention." *Journal of Environmental Psychology* 15: 77–85.

Wells, N. M. 2000. "At Home with Nature: Effects of "Greenness" on Children's Cognitive Functioning." *Environment and Behavior* 32: 775–95.

Wells, N. M., and G. W. Evans. 2003. "Nearby Nature: A Buffer of Life Stress among Rural Children." *Environment and Behavior* 35, no. 3: 311–30.

Wells, N. M., and K. S. Lekies. 2006. "Nature and the Life Course: Pathways from Childhood Nature Experiences to Adult Environmentalism." *Children Youth and Environment* 16, no. 1: 1–24.

Robin Moore and Nilda Cosco

STORIES FROM THE GARDEN

Nature Play for Young Children

Nilda Cosco, Ph.D., is Education Specialist, The Natural Learning Initiative, and Research Associate Professor in the College of Design, NC State University. Cosco's interests cover the impact of the built environment on the health and well-being of children and families, including the influence of nature on learning.

Robin Moore is Professor of Landscape Architecture, Adjunct Professor of Family and Consumer Sciences, and Director of the Natural Learning Initiative, North Carolina State University. He holds degrees in Architecture, London University, UK, and City and Regional Planning from MIT.

"I don't know why, but she immediately calms when I sit her down in front of the window," the childcare center teacher said, referring to the 12-month-old who, only moments before, had bawled her head off when her mother left for work. We are chatting with the teacher of an infant classroom. Pressing up against the window, a bed of perennials is in full summer bloom: black-eyed Susans, coneflowers, giant shasta daisies, anise, flags, all kinds of colors, textures, fragrances, and relationships to insects and birds. This was a only a sample of one "goodbye-in-the-morning-trauma"; however, the pre- and post-experimental treatment conditions were excellent and the results strongly indicative of a "therapeutic landscape effect." Play in natural settings offers children friendship, comfort, and recovery from the stresses of contemporary childhood.

The year was 1996, and the perennial bed was part of the first infant garden installed in a local childcare center by co-author Moore and his landscape architecture students. It was part of a renovation of the center's outdoor environment, including the toddler and preschool "play yards" or "play gardens." The center director and lead teachers requested the renovation because they knew there was a better design than dusty grass, half a dozen shade trees, dead-end paths, and brightly colored, manufactured play equipment.

In the mid-1990s, no literature or guidance was available for childcare center playgrounds, even for one that served families of a high-grade, high-tech company. The renovation fixed obvious problems such as the lack of shade (in hot North Carolina). They added "looped" wheeled-toy pathways for toddlers and preschoolers, wa-

ter play, and nature as requested by the teaching staff. The "nature" part was easy for the team of horticulture and landscape architecture students involved in the project. They chose perennials, ground covers, vines, and shrubs for the sensory stimulation they offered children. Other considerations included appropriate scale, maintenance, and nontoxicity.[1] The play area already has been through a second cycle of renovation, including building of a semi-covered outdoor classroom.

The rich landscape of three play yards offers fascinating and productive research settings for writers and students from local campuses. Co-author Cosco conducted dissertation research at this site and discovered statistically significant activity attributes of this closely packed environment that afford more physically active play.[2] Nature provides daily engagement for the children, who spend up to ten hours a day, five days a week, and fifty weeks of the year at the center. For a majority of children, this daily environment must satisfy their needs for sensory stimulation, social development, and cognitive challenge by presenting new opportunities for exploration and discovery. The natural world is the only way to satisfy these needs every day because it is alive and constantly changing.

Grasshopper Surprise

A year-old boy in diapers notices a grasshopper on one of the flagstones. He observes it for

a minute before approaching to pick it up. It hops into the grass but the boy, visually tracking it, toddles closer. The grasshopper leaps again, landing on top of a log, a meter from the flagstone. The child follows, fascinated for a minute or two, but comes too close. Now the insect hops into the flowerbed and finds a more substantial refuge. The boy, still intrigued, is no match for the grasshopper. Several days later, we notice the child crouching with arms flung back as if about to jump. Following the theory of perceptual learning, the jumping grasshopper can be considered an *event* affording the child's observation of a small animal and experimentation of his own movements, apparently stimulated by those of the grasshopper.[3]

Lessons from Pansies

In the same infant garden, another toddler collects pansy petals. He carefully removes them from the flower head one after the other and places them in his red bucket, learning that the world is made of groups of units. He follows a rhythmic sequence without interruption. When he is finished, he looks into his bucket, takes one of the petals, and tries to "reinsert" it onto the flower. It doesn't work! Thus he learns some actions are not reversible.

The "Violet Thing"

For three- or four-year-olds, the outdoors can provide daily adventures and problem-solving challenges. Fascination with nature starts at a very early age if children are given freedom to explore. A group of preschoolers is trying to get their hands on what they call the "violet thing" (violet hyacinth bean pod), from several hanging off the "vine teepee" in the garden. The children are carefully planning a strategy to grab the pod: It is hanging too high to reach from the ground. They pile up plastic blocks and add two large Tonka toy trucks to step on. After several failed attempts, one positions himself like a cat ready to pounce, jumps from the rickety pile of toys, grabs the pod, pulls it down, breaks it open, and disdainfully exclaims, "it's green inside!" His hypothesis negated, he discards the useless object he imagined would be purple.

Worms Looking for Their Mum

A girl is collecting small worms in a plastic cup from the wet area around the drinking fountain.

Two boys join her. The girl explains that the worms are looking for their mums. She walks around the play area with the cup, showing other children the worms and explaining their story. It was remarkable to find out that this girl had a difficult time saying goodbye to her own mother that morning. The re-enactment of a separation and reunion episode may have helped her to calm her anxiety.

Although common, most "stories from the garden" are not recorded or even noticed by caregivers. However, their influence on children's development is undeniable. Anecdotes and empirical investigations are beginning to indicate the power of nature and the possibility of harnessing it through design in order to integrate it into the lives of children.[4]

Our observations and research support the findings of other scientific research, notably that of Patrik Grahn and his colleagues in South Sweden and at the University of Illinois, that identify a significant relationship among nature and physical, social, psychological, and cognitive development of children.[5]

One such finding relates to attention span. Nature focuses children's attention, acting as a preventive mechanism or antidote to attention deficit disorders. These have become prevalent especially in the United States, where children consume 80 percent of the world's supply of Ritalin, an ADHD drug.[6]

Research suggests that play in nature could be a positive treatment and a substitute for drugs. Scientific research on the impact of "nearby nature" on the adult population reinforces these tentative conclusions. Psychologists Rachel and Stephen Kaplan emphasize the importance of "nearby nature" and its potential for inducing "focused attention" and psychological restoration for adults.[7] For children, nature needs to be literally hands-on and can produce similarly powerful effects.

Spontaneous interaction with the living environment encourages the desire to learn about plants, animals, and natural processes. Group explorations improve cooperation, strategic thinking, language, and knowledge of the natural world. Diverse environments accommodate the needs of different learning abilities. Teachers as facilitators allow children to enjoy complete experiences without interruption, a role that contributes to the ability to concentrate.

Opportunities to explore plants and animals help children to develop a reciprocal relationship with the world around them. Playing outdoors has a healing effect; the power of nature's regenerative processes supports personal development as well. The only necessary ingredients are an interactive environment and the freedom to enjoy it.

Notes

1. For a more complete set of selection criteria for children's gardens, see R. Moore, *Plants for Play: A Plant Selection Guide for Children's Outdoor Environments* (Berkeley: MIG Communications, 1993).

2. N. Cosco, "Motivation to Move: Physical Activity Affordances in Preschool Play Areas," Ph.D. dissertation, School of Landscape Architecture, Edinburgh College of Art, Heriot Watt University, 2006.

3. J. Gibson, *The Ecological Approach to Visual Perception* (Boston: Houghton-Mifflin, 1979); E. Gibson and A. Pick, *An Ecological Approach to Perceptual Learning and Development* (New York: Oxford University Press, 2000).

4. Cosco, "Motivation to Move."

5. P. Grahn, F. Mårtensson, B. Lindblad, P. Nilsson, and A. Ekman, "Ute på Dagis" ["Out in the Preschool"], *Stad and Land* 145 (1997); A. F. Faber Taylor, F. Kuo, and W. Sullivan, "Coping with ADD: The Surprising Connecting to Green Play Settings," *Environment and Behavior* 33, no. 1 (2001): 54.

6. T. Woodworth, "Statement before the Committee on Education and the Workforce Subcommittee on Early Childhood, Youth and Families," U.S. Drug Enforcement Administration, May 16, 2000, http://www.house.gov/ed _workforce/hearings/106th/ecyf/ritalin51600 /woodworth.htm; http://www.drugabuse.gov /infofacts/ritalin.html.

7. R. Kaplan and S. Kaplan, *The Experience of Nature: A Psychological Perspective* (Cambridge, U.K.: Cambridge University Press, 1989).

8. Winnicott, D. W. (1964). *The Child, the Family, and the Outside World*. Middlesex, England: Penguin Books Ltd.

Louise Chawla and David Driskell

HAVING A SAY ABOUT WHERE TO PLAY

A Serious Way to Learn Democracy

Louise Chawla is a Professor in the College of Architecture and Planning at the University of Colorado at Denver and Health Sciences Center, where she serves as a member of the Executive Committee of the Children, Youth and Environments Center for Research and Design.

David Driskell holds the UNESCO Chair in Growing Up in Cities in the Department of City and Regional Planning at Cornell University. He is a practicing planner with extensive experience in community participation.

For Expert Advice on Play, Ask a Child

Most people agree that young people need places to gather and play beyond the boundaries of their homes and yards. After all, providing recreation for children and youth is one of the main missions of parks and recreation departments in cities and towns across the nation, just as ensuring public open space and park areas is a core value of every city's planning department. Staffed by trained professionals, these departments have the lead responsibility for planning and implementing places and programs for play. What could children have to say about places to play that experts don't know already? And further, what possibly could be the value of involving young people in the design and management of places for play?

Until we listen to and involve young people, we have no way to answer these questions.

Adults certainly have their areas of expertise. They have the information on tax revenues, budget allocations, national standards, and population growth projections. But nobody knows better than young people themselves how possibilities for play "play out" at the level of their own communities. Children and their parents are the experts on local resources and risks, barriers and opportunities, family rules and daily routines. Children themselves are best qualified to tell us what is considered most fun if you are a boy or a girl; six or twelve or sixteen years old; fifteenth-generation African American, fifth-generation Irish American, or a new immigrant from Somalia, Cambodia, or the Dominican Republic. Children know the intricacies of their local environment and culture, which help determine not only the places that are available to them, but also the places where they feel safe and comfortable. Just as important, young people can bring energy and new ideas to the work of creating better public places for all ages.

This essay advocates for young people's direct participation in documenting where they play and gather with friends and then working with community organizations and local governments to improve recreation opportunities. We review research that suggests that this kind of direct participation in civic action is one of the best preparations for a life of democratic engagement. Through examples from a six-neighborhood program in New York, we will show young people taking steps to learn democracy by doing it, and share their recommendations to improve conditions for play in the city.

One outcome that these examples illustrate is that young people's experience challenges many adults' assumptions about planning for play. Although the young adolescents in this New York program described a wide range of places where they go to play, do sports, or hang out, their broad-ranging critique of their local environments often focused on issues not specific to play but nonetheless central to their ability to explore and have fun in public spaces. They often identified a local park as both a favorite and least-favorite place: one of the few public places available to them, and valued as such; but too often poorly designed, poorly managed, and poorly maintained. These lost spaces can be reclaimed not only as essential spaces for young people, but as opportunities for demonstrating democracy in action. As the examples that follow show, young people have the capacity, interest, and energy to be partners in transforming neighborhood spaces for play as well as in addressing related neighborhood issues.

From Consultation to Participation

The New York examples are all part of Growing Up in Cities (GUiC), an international action research initiative affiliated with UNESCO that engages children and youth in evaluating where they live, imagining and planning improvements to local places, and working in partnership with adults to realize their plans.[1] In most of its locations around the world, the project focuses on young adolescents from the ages of ten through fourteen, an age group that stands on the verge of adulthood, with considerable capacities to contribute to change, but still dependent on the resources of their immediate surroundings. In the low-income communities where the project typically is implemented, accessible resources for play need to be right at hand. Few participants have opportunities to go away for summer vacations or holidays, or even to travel to attractions in distant parts of their cities. For most of them, either they have affordable, safe places to play nearby, or none at all.

Kevin Lynch, the urban planner and designer who conceived of GUiC in the 1970s, anticipated that children's reports about the outdoor places they use usually would be at odds with adults' assumptions. When he introduced the project, he expected to learn about "the misperceptions of planners," as well as to show how to develop local research capabilities and mobilize public support to inform local and national policies related to children.[2] Unfortunately, the first round of project sites in Australia, Argentina, Mexico, and Poland confirmed his prediction that planners would tend to misjudge children's needs and the impact of their policies. Since the project was revived in 1995, new sites around the world continue to demonstrate that this re-mains true all too often.

In the summer of 2005, GUiC was introduced in six sites in New York in the boroughs of the Bronx, Brooklyn, Manhattan, and Queens. Coordinated by the office of the UNESCO Chair for Growing Up in Cities at Cornell University and facilitated by university students in partnership with site-based schools and community organizations, the project brings young people together around shared goals to improve local conditions. The issues that have emerged typically revolve around safety as well as the creation, design, and management of places to play, rest, dream, and hang out with friends. As at other contemporary sites, the work reflects transformations in public perceptions of children's rights and capabilities since Lynch first proposed GUiC to UNESCO in 1970.

When Lynch decided to ask young adolescents how they used and evaluated their cities, he was drawing on a tradition of advocacy planning that brought planners together with grassroots groups to help community residents formulate and advance their ideas about local problems and potential solutions. What was radical was that he proposed to enlist children in this process in order to understand their lives in urbanizing areas of particular relevance for planning policy. In the approach that he developed, children began by drawing their images of their neighborhoods and their cities and talking about where they went, what they did, the places that they liked

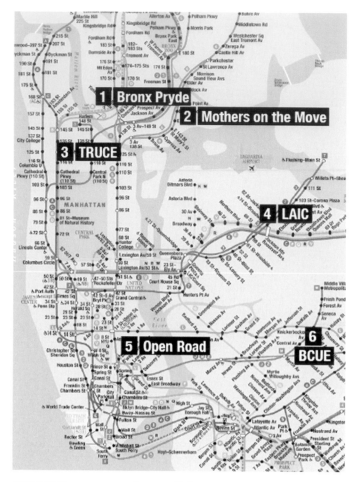

GUiNYC partners and map of sites

prove their communities and that government officials would listen. In Australia and Argentina, where project facilitators presented young people's recommendations to local councils, officials paid no heed. In the 1970s, the idea that children could have something worthwhile to say about how to create more livable cities was still a generation ahead of its time.

What drives GUiC today is a growing recognition, nationally and internationally, that successful community development requires local residents' participation—including the participation of children and youth. This recognition is embodied in a number of important international documents, the most important of which is the Convention on the Rights of the Child (CRC). In 1989, the United Nations adopted this document, which articulates children's rights to protection, the provision of basic needs, and participation in decisions that affect their lives.[3] In particular, Article 31 of the CRC recognizes "the right of the child to rest and leisure, to engage in play and recreational activities appropriate to the age of the child and to participate freely in cultural life and the arts." All of the member nations of the United Nations have ratified the CRC with the exception of the United States and Somalia, but the Convention is accepted so widely that it has assumed the force of customary law as a worldwide standard of government obligations to promote children's well-being.

The mehods that Kevin Lynch introduced still

best, places they avoided or feared, and their expectations and hopes for how their locality would change. Small groups of participants also led researchers on walking tours. In addition, researchers collected maps, observed children's activities in streets and parks, took photographs, and spoke with parents and officials about their views of how their city functioned for children and how it was changing.

Lynch hoped that children would then use this rich base of information to propose how to im-

Photography is one GUiC method used by young people as they explore and document their local area. Here, two young people in the Lower Eastside use a "photoframe" exercise to highlight places in their neighborhood that they define as "teen-friendly" or "unfriendly" as well as places that are "safe" or "dangerous." *Credit: Open Road of NY/GUiNYC*

remain a core part of GUiC. However, today there is also a commitment to ensure that local projects move from the initial stage of research to take action on young people's ideas.[4] This commitment reflects a significant shift from a model of advocacy planning, in which adult professionals consult with a community and then act on its behalf, to a model of participatory action research in which communities—including young people—are partners in both research and action.

Schools of Democracy

When young people in the Growing Up in New York City (GUiNYC) project documented where they went to play and relax and identified how to make public places more attractive or accessible, they enrolled in a new contact sport:

democracy. By bringing young people together around issues that matter to them, in partnership with adults who already are seasoned in processes of community development, GUiC deliberately seeks to create "schools of democracy" in the sense that the Frenchman Alexis de Tocqueville first used this term.[5] When de Tocqueville traveled across the United States in 1831, he observed that voluntary community associations were one of the new nation's most distinctive characteristics, and he called them schools of democracy because they enabled people to practice the skills and values that a well-functioning democracy requires.

Adults who create opportunities for young people to "learn by doing" can draw on more than 50 years of research on political socialization, which investigates how children and youth develop knowledge and interest about government and politics and a willingness to engage in civic life. Several of the leading researchers in this field have concluded that one of the most effective ways for young people to learn how politics works and why it matters is to take action on local issues.[6] This learning-by-doing model contrasts with the traditional teaching of civics, which drills students on the branches of government, the succession of the presidents, and how a bill becomes a law in Congress, with little or no attention to local government and community decision-making.

As the experience of GUiC in New York and elsewhere shows, when children and youth get involved in issues at local levels, their engagement not only helps improve the design and management of public spaces, but also contributes to their development of democratic skills and values. By taking on local issues that concern them, young people learn how to gather evidence, analyze it, organize themselves, negotiate differences, find allies, and engage with civil society and government representatives to work for the common good. The issues that concern children may change as they grow up, but at any age, these remain the bedrock skills of democratic citizenship.

A number of studies in the field of political socialization demonstrate that people who serve in community organizations in childhood and adolescence are more likely to contribute to civic organizations in adulthood and maintain an interest in politics.[7] Further, young people are most likely to develop a sense of civic obligation when service activities include opportunities for public action.[8] Unfortunately, survey data in the United States show that children in urban areas with high rates of poverty are significantly less likely to report community service than their peers in suburban or rural neighborhoods.[9] They are also less likely to see adults model civic behaviors such as voting and membership in voluntary associations.[10]

Despite what we know about how to encour-age political engagement among young people, the overall trend of young people's participation in political activities is not encouraging. For example, in a recent survey of fourteen year-olds in 28 democracies, including the United States, four out of five students reported that they did not intend to participate in conventional political activities when they became adults, such as joining a party, writing letters to newspapers, or standing as a candidate for a local office.[11] Most said that they did intend to vote; but in the United States, election participation by 18- to 24-year-olds declined from 52 percent in 1972 (the first year after the voting age was lowered to 18) to 37 percent in 2000.[12] Voting by this age group showed an upswing in the 2004 presidential election, but at 42 percent, it still fell significantly below the rates of older ages.[13]

One bright spot in young people's civic engagement is their interest in the environment and social issues. In the 28-nation survey, students were likely to endorse participation in environmental or community organizations as a way to express citizenship.[14] In another survey in seven nations, including the United States, one of the most frequent forms of civic engagement that adolescents claimed was protection of the environment.[15] For many, environmental action has become a route into political action.

One of the most striking aspects of decades of research on political socialization is that conclusions converge about the mechanisms that pro-

Young people in several of the GUiNYC sites focused on environmental actions as their top priorities, including neighborhood cleanups and park improvement campaigns, such as the "Prove It with Improvements" or PIWI campaign developed by young people in the Lower Eastside. *Credit: Open Road of NY/GUiNYC*

mote political knowledge, interest, and behavior, whether findings are drawn from large-scale surveys or qualitative interviews. One of the most potent factors associated with the development of democratic values and civic commitment is a family culture of social responsibility and political interest.[16] Although projects like GUiC connect with children through schools and community institutions beyond the home, this finding underscores the importance of involving parents in their children's initiatives whenever possible, or at a minimum, keeping them well informed and supportive of their children's efforts. This is of particular importance when working with young people whose families are not politically active, as is often the case for young people whose parents are undocumented immigrants

while they themselves may be legal citizens.

Other major factors associated with the development of political knowledge, interest, and action include:

- opportunities to discuss political issues, hear a variety of perspectives, and feel that one's own ideas receive attention;
- direct confrontations with problems in the public domain, such as social inequities or the degradation of the environment;
- opportunities to tackle problems and practice activism;
- supportive social networks that show young people that their efforts are valued and that they are not alone in their work.

Using examples from GUiNYC, the remainder of this chapter describes how each of these factors associated with political development can be integrated into program activities with young people, so that community programs focused on the local environment can function as deliberate and effective "schools of democracy." Although this chapter features GUiNYC, the principles and processes that it describes could be applied to any project that involves young people in collective action to create better conditions in their communities.

Open Discussion and Deliberative Debate

Freedom to associate and share views on political matters is one of the most basic civil liberties, but in addition to being an essential criterion of democracy, it is a means for young people to cultivate an interest in politics. Its importance is shown by more than 25 years of research in civics education. "Rote and ritual" approaches, like saluting the flag or memorizing how a bill becomes law, have little effect, but what repeatedly *is* associated with students' political knowledge and interest are classes characterized by an open climate for the discussion of public issues.[17] When students say that they feel comfortable expressing their opinions about political issues in class, and multiple views get explored, they tend to score high on political interest and knowledge and a sense of political efficacy, and report the most political behaviors, such as following current events in the news and talking about political topics outside of school.[18]

Many teachers, however, deliberately steer clear of these topics, fearful of stirring up conflict and controversy. It then falls to after-school and out-of-school programs like GUiNYC to make time for young people to talk together about issues in the public realm, including opportunities for play and recreation in public places. While it is true that one of the guiding principles of CUiC is "Don't just talk about it—do something!" an equally important principle to remember is "Don't just do something—talk about it!" Chances to combine action with reflection are also central to John Dewey's philosophy of edu-

cation for democracy.[19]

Research on moral development suggests why open discussion is so important. Numerous studies show that children tend to progress to higher levels of moral reasoning when they have opportunities to hear and consider a range of perspectives, including levels of reasoning a step or two above their own.[20] This is especially true when children have chances for "reasoning that operates on the reasoning of another": not merely restating what another person says, but transforming it by clarifying it, extending it, critiquing it, integrating it into their own thinking, or seeking compromises or common ground.[21] Children feel especially free to do this in the fairly symmetrical give-and-take of discussions with peers.

In the GUiNYC sites, opportunities for young people to discuss their ideas and priorities and negotiate differences of opinion were a central feature of program activities. Following two weeks of neighborhood exploration through interviews, walking tours, photography, and mapping, participants worked together to agree on shared priorities and decide upon a course of action. While they often made final decisions through a group vote, they first discussed the relationships among various issues as well as trade-offs between different suggestions for action, taking time for all opinions to be voiced, heard, and considered.

To guide discussions, each group was asked to

Young people at GUiNYC's site in Queens present and defend their ideas to their peers as they work as a group to identify a priority action project. *Credit: LAIC/GUiNYC*

consider things they could do themselves without any help, as well as things they could do if they had adult assistance or additional resources, and things they needed adults to do for them. They also were asked to consider different kinds of actions: changing the physical environment, changing people's attitudes, and changing policies.

In Queens, young people had the idea of creating a mock courtroom in which each small group would present their case for why a particular issue and action should be given highest priority by the entire group. During their presentations and cross-examinations, they drew on the strategies, language, and dramatic effects many of them knew well from television programs. After all arguments had been heard and the relationships and trade-offs among different ideas had been debated, the "jury" deliberated and reached a consensus verdict. They decided to undertake

two action projects—a community mural and a neighborhood clean-up—so that everyone could work on at least one project that they felt was important.

For these young people, "play space" meant "hang-out space." Creating a safe space for them to hang out was their highest priority, but they felt that it was something they needed to work on in the long term, while their two short-term projects would be good steps in that direction. The mural was to be an expression of youth voice, youth issues, and the positive power of young people to make a difference in their community. The neighborhood clean-up had as much to do with taking care of the local environment as it did with creating a neighborhood that expressed a positive attitude toward its residents, including young people. As one young person noted, "All the litter makes it feel like this is a place where nobody cares about you."

Confronting Problems and Practicing Collective Action

If public discourse is the lifeblood of democracy, then personal experiences in the public realm are the flesh and bones that give young people something to think about and discuss. A number of studies show that participation in community service, political volunteering, and membership in school organizations in childhood and adolescence are associated with higher rates of community service, political volunteering, and voting in adulthood.[22] In the survey of adolescents in seven nations, community volunteering was one of the factors most strongly related to civic interest.[23] According to the authors of a report on the survey, "Experiences of membership in institutions beyond the family are necessary for the social integration of young people into a political community and for their identification with a common good."[24] These findings come from young people's involvement in a variety of activities, from social programs like tutoring or service in a homeless shelter to environmental clean-ups and campaigns.

Young people claim that through these activities, they gain increased confidence, the ability to speak in public and exercise leadership, and greater facility to deal with people and accept them for who they are.[25] In a questionnaire study of 269 young people aged 13 to 20 who were involved in a variety of municipal youth projects in Austria, from 85 to 88 percent said that they increased their abilities to work in teams, adopt more realistic perspectives, and cope with problems.[26] At the same time, this study underscores how important it is for adults to partner with young people in their efforts. Although 85 percent of the youth believed that participation had strengthened their democratic consciousness, 56 percent stated that they had become more disinterested in politics—exactly the same percentage who said that they had the impression that their efforts were not taken seriously by adults, in particular politicians. An evaluation of a GUiC initiative in South Africa exposed the same risk.[27] Three years after the Greater Johannesburg Metropolitan Council commissioned a four-district study of children's public space needs, young participants were recontacted and interviewed. Although they still expressed appreciation for the experience of expressing their views, they believed that the government should not have wasted their time unless it seriously intended to act on at least some of their recommendations.

It is possible that young people who become involved in political and service organizations in childhood are already significantly different from nonvolunteers, and simply carry these special characteristics into adulthood. A long-term follow-up of a special program in a Pennsylvania high school, however, suggests that political involvement may alter participants in lasting ways.[28] For four consecutive years, the teacher of a senior social studies class involved his students in assisting the City Planning Commission to prepare a master plan for anticipated growth. Thirty years later, alumni of these classes were compared with other seniors who happened to get assigned to conventional classes, but who were otherwise similar. Over the intervening 30 years, members of the planning project were four times more likely than nonmembers to have belonged to volunteer groups and twice as likely to have been officers in civic and service organizations.

A more recent demonstration that participation in city planning can change civic habits is the Youth Planner initiative in Hampton, Virginia.[29] In 1992, the City Council of Hampton established a new city department, the Coalition for Youth, whose responsibilities include ensuring that young people in the city will be "seen, heard, and respected as citizens of the community." To achieve this goal, two high school students work alongside other members of the planning department as paid part-time staff, regularly conducting surveys and focus groups with their peers about issues of concern, keeping other young people informed about opportunities for community engagement, and facilitating a Youth Commission with the authority to represent issues of importance for children and youth, recommend policy, and appropriate funds. In the 2004 election, the voting rate of eligible young adult voters in Hampton exceeded the national average by 29 percent.

The power of jumping into action on community issues—even being thrown in—was illustrated dramatically by one of GUiNYC's school-based sites, where a number of young people were "assigned" to participate due to their poor academic performance. For the GUiNYC facilitators, this was an unwelcome development, as a core principle of the project is that participation should be entirely voluntary.

Being placed into the program to fulfill summer-school requirements was inconsistent with this principle. Nonetheless, the program continued with approximately half of the participants being "placements" rather than volunteers.

One lesson that quickly emerged was the value of getting out of the classroom and into the neighborhood. In the classroom, interactions were extremely difficult. Many of the young people showed challenging behaviors and a significant lack of motivation, and site leaders reacted by focusing on establishing control. However, as the group moved from the classroom to a neighborhood activity, individual and group dynamics were transformed immediately. A young man who 30 minutes earlier had threatened to cut a fellow student now was skipping down the sidewalk with the same student, chasing a butterfly. Young people who had very little to say in the classroom became effusive in their descriptions of what was happening on each block—what they had seen, what they had heard, and even ghost stories from aunts, cousins, and grandparents about particular abandoned properties. Even the site leaders were noticeably more relaxed, with much more positive interactions with the young participants.

As the summer proceeded, many of the young people at this site became increasingly engaged in program activities, concluding their summer with a group action that included a press conference for local media and elected officials. Young

Young people in the South Bronx present their neighborhood evaluation results and ideas for action to a press conference that included a local television news channel, two radio stations, and several elected officials. *Credit: GUiNYC*

people who five weeks previously were too shy or disinterested to give their name in front of a group of their peers were now standing in front of a news camera and reading their statements about issues in their neighborhood and their ideas for change. At the beginning of the summer, just over 30 percent stated that they thought they could make a difference in their neighborhood. At summer's end, 85 percent felt that way.

As school started in the fall, these same young people lobbied their principal to form an after-school club so that they could continue their work together. The principal not only created the club, but also committed their school to a second summer of research and action. She now refers to the GUiNYC group as a leadership team. With the support of university interns and community partners, young people in this group currently are working with the New York Parks and Recreation Department to secure a vacant property in their neighborhood to create a community garden that also will serve as an outdoor classroom and a place to relax with friends.

Building a Spirit of Solidarity

A family culture of social responsibility, opportunities to discuss public issues, personal confrontations with the reality of these issues, and initial experiences with civic involvement are all factors that motivate young people to take action for the common good. But what sustains them in this path? In interviews, Canadian youth from ages 16 to 20 who were nominated by community agencies as exemplary volunteers were presented with this question.[30] Some spoke of the satisfaction of making a difference when they experienced positive outcomes from their work. Mostly, however, they spoke about social support: family members or friends who encouraged their involvement, the new relationships that they formed in the course of their work, and a feeling of belonging and appreciation in their service organization. Some also observed that, in the course of their work, civic responsibility became part of their sense of identity. It became part of the way others viewed them and integral to their own understanding of who they were.

These answers echo reflections by adult activists for social justice and the environment when they have been asked to review their lives.[31] Most speak of having witnessed exemplars of care for the environment or social justice when they were children or young adults—often parents or other family members. After initially taking action in causes that caught their interest, their commitment deepened, along with a growing sense of solidarity with their organizations and with other activists in the same cause. Supportive social relationships both led them into civic action and sustained them there.

Similar sentiments were expressed by the young people who participated in the first summer of the GUiNYC project. In interviews, questionnaires, and focus groups at the end of the summer, young people talked about how much they enjoyed making new friends and working together to make a difference in their neighborhoods. Some of the new friendships most valued by young participants were those with the older high school youth who helped facilitate activities at many of the sites. Similarly, these older youth valued being mentors and role models, and enjoyed spending time with the younger middle-school participants, often surprised by the resourcefulness and ideas of those they viewed as being from "the next generation."

One particularly striking example of relationship building and a spirit of solidarity emerged from the GUiNYC site in Queens, in which a community-based organization partnered with a local school. Roughly half of the participants came from each group. They represented different socioeconomic backgrounds: stable middle- and working-class families on the side of the school; and on the side of the community organization, a number of households where parents were low-income immigrants. During the first week of the program, tensions ran high and there were several disputes. By the end of the summer, not only had the young people forged friendships between the two groups, but they had developed a genuine commitment to each other. When young people at the school decided to form an after-school club to continue their work, they told the school administration they would do so only if those from the community organization could also participate. Young people from the school also have visited the offices of the community organization on numerous occasions, and joined several immigrants' rights rallies and marches.

When the GUiNYC project director visited each of the six sites seven months after the summer project activities had stopped, he was surprised to find that young people's enthusiasm for their work not only was intact, but that it had found many avenues of expression in the intervening months. Participants had formed after-school clubs at two sites and had undertaken various other follow-up activities at five of the six sites. Several of their initiatives involved play and recreation. On the Lower Eastside, young people had moved forward with their plans for organizing and launching a youth-led parks improvement campaign, which they named the PIWI Campaign (Prove It With Improvements). They also started working with a partner organization to start a new site in northern Harlem. In Queens, young people's initiatives included finding a permanent location for their community mural and developing a safe youth hang-out space. In the South Bronx, a site is nearly secure for young people to create a youth-designed and managed community garden.

Behind all of these activities, a number of changes—subtle and profound—have developed in the adults and organizations involved, including the university faculty and students. They too have developed new relationships and friendships that are creating new opportunities for collaboration, learning, and action. Along with young people, many of the adults have valued the collaborative nature of the project, and the feeling of being part of something larger than oneself or one's own neighborhood. Feeling connected to the citywide project coalition and the international initiative of CUiC has helped young people see their world and themselves differently. They are a part of a whole, with confidence that each part has something significant to offer in making positive change in their community and their world.

Young people in Queens used a community mural project to express some of the values they agreed upon as a group, including the value of diversity, the importance of youth voice and participation, the need to protect the environment, and the connections between their neighborhood and the world at large. *Credit: LAIC / GUiNYC*

Notes

1. For an introduction to Growing Up in Cities, see Louise Chawla, ed., *Growing Up in an Urbanising World* (London/Paris: Earthscan Publications/UNESCO, 2002); and David Driskell, *Creating Better Cities with Children and Youth* (London/Paris: Earthscan Publications /UNESCO, 2002).

2. Kevin Lynch, *Growing Up in Cities* (Cambridge, Mass.: MIT Press, 1977).

3. The full text of the Convention on the Rights of the Child is available at www.unicef.org/crc /crc.htm. It defines a "child" as anyone below the age of 18.

4. L. Chawla, N. Blanchet-Cohen, N. Cosco, D. Driskell, J. Kruger, K. Malone, R. Moore, and B. Percy-Smith, "Don't Just Listen—Do Something! Lessons Learned about Governance from the Growing Up in Cities Project," *Children, Youth and Environments* 15, no. 2 (2005): 53–88 (retrieved 2/1/06 from http:// www.colorado.edu/journals/cye/).

5. A. de Tocqueville, *Democracy in America* (1835; reprint, New York: New American Library, 2001).

6. P. Conover and D. Searing, "Democracy, Citizenship, and the Study of Political Socialization," in *Developing Democracy*, ed. I. Budge and D. McKay (London: Sage, 1994); R. G. Niemi and J. Junn, *Civic Education: What Makes Students Learn* (New Haven: Yale University Press, 1998); J. Torney-Purta, J. Schwille, and J. Amadeo, eds., *Civic Education Across Countries* (Amsterdam/Washington, D.C.: International Association for the Evaluation of Educational Achievement/National Council for the Social Studies, 1999).

7. J. Younisss, J. A. McLellan, and M. Yates, "What We Know about Engendering Civic Identity," *American Behavioral Scientist* 40 (1997): 620–31.

8. E. Reidel, "The Impact of High School community Service Programs on Students' Feelings of Civic Obligation," *American Politics Research* 30, no. 5 (2002): 499–527.

9. R. Atkins and D. Hart, "Neighborhoods, Adults, and the Development of Civic Identity in Urban Youth," *Applied Developmental Science* 7, no. 3 (2003): 156–64.

10. D. Hart and R. Atkins, "Fostering Citizenship in Urban Youth," *Applied Developmental Science* 6 (2002): 227–37.

J. Torney-Purta, R. Lehmann, H. Oswald, and W. Schultz, *Citizenship and Education in Twenty-eight Countries* (Amsterdam: International Association for the Evaluation of Educational Achievement, 2001).

12. Y. Rosenberg, "Lost Youth," *American Demographics* 26, no. 2 (2004): 17–19.

13. CIRCLE (Center on Information and Research on Civic Learning and Engagement), "Youth Voting in the 2004 Election," *Social Education* 69, no. 1 (2005): 33–35.

14. Torney-Purta et al., *Citizenship and Education*.

15. C. Flanagan, B. Jonsson, L. Botcheva, B. Csapo, J. Bowes, P. Macek, I. Averina, and E. Sheblanova, "Adolescents and the 'Social Contract': Developmental Roots of Citizenship in Seven Countries," in *Community Service and Civic Engagement in Youth,* ed. M. Yates and J. Youniss, 135–55 (New York: Cambridge University Press, 1998).

15. For a review, see Sheldon Berman, *Children's Social Consciousness and the Development of Social Responsibility* (Albany: State University of New York Press, 1997).

17. C. L. Hahn, *Becoming Political* (New York: State University of New York Press, 1998); Niemi and Junn, *Civic Education*; J. V. Torney, A. N. Oppenheim, and R. F. Farnen, *Civic Education in Ten Countries* (New York: Halsted Press of John Wiley, 1975); Torney-Purta et al., *Citizenship and Education in Twenty-eight Countries.*

18. Reviewed in Hahn (1998), pp. 179–81. See also Torney-Purta et al., *Citizenship and Education in Twenty-eight Countries.*

19. J. Dewey, *Democracy and Education* (New York: Macmillan, 1916).

20. L. Kohlberg, "Moral Stages and Motivation," in *Moral Development and Behavior*, ed. T. Lickona, 31–53 (New York: Holt, Rinehart and Winston, 1976).

21. M. W. Berkowitz and J. C. Gibbs, "Measuring the Developmental Features of Moral Discussion," *Merrill-Palmer Quarterly* 29, no. 4 (1983): 399–410; W. Damon and M. Killen, "Peer Interactions and the Process of Change in Children's Moral Reasoning," *Merrill-Palmer Quarterly* 28, no. 3 (1982): 347–67.

22 Youniss, McLellan, and Yates, "What We Know about Engendering Civic Identity."

23. C. Flanagan, J. Bowes, B. Jonsson, B. Csapo, and E. Sheblanova, "Ties that Bind: Correlates of Adolescents' Civic Commitment in Seven Countries," *Journal of Social Issues* 54, no. 3 (1998): 457–75.

24. Ibid., 458.

25. S. M. Pancer and M. W. Pratt, "Social and Family Determinants of Community Service Involvement in Canadian Youth," in *Roots of Civic Identity*, ed. M. Yates and J. Youniss, 32–55 (Cambridge: Cambridge University Press, 1999); D. Roker, K. Player, and J. Coleman, "Exploring Adolescent Altruism: British Young People's Involvement in Voluntary Work and Campaigning," in *Roots of Civic Identity*, 56–72.

26. B. Riepl, "Political Participation of Youth in Austria," in *Political Participation of Youth Below Voting Age*, ed. B. Riepl and H. Wintersberger, 23–61 (Vienna: European Centre, 1999).

27. J. Clements, "How Crazy Can It Be? An Assessment, Three Years Later, of Outcomes from a Participatory Project with Children in Johannesburg," *Children, Youth and Environments* 15, no. 2 (2005): 105–16 (retrieved on June 7, 2006 from www.colorado.edu/journals/cye).

28. J. Beane, J. Turner, D. Jones, and R. Lipka,

Long-Term Effects of Community Service Programs, *Curriculum Inquiry* 11, no. 2 (1981): 143–55.

29. C. Carlson, "Youth with Influence: The Youth Planner Initiative in Hampton, Virginia, *Children, Youth and Environments* 15, no. 2 (2005): 211–26 (retrieved 6/10/06 from http://www.colorado.edu/journals/cye).

30. Pancer and Pratt, "Social and Family Determinants of Community Service Involvement in Canadian Youth."

31. A. Colby and W. Damon, *Some Do Care* (New York: Free Press, 1992); L. Chawla, "Life Paths into Effective Environmental Action," *Journal of Environmental Education* 29, no. 3 (1999): 11–21; S. Zavestoski, "Constructing and Maintaining Ecological Identities," in *Identity and the Natural Environment*, ed. S. Clayton and S. Opotow, 297–315. Cambridge, Mass.: MIT Press, 2003).

Stuart Brown

PLAY AS AN ORGANIZING PRINCIPLE

Clinical Evidence, Personal Observations

Stuart Brown is the founder-president of the National Institute for Play (www.nifplay.org). He has made a life odyssey of the study of play as an organizing principle, attempting to bring a rich, highly diverse, anciently derived, natural process into a focus through his own life experiences, many of which have been viewed through the lens of biology and human behavioral science.

Background

I am a physician-psychiatrist by training and practice, but more recently I have engaged in independent scholarship, educational film production, and popular writing. I generally rely on clinical observation to demonstrate a phenomenon and then go searching for "explanations" that best explain and characterize it. The general subject of *play* in animals and humans gradually has emerged as a broad category of behavior that warrants a fresh look (Brownlee 1997). Play is generally easy to recognize, but very elusive and difficult to define. The views given here offer the play enthusiast and student fresh ways to see the subject and are designed to stimulate personal examination of the culture and biology of playfulness.

As children, all safe and well-fed kids *experience* play as important. From the moment of an infant's earliest post-feeding nipple play, play occurs naturally and is the engine that drives much of the spontaneous activity of our childhood. It energizes children worldwide and fosters a child's play culture, which differs in form and language from that of the adult (Sutton-Smith 1974, 1972).

The play of my childhood was open. I enjoyed roughhousing with my peer group, nonorganized school games, afternoon unsupervised play, and exploratory roaming, all without much adult oversight. The internal narratives that defined my childhood sense of reality were similar to those depicted in some of the writings of Sutton-Smith (McMahon and Sutton-Smith 1995; Sutton-Smith et al. 1995). These early, private, stream-of-consciousness childhood stories are considered outrageous by the prevailing adult culture (Sutton-Smith 1981). Though culturally sculpted, the spontaneous narratives and stories of children appear structurally similar now to those of thirty or forty years ago (Sutton-Smith et al. 1995).

I also was fortunate enough to have parents who interfered little with the spontaneity of play and had an extended family who prioritized childhood and adult play highly, a condition not unusual in the 1940s. Play was unquestioned and never viewed analytically, but was honored as important, except in temporary pious moments of throwbacks to Puritanical cultural over-control. Most adults have significant amnesia regarding

their own play unless systematically summoned to recall it. They tend to become threatened by the very behavior they once spontaneously enjoyed (Sutton-Smith 1993; Pellegrini 1989).

Adults tend to compartmentalize their lives into work-play divisions, which is not the way of children. For children, virtually all of their nonsurvival activities are play. This sparse description of childhood play is not meant to be an ideological pitch for an impractically permissive societal approach to play management, but rather should serve as a partial description to open the door of memory to individuals' natural history of play. This process often positively shifts adults to re-evaluate their attitudes toward play in their own and their children's lives.

I do not recall any specific transitional moments when duty, responsibility, productivity, and other "adult" behaviors became more rewarded than play, or exactly why or when a work-play separation occurred, but it did, and it seemed normal.

Medical Studies and Play

My first awareness that play warranted clinical explanation came while I was a medical student rotating through the hospital pediatric services, observing and helping to care for desperately ill infants and children. As sick children began to recover, often the first signal of their return to wellness was their erupting sense of humor or other signs of spontaneous play. Their playful ways were frequently the most reliable signs of impending recovery and often preceded positive changes in temperature levels or laboratory findings. Now, hospital pediatric departments regularly provide play areas and programs for inpatients, recognizing the role of play in the healing process.

When a rubella (viral German measles) epidemic hit Houston, the Texas Medical Center mobilized to assist the victims. With David Freedman as the principal investigator, the center began to follow the development of the disease in many seriously ill, congenitally infected babies. As they slowly recovered, we used then state-of-the-art technology to examine the emergence of audition, sight, pain perception, and other developing modalities that had been damaged by the viral assault (Brown and Freedman 1970). Most of these infants were affected profoundly by their disease and suffered central nervous system damage as well as peripheral defects. Many were clinically deaf and blind, often incapable of vocalizations or even of withdrawal responses to pain. As the virus was cleared by their developing immune systems in the presence of loving and concerned parents, those who did not suffer profound irreversible damage slowly began to recover. This "slow-motion" recovery allowed windows of observation normally obscured by already-completed fetal maturation, or missed due to the normal avalanche of developmental changes during the first months of extra-uterine life. By measuring brain activity using noninvasive electroencephalogram (EEG), we were able to recognize the first signals that these disease-compromised babies were capable of detecting and integrating sight, sound, or pain. We used this information to intervene therapeutically at the earliest moment to provide the best prognosis for these infants. During the times the virus was most active, the signs of recognition were absent. In uninfected newborns, definite visual, auditory, and pain responses generally already are intact at birth and change progressively and rapidly as maturation occurs. During this special time of observed recovery in the rubella kids, I incidentally noted that play behavior preceded the EEG establishment of perceptual awareness.

Play, as it emerged in this late-1960s research setting, was a positive prognostic sign that differentiated those whose nervous systems would integrate and heal from those who were damaged permanently. Play was a sign of impending cognitive and perceptual normalcy in healing children. The possibility that play behavior itself may have a sculpting action on neural patterning warrants further research. The notion fits well with the growing body of play-related neuroscience that is the result of major new technologic capabilities.

Mass Murderers and Play

During the rubella studies, I was appointed to a research team assigned to understand the motives and life of the Texas Tower mass murderer Charles Whitman. After killing his wife and mother, this 25-year-old architectural engineering student at the University of Texas–Austin mounted the campus tower and with deadly accurate fire killed 17 and wounded 31 before being gunned down by vigilante and police crossfire. Whitman had been a model student, a supposedly loving husband and son, at age 12 the United States' youngest Eagle scout, an NROTC scholarship recipient, and an ex-Marine. John Connally, then governor of Texas, who had been wounded in the Kennedy assassination, was urgent in his insistence that we discern what made Whitman tick. The Texas legislature fully funded a task force to find answers. In the late 1960s, fear reigned that assassins and havoc were taking over society.

That in-depth study allowed us to dissect Whitman's psychobiology intricately. We called in a broadly based, multidisciplinary group of distinguished consulting experts, ranging from pathologists, toxicologists, neuroanatomists, and neurologists, to graphologists, sociologists, neuropsychologists, and other specialists. We conducted field interviews that reconstructed Whitman's life in as much detail as possible and catalogued every available aspect of his behavior. Our investigation included the written and verbal recollections of the family doctor who delivered him and cared for his mother (for example, we learned that she was kicked in the stomach by Whitman's father when six months pregnant with Charles). We conducted extensive interviews with his large family, examined childhood drawings, and collected nursery school anecdotes. We systematically organized lore from friends, dissected his lengthy diaries, gained access to his medical and military records, and reviewed home movies, school records, snapshots, and so on. As we re-created his life, we began to gain a consistent recognition of his personal ecology and development, weighing as many factors that defined and predicted his behavior as we could.

The full compilation of data was compelling. The task force concluded that the conditions that led to his violent and tragically destructive behavior were set in motion early by specific family experiences, which included physical and emotional abuse, play deprivation, paternal over-control, practice with weapons, and other factors. Viewing his last months with the information gleaned from our field interviews and from the autopsy and tissue studies, we felt that the crescendo of drama related to his parents' chronically abusive relationship became his perceived responsibility, and was the major precipitating stress leading to mass murder. By three months before the tower tragedy, he was having homicidal fantasies that he shared with a campus psychiatrist. Although he maintained a Mr. Clean public image, evidence of decompensation could be found. He was receiving daily phone abuse and demeaning diatribes from his father, culminating in a particularly cutting conversation the day before his ascent of the tower. We interpreted the final violent and suicidal acts as being triggered by his sense of powerlessness, humiliation, and entrapment. His inability to find coping techniques through play, humor, safe reciprocal friendships, and other distancing and stress-lowering habits were striking findings agreed upon by all members of our team as extremely significant. We originally had expected to discover a brain tumor and drugs as primary causal agents, but our intensive investigation weighed abuse and play deprivation as the major factors placing him and his future victims at risk.

The Whitman study led to a more organized selected pilot study of 26 young murderers who were interviewed throughout the state of Texas (Brown and Lomax 1969). By design, we chose to examine young males whose only crime had been homicide, and who had been convicted less than two years prior to our study. The study group was surprisingly culturally heterogeneous. We selected a comparative group of young males with similar demographics from a large epidemiological study of medical care then underway in Texas. We interviewed all participants with a structured format. In the young male murderers, we found that significant physical abuse had occurred in 90 percent of the cases. Findings we were not expecting were play deprivation and/or major play abnormalities, which also occurred at the 90 percent level. The nonhomicidal group showed abuse and play abnormalities at below the ten percent level. Play began to be seen as more important, but exactly how and why was not clear.

What these studies repeatedly revealed, and what struck our research team as unexpected, was that *normal play behavior was virtually absent throughout the lives of highly violent, anti-social men,* regardless of demography. Although physical abuse (largely paternal) and social deprivations were significant in predicting chronic risks for violence in the homicide studies, absent or abnormal play was in league with later social and personal tragedy in the group of murderers. These were not the findings in the comparison group. Although individuals in the control group reported many stressful life experiences, their capacities to engage a repertoire of coping capacities were related to the richness and variety of play experiences, particularly those early in life. Although these conclusions lacked sufficient numbers and rigorous methodology to become part of established mainstream social-behavioral science, they still remain reasonable.

Following the human studies on homicide, I read in the *National Geographic Magazine* of the murder-cannibalism by Gombe female chimpanzees Passion and Pom. Having previously learned of other chimpanzee-human similarities, and knowing of Jane Goodall's long-term detailed observations of the Gombe Stream chimpanzees, I wrote to ask her about the chimpanzee homicide. She responded that both Passion and Pom were ineffectively mothered and that she had observed that their early play and later socialization patterns were constricted. Dr. Goodall and I since have engaged in rich discussions about play and its relationship to violence. She once wrote, "Play is a signal that nature's wisdom is being enacted."

Play Research in the Clinical Setting

I left clinical research shortly after completing these studies and became a clinician-administrator in a teaching hospital, curious about and sensitized to the importance of play, but involved more as a traditional clinician with urgent patient and administrative responsibilities. As a private practitioner over a 20-year duration, I conducted an estimated eight thousand detailed patient interviews. In as many ways as practical, I delved into each patient's play history, play patterns, imaginative playmates, friendships, pet involvements, toy use, and pleasurably repetitive activities of any sort: physical, emotional, musical, fantasy, solo, or social. From these anecdotal sources, filtered through the growing information base about how humans develop and socialize, I gradually have come to see play as a separate form of behavior, operating broadly in the development and sustenance of grace and movement, cognition, and socialization.

In 1986, I received a small grant from the Cooper Foundation to survey selected special educational environments and interview a few "genius" scientists, looking for the seeds and harvests of creativity. In such nonpathologic environments, I found playfulness to be the constant companion of kids learning creatively; it remained active in those scientists whose productivity remained high and varied as they aged. I now perceive healthy, varied play in childhood as essential for the development of empathy, social altruism, and social behaviors enabling the player to handle stress, particularly humiliation and powerlessness. I also have found that general well-being and play are partners, and that play accompanies the most gifted adult achievements. A flowing sense of humor and the capacity for engagement in play are important for all of us. From my clinical practice, I have seen that a return to play in depressed and stressed adulthood promotes personal healing.

Of course, since play is linked so integrally and may even borrow from other behaviors, and because rigorous research criteria defining play are lacking, no specific conclusions about play or its absence in the causality of violence and antisocial behavior was then, or is now, fully warranted. But it appears that we all pay a high price for seriously neglecting play. Lives without play, examined in the context of the private and academic practice of clinical psychiatry, often were surrounded by states of high accomplishment, but they lacked the exuberance that accompanies a buoyant sense of empowerment or mastery. Depression, over-control, driven ambition, envy, proneness to addiction, and ecological havoc may accompany the play-deprived life. In one form or another, play-starved adults, even if economically prosperous, were found to live in a narrower, more stereotyped world, and play-deprived children are the tragic forerunners of social and personal breakdown. I believe these clinical conclusions are reinforced by many detailed biographies of famous and infamous historical characters, such as Erik Erikson's of Luther and Flood's of Hitler, whose play life was deficient and aberrant from earliest description (Erikson 1949; Flood 1989).

The Evolution of Play

I had the good fortune to spend time as a research fellow studying the evolution of the universe at the Center for the Story of the Universe in San Francisco under the tutelage of physicist-cosmologist Brian Swimme. I wanted to discern how play could be seen within the context of the evolution of complex life. Immersed in the universe story and major theories from the Big Bang on, I began to think of play differently. "New" forms of behavior such as sleep and play are fundamentally stabilizing complex systems. An examination of their origins and elaboration of them offer a theoretical foundation for their serving as stabilizing entities for intricate evolving nervous systems.

I soon realized that the leap from the conceptual to the clinical was too great for direct confirmation. Eager to see authentic play in the wild, I made the decision to study animals at play and again contacted Jane Goodall. She encouraged me to look up Mary Smith, then a Senior Editor of the National Geographic Society. By 1991, I was under contract with them to write an article and to consult and co-produce a TV program on animals at play, all of which were completed in 1995 (Brown 1994, 1995a).

The experience of worldwide observation of animals in the wild and time spent with talented ethologists who watch and learn from their subjects in the field enlarged my understanding of play as a broad evolutionary phenomenon in all smart animals. Certain evolutionary components have to be in place, I learned, for play to occur. First and foremost are a highly complex brain and central nervous system. Play is limited primarily to warm-blooded, smart animals. Specific evolutionary pathways leading to play behavior are obscured by the drama of time and variability, but this conclusion does not lessen the presence or significance of play as a persistent, growing phenomenon in nature. My opinions about play began to extend beyond clinical guesses to speculations about its evolutionary roles. I believe its presence promotes quickness, adaptability, and flexibility. It nullifies the rigidity that sets in after successful mastery of a new behavior. It may have an engineering role in the evolution of complex behaviors.

Nature has provided the brains of big-cortexed, warm-blooded, high-energy-storing birds and mammals an extra "uncommitted" supply of neurons and connections. These exist in addition to more primitive structures that have been passed on by ancient forebears. Cold-blooded creatures, on the other hand, are without such networks, and are controlled from within their physiology. They expose themselves to the sun to get warm and turn down their metabolic demands when they are no longer hungry.

Players, regardless of external circumstances, have a stable brainstem and hypothalamus supported by energy reservoirs that free these uncommitted neural networks to explore the world actively. They are active in engaging the world, and in early development, play is the prime organizer of that engagement. Systematic studies of the cortical architecture of creatures as their cortices enlarge with increasing phylogenetic complexity reveal more neural networking that is not directly hooked into specific reflex-like functioning. Behaviorally, this phenomenon is accompanied by an increase in complex behavior, particularly interactions with others. Vocalization and subtle signaling by body and facial expressions, some of the basic hallmarks of play, emerge and lead to a sense of self and others. In addition to play behavior, larger cortices reflect the capacity for greater cognitive variety.

Playing creatures have or develop the capacity to receive, integrate, remember, and contextualize internal and external signals. They are not always looking for a fight, sex, or food, nor are they warily looking over their shoulders for the next-higher food-chain representative. Safe and well-fed, they play. How they play and what constitutes play behavior become less controversial as play information accumulates. The external signals that herald play across species powerfully affect behavior. Humans understand that when a dog bows while tail wagging, he wants to play; a raven gets the message as well. Human and raven usually respond in an enlivened way to the dog's signal.

Why creatures play remains as scientifically unanswered as why sleep and dream exist. Yet play behavior is as fundamental in the lives of players as sleep is in the lives of sleepers. Perhaps play acts like other fundamental organizers in nature; perhaps it functions as an "attractor," a stabilizer, as the matchmaker to new, evolutionarily acquired, emergently stabilizing capabilities within immensely complex brains.

In his theory of neuronal growth selection, Edelman (1992) describes how perceptual categorization, memory, affect, and more, combine to form cortical maps. By becoming sequentially organized into useful adaptive patterns, play may establish new and dynamically interconnected maps each time. Two players mutually develop cooperative, nondominating behavior that evolves as a unit. The play signals given and received have meaning to the players, are unambiguous, and necessary for their development. Yet the interplay between the maps, the "scenes" they contain, is highly individualistic. These maps, the character of which Edelman elaborates as possessing "re-entrant connectivity," remain present and available for modification throughout life, but accumulate most rapidly in infancy and youth. They are also "value-laden" and certainly could form the major cartography of learning. Furthermore, stable socialization patterns are learned during repetition of roughhousing or other social species-specific acts of playfulness. The implications of this fact, if true for humans, should give all educators pause as they plan curricula.

My surmise, integrating Edelman's thought with clinical observation, is that play-deficient creatures suffer from "value-laden adaptive map deficiency." As each map yields new functions, new kinds of memory, and a series of new, inner-value-laden scenes, the player may begin (depending on its evolutionarily derived cartography capabilities) to develop a rudimentary sense of self and others (Edelman 1992; Bekoff 1972; Gopnik 1993). Accumulation of play experience allows the scene-makers to use the new scene and compare it with previous scenes.

Jane Goodall, writing in *ReVision*, describes one chimpanzee's symbolic play and joking in ways that are consistent with a developing rudimentary internal stream-of-consciousness (Goodall 1995). Combined with pretense and symbol manipulation, this chimpanzee narrative was shared between the chimpanzee and her caretaker (Lyn, Greenfield, and Savage-Rumbaugh 2006). I can think of similar though less complex episodes while engaged in play and pretense with my Labrador retriever, Jason.

Cortical Play Maps

Brian Sutton-Smith's (1981) longitudinal crosscultural observations of the play and games of children and his review of their growing narratives, beginning with fragmented nonsense stories to privately generated dramas with full structure, give credence to including narrative as a form of imaginatively created series of interconnected cortical play maps. It seems possible, then, that children's narrative representations, their stories, may comprise a significant part of their inner conscious reality. By looking at play as a generator of dynamically integrated, affect-laden cortical maps of increasing complexity, play can be considered a major organizer and sustainer of humans' dynamic sense of reality.

Creatures who do not play may have an inflexible, narrow, more lizard-like and stereotyped sense of "self" and reality. In a cold-blooded reptile of small cortex, no options for complex cooperative play are likely. In the murderers previously cited, inflexibility in the presence of

91

stress, narrowed repertoire of behavioral responsiveness, and the inability to modulate or have a context for control of strong surges of affect (rage, shame) could be attributed to "play-map deficiency" from abuse and deprivation.

Part of the appeal of Edelman's ideas and the reason I enjoy incorporating them into play theory is because they are validated by their illumination of otherwise obscure clinical neurological syndromes. Oliver Sacks vividly describes some of the strangeness that brain lesions produce, many of which lacked a comprehensive theoretical basis before Edelman (Sacks 1993). Localized "map deficits" can explain what occurs in brain trauma, stroke, tumor, or degenerative diseases, and correlate well with the effects of chronic abuse or deprivation—all may result in cognitive and socialization dysfunction. The "intimate reciprocal relationship in animals as they play" and their capacity to communicate value-laden intentions ("what follows is play and will not harm you"), so adroitly written of by Marc Bekoff (1972), harmonize with theories of the qualia (values) that Edelman writes of in his discussions of animal primary consciousness (Edelman 1992).

Sutton-Smith's seminal writings on children involved in games and his observations about the efficacy of sequentially more complex group-game play can be linked to an evolutionary play ladder. He sees children's development of the capacity for later adult-unified behavior as dependent upon their successfully mastering such unifying games as ring-around-the-rosy. Children's games also teach the game-player how to accept authority, learn strategy, win, lose, handicap oneself in the service of the game, and much more. Competent group behavior requires learning in group-play situations in childhood. The "intimate reciprocal" relationships established as basic and essential in animal play operate just as importantly in human group play, games, and in one-on-one social play. We, too, may be the legatees through play of mutually developing cooperative units aiding survival and adding joy.

Just as Charles Whitman was not taught the requirements of intimacy and playfulness as a child, the game- and rough-and-tumble play–deprived child may well become the socially dysfunctional adult who cannot handle the complexities inherent in the adult world. Despite lacking a proven theoretical base, the establishment of playfulness has been used effectively in the business world to enhance well-being, productivity, and creativity on the job (Weinstein 1996). Wise parents, gifted teachers, and fulfilled adults continue to live play-filled lives. Stories of play, whether personal or professional, will continue to enchant, beguile, and inspire us. Within them lie the energies for discovering more vital and meaningful lives.

Works Cited

Allen, C., and M. Bekoff. 1992. *Essay on Contemporary Issues in Ethology: Intentional Icons: Towards an Evolutionary Cognitive Ethology.* Berlin and Hamburg: Paul Parey Scientific Publishers.

Bekoff, M. 1972. "The Development of Social Interaction, Play and Metacommuniction in Mammals: An Ethological Perspective." *Quarterly Review of Biology.*

Bekoff, M., and J. Byers. 1997. "Intentional Communication and Social Play: How and Why Animals Negotiate and Agree to Play." In *Animal Play: Evolutionary, Comparative and Ecological Perspectives.* Cambridge and New York: Cambridge University Press.

Berry, T., and B. Swimme. 1992. *The Universe Story.* New York: Harper Collins.

Brown, S. L. 1987. *The Hero's Journey: The World of Joseph Campbell.* PBS documentary.

———. 1994. "Animals at Play." *National Geographic Magazine* 186: 2–35.

———. 1995a. "Play, the Nature of the Game." *National Geographic Explore.* TBS documentary.

———. 1995b. "Through the Lens of Play." *ReVision Magazine* 17, no. 4 (Spring): 2–12, 35–42.

Brown, S. L., P. J. Bohnert, J. P. Smith, and A. D. Pokorny. 1968. *Alcohol Safety Study: Drivers Who Die.* Prepared under contract with the U.S. Department of Transportation, National Safety Bureau, No. FH-11-6603, Baylor University College of Medicine.

Brown, S. L., and P. Cousineau. 1990. *The Hero's Journey.* San Francisco: Harper.

Brown, S. L., and D. A. Freedman. 1968. "On the Role of Coenesthetic Stimulation in the Evolution of Psychic Structure." *Psychoanalytic Quarterly* 37: 418–38.

———. 1970. "A Multi-Handicapped Baby: The First Eighteen Months." *Journal of the American Academy of Child Psychiatry* 9, no. 2.

Brown, S. L., and J. Lomax. 1969. "A Pilot Study of Young Murderers. *Hogg Foundation Annual Report.* Austin, Tex.: Hogg Foundation.

Brown, S. L., and A. Tilby. 1992. *The Soul of the Universe.* BBC Television.

Brownlee, S. 1997. "Play: It's Not Just Fooling Around." *US News and World Report:* 45–48.

Burghardt, G. M., B. Ward, and R. Rosccoe. 1996. "Problem of Reptile Play: Environmental Enrichment and Play Behavior in a Captive Nile Softshell Turtle, *Troinyx triunguis.*" *Zoo Biology* 15: 223–38.

California Academy of Sciences. 1992. Symposium: Neoteny and the Evolution of the Human. San Francisco.

Da Masio, A. 1994. *Des Cartes Error.* New York: Avon Books.

Edelman, G. 1992. *Bright Air, Brilliant Fire.* New York: Basic Books.

Erikson, E. 1949. *Young Man Luther.* New York: Norton.

Flood, C. 1989. *Hitler, the Path to Power*. Boston: Houghton-Mifflin.

Goodall, J. 1995. "Chimpanzees and Others at Play." *ReVision* 12, no. 4 (Spring): 14–20.

Gopnik, A. 1993. "Psychopsychology." *Consciousness and Cognition* 2: 264–80.

Lewin, R. 1992. *Life at the Edge of Chaos: Complexity*. New York: Macmillan.

Lyn, H., P. Greenfield, and S. Savage-Rumbaugh. 2006. "The Development of Representational Play in Chimpanzees and Bonobos: Evolutionary Implications, Pretense, and the Role of Interspecies Communication." *Cognitive Development* 21: 199–213.

McMahon, F., and B. Sutton-Smith. 1995. "The Past in the Present: Theoretical Directions for Children's Folklore." In *Children's Folklore: A Source Book,* ed. B. Sutton-Smith, J. Mechling, T. Johnson, and F. McMahon. New York: Garland.

Meeker, J. 1997. *The Comedy of Survival*. Tucson: University of Arizona Press.

Pellegrini, A. D. 1989. "Elementary School-children's Rough-and-Tumble Play." *Early Childhood Research Quarterly* 4: 245–60.

Sacks, Oliver. 1993. "Making Up the Mind." *New York Review of Books,* April 8, 42–49.

Sutton-Smith, B. 1972. *The Folkgames of Children*. Austin: University of Texas Press.

———. 1974. "The Anthropology of Play." *Association for the Anthropological Study of Play* 2: 8–12.

———. 1981. *The Folkstories of Children*. Philadelphia: University of Pennsylvania Press.

———. 1993. "Dilemmas in Adult Play with Children." In *Parent-Child Play Descriptions and Implications,* ed. K. McDonald. New York: State University of New York Press.

Sutton-Smith, B., J. Mechling, T. Johnson, and F. McMahon, eds. 1995. *Children's Folklore: A Source Book*. New York: Garland.

Waldrop, M. M. 1992. *Complexity: The Emerging Science at the Edge of Order and Chaos*. New York: Simon & Schuster.

Weinstein, M. 1996. *Managing to Have Fun*. New York: Simon & Schuster.

III. ROOTING FOR IMAGINATION

At home, at school, everything is oriented toward sports and what we call rules-based activity, so children have very little opportunity to just go to the park and organize their own game, or go into the woods.

For me, play is like a fountain of life, maybe even a fountain of youth, that comes bubbling up from us. Play takes any situation which we may look at in a grim, serious way as an adult, but as a child you start to play with it. You turn it around, you turn it on its head, you look at it in different ways out of this wellspring of creativity and life that's in us.

When you're playing, you usually are very concentrated, very focused, and you're really getting new life rather than being drained of life. And what happens when you don't play is that the wellspring is there, it's always there in us, we never lose it, but it gets clogged up with rubble,

> We never lose this wellspring, but it gets clogged up with rubble, and so it's not flowing very freely.

and so it's not flowing very freely. And the amazing thing with adults is when you work on this a little bit, and you clear the rubble, you suddenly discover that you have a playful nature, that it's still there, it's in us all our lives. In some people it's evident and in some people it's covered over, but it's always there.

So this wonderful wellspring, when it comes out, you freely chose how you want to use it, and what you want to do with it, and you direct it yourself, and you do it because you want to do it. Play is not something that lends itself well to somebody else's agenda. It stops being play. It may be learning in a playful way. That's better than learning in an unplayful way, but it's not pure play, and pure play is essential.

Joan Almon, Co-Founder and Director, The Alliance for Childhood. Quoted from film interview, *Where Do the Children Play?* (2007)

Jane P. Perry

CHILDREN'S EXPERIENCE OF SECURITY AND MASTERY ON THE PLAYGROUND

Jane P. Perry is an ethnographer, teacher, and research coordinator at the Harold E. Jones Child Study Center at the University of California, Berkeley. Her co-authored forthcoming book, *Children Making Sense: A Curriculum for the Early Years* (Pearson Education) advocates for play. See Jane's work at www.redroom.com/author/jane-p-perry.

[Andreas, Sean, Chase, and others gather around a water spout.]

Andreas: *[Peers into the darkened hole.]* Are you down there, Butty?

[Butty is the name Andreas gave to a snail he brought into the classroom several weeks ago. At that time, the children occupied themselves in caring for Butty, building a home for Butty with blocks, finding danger in the world from which Butty needed protection, and nestling Butty in the shade during the children's nap. Butty escaped while they slept.]

Michael: *[Arrives with a centipede on his wrist. He positions it in front of the spout hole.]* Look what I have.

Andreas: I hear something! Butty! Butty, are you down there?

Chase: *[Finds a string in the grass and peers at Morgan and Janelle, who are in the sand making a "lake" with a hose draped into a gutter.]* Hey, it's a little thing for if Butty drowns we can save him. *[Chase jumps from the grass into the sand, standing on the bank of the lake.]*

[Michael floats a boat in the lake. His centipede is in the boat.]

Chase: It's a saving boat. A saving boat!

Michael: It's not a saving boat.

Chase: *[Undeterred.]* We need a saving boat to save Butty. *[He fetches another boat and floats it to the side.]* Mine is parked on shore. *[His string sinks into the lake.]* Whoever finds the string wins the Olympics.

Janelle: *[Morgan runs off for the art table as Janelle registers Morgan's leave-taking, disapprovingly.]* Not nice.

Andreas: Okay, I'll find the string,.

Chase: Whoever is the winner is the goodest.

Morgan: Here, Chase. *[Morgan returns with a freshly cut piece of string.]*

Chase: Okay, I need to tie it onto my boat. We need to find Butty.

Emma: Where's Butty?

Chase: In the water. Butty! Butty!

Emma: Did Butty drop in the water?

Chase: Yeah.

Andreas: Let's drain all the water. *[Andreas pulls the hose out of the gutter.]* Now the water is draining out.

Chase: Hey, we need water. If there is no water, the boats won't be able to rescue Butty!

[Sean returns the hose to the gutter. Andreas begins to block the water with shovelfuls of sand.]

Morgan: *[Turns to Andreas, speaking in a baby voice.]* Andreas, I know where Butty is. Butty outside of classroom.

Andreas: Okay.

[The game continues as the kids excavate water channels to direct a stream and pack "cement" against its sides to control the current.]

Play and Learning on the Playground

The playground is where children go to make sense of their world.[1] The outdoors, with its flexibility in space and noise, where imagination is complemented by nature, children explore early peer-culture themes of life and death, danger and safety, power and control.[2] It is a place of vivid physicality: ball and trike play, climbing, running, rolling, spinning, full-body digging, and construction. Because young children learn with their whole bodies, the playground is a place for significant growth in social, emotional, language, and cognitive development as well.[3] The playground allows adults to focus on children's development because the behavior is directed by them. The teacher observes, records, and reflects on children's intentions and next steps, then guides learning based on these observations and reflections.

Along with physical skills, children on the playground use their abilities in language, turn-taking, appreciating another's point of view, problem-solving, and representational thinking, all while juggling notions of fantasy and reality.[4] Children practice articulating a plan and communicating that plan to others. Their games have rules. They practice negotiating, experiment with affiliation, teasing, taunting, and the nuanced reactions to all three.[5] Children are scientists, ever curious: *what happens if I do this?*[6] Learning on the playground is a process of initiative, discovery, and inventiveness.

Learning necessarily involves the risk of moving from the known to the unknown. Children on the playground recognize this feeling as they experiment with their independence. Andreas, new to self-control, is understanding what it feels like to nurture another. Chase is interested in the drama of a rescue, not needing a real snail to reenact previous play about unpredictable dangers. Michael has different ideas for this game, but is not prepared to verbalize them yet. Emma, walking into the middle of this play scene, needs little introduction—Butty is a figure of myth in the classroom community. Morgan subtly orchestrates the addition of others to her lake game, fetching a new string when the prop is needed and adeptly shifting status by adopting a baby voice to gain Andreas' acceptance of continued water flow. These interactions are not unusual. Children on the playground create scenarios to establish security and experience mastery. Teachers recognize the risk involved by focusing on what children are trying to do, and including children in planning a reasonable means towards accomplishment.

Negotiation between Peer and Teacher Cultures

Learning is a negotiated process between the intentions of children in their peer-play culture and the intentions of teachers in their teaching culture.[7] Two themes dominate children's peer play culture: a strong desire to be in the company of other playmates, and a drive to challenge authority and gain control over the process of learning.[8] Play often is initiated by a confirmation of affiliation: "We're friends, right?" "Right!" New ideas involve securing agreement from companions: "Pretend we're building a house, okay?" "'kay, and then we can put bears inside, right?" Running and chasing solidify children's experience of affiliation, often when children are new to playing with peers. Requests for play frequently are met by resistance, establishing a precedent for vigilance if play with others is desired. Termination of a play interaction frequently occurs without warning or recognition, leaving a playmate unpredictably without a partner (Janelle registers disapproval when Morgan switches her attentions to Michael's need for string). Vigilance and unpredictability add a quality of fragility to playground play.[9] Children respond with play routines intended to secure participation and some measure of control.

A teacher who recognizes that children's need for control springs from their desire to experience security and mastery can become an ally in children's learning. The desire to control can mean that access to playmates becomes a challenge. It is much more powerful in the primitive world of first interactions to reject rather than accede.

[Jong is chasing a group of four girls. They flee into a playhouse. When Jong attempts to enter, they shriek.]

Girls: No! You can't come in! We're not playing with you!"

Perry: *[I approach and poke my head into the doorway.]* Where's your door bell?

Niesha: *[Steps forward, ready to take up this overture.]* It's right here. *[She points to a slight indent in the exterior wall.]*

Perry: *[I elaborate as they welcomed Jong in.]* Do you have any tea? Any tea and cookies for your guest?

Emma: Oh, yes!

Jong: *[Enters and sits on the floor at the feet of the four others.]* I've never played with so many kids before.

On the playground, an attentive teacher can help address children's developing social and intellectual skills by using children's desire for affiliation and control as incentives to practice next steps.

The playground can challenge children who feel safer in the less physically demanding and more established, adult-attended environment of the indoors. A teacher looking at playground behavior through the lens of the peer culture can help reestablish security and acknowledge the mastery of new accomplishment. What looks like Jong's bullying is an attempt to secure fragile allegiance. A teacher can offer a switch from the "run-away" routine to a "running-with" game that recognizes children's affiliative needs in peer-play customs.

Provocation can be a primitive attempt at initiating play, something the teacher can articulate ("I think Janelle wants to play. What could she be?").[10] Provocation can occur when children inadvertently transgress the peer-culture protocol.

Michael: *[Greets Natalia warmly on the playground blacktop]* Hi Natalia Batalia!

Natalia: *[Face shadows.]* No! *[Turning away.]*

Michael's greeting, a playful game of rhyme that his father uses with him, has not generalized to peer play and is received by Natalia as a slight. The teacher on the playground can model flexible thinking, such as the "you have a visitor" switch, or help to smooth over peer culture violations ("Oh, Michael likes rhyming games. That's fun: Jane, train, rain!").

As a bartering chip in the negotiation process, teachers offer special privileges like lingering with toys, friends, or play spots to encourage intentional planning ("The climbing structure is their hyena den right now. They'll let you know when they are done."). Children may need the security of adult coaching in how to use play areas before experiencing the feedback of self-direction.

Conclusion

Children crave security and mastery as they play and learn. Active outdoor playgrounds with fewer adult constraints can be perfect learning environments because they offer children the opportunity to direct their own initiative and inquiry.[11] Adults observe, reflect, and facilitate children's intentions where playground cues are flexible: a climbing apparatus or sand box presents physical challenges, but the theme of play must be invented, directed, and negotiated with others.[12] The degree of interpretation required on children's part suggests that demands are made on cognitive and socialization skills based on the explicitness of playground cues. During outdoor play, when cues are open-ended and children are involved in negotiating idiosyncratic personal symbols and plans, interactions by necessity become more complex. The Butty game involved informative and timed verbal commentary, subtle directives and queries, and the use of props to tether the imaginative theme and propel progress. Children established security by mastering danger, where danger was not dispensed with but was controlled with props and constructive plans.

Children can perform with greater competence playing in the company of others than just alone.[13] Their individual skills, buttressed by the collaborative efforts of the group, support their next steps. By appreciating outdoor play routines as an integral feature of the peer group, teachers meet children's need for involvement by creating and protecting outdoor spaces for children's self-directed interpretation and negotiation. Teachers help children distinguish between pretend and actual fighting through facilitating the encoding and decoding of interactive signals. Teachers cue players as to when chasing means that a peer wants to play. Teachers arrange outdoor play space so that playgroups can separate into manageable numbers supporting realistic opportunities for negotiation. Outdoor play offers experience in critical intellectual skills while capitalizing on physical maturation. Look to the playgrounds, where children go to experience security and mastery and gain clarity of selfhood necessary to navigate life.

Notes

1. J. P. Perry, *Outdoor Play: Teaching Strategies with Young Children* (New York: Teachers College Press, 2001).

2. W. A. Corsaro, *Friendship and Peer Culture in the Early Years* (Norwood, N.J.: Ablex, 1985); W. A. Corsaro, *We're Friends, Right: Inside Kids' Culture* (Washington, D.C.: The Joseph Henry Press, 2003).

3. M. J. Kostelnik, A. K. Soderman, and A. P. Whiren, *Developmentally Appropriate Curriculum: Best Practices in Early Childhood Education* (Upper Saddle River, N. J.: Pearson Education, Inc., 2004).

4. J. Frost, D. Shin, and P. Jacobs, "Physical Environments and Children's Play." In *Multiple Perspectives on Play in Early Childhood Education,* ed. O. Saracho and B. Spodek, 255–94 (Albany: SUNY Press, 1998); A. D. Pelligrini, "The Effects of Exploration and Play on Young Children's Associative Fluency: A Review and Extension in Training Studies," in *Child's Play: Developmental and Applied,* ed. T. D. Yawkey and A. D. Pellegrini, 237–53 (Hillsdale, N.J.: Erlbaum, 1984); A. D. Pelligrini, "Play and the Assessment of Children," in *Multiple Perspectives on Play in Early Childhood Education,* ed. O. Saracho and B. Spodek, 220–39 (Albany: SUNY Press, 1998); J. P. Perry, *Outdoor Play*; J. P. Perry "Making Sense of Outdoor Pretend Play," *Young Children* 583 (2003): 26–30.

5. D. Keltner, L. Capps, A. M. Kring, R. C. Young, and E. A. Heery, "Just Teasing: A Conceptual Analysis and Empirical Review," *Psychological Bulletin* 1272 (2001): 229–48; K. Gallas, *Sometimes I Can Be Anything: Power, Gender and Identity in a Primary Classroom* (New York: Teachers College Press, 1998).

6. A. Gopnik, A. N. Meltzoff, and P. K. Kuhl, *The Scientist in the Crib: What Early Learning Tells Us about the Mind* (New York: Perennial Press, 1999); C. Seefeldt, *How to Work with Standards in the Early Childhood Classroom* (New York: Teachers College Press, 2005).

7. W. A. Corsaro, *Friendship and Peer Culture in the Early Years;* W. A. Corsaro, *We're Friends, Right;* F. Erikson, *Talk and Social Theory: Ecologies of Speaking and Listening in Everyday Life* (Cambridge UK: Polity Press, 2004); S. B. Heath, *Ways with Words: Language, Life and Work in Communities and Classrooms* (New York: Cambridge University Press, 1983); F. Hughes, "Sensitivity to the Social and Cultural Contexts of the Play of Young Children," in *Major Trends and Issues in Early Childhood Education: Challenges, Controversies, and Insights,* ed. J. Isenberg and M. Jalongo, 126–35 (New York: Teachers College Press, 2003); J. P. Perry, *Outdoor Play;* H. B. Schwartzman, *Transformations: The Anthropology of Children's Play* (New York: Plenum Press, 1978).

8. N. King, "The Impact of Context on the Play of Young Children," in *Reconceptualizing*

the *Early Childhood Curriculum,* ed. S. Kessler and B. Swadener, 43–61 (New York: Teachers College Press, 1992); W. G. Scarlett, S. Naudeau, D. Salonius-Pasternak, and I. Ponte, *Children's Play* (Thousand Oaks, Calif.: Sage Publications, 2005); B. Sutton-Smith, "Conclusion: The Persuasive Rhetorics of Play," in *The Future of Play Theory: A Multidisciplinary Inquiry into the Contributions of Brian Sutton-Smith,* ed. A. Pellegrini, 275–98 (Albany: SUNY Press, 1995).

9. J. P. Perry, *Outdoor Play.*

10. J. Van Hoorn, P. M. Nourot, B. Scales, and K. R. Alward, *Play at the Center of the Curriculum,* 4th ed. (Upper Saddle River, N.J.: Pearson Education, Inc., 2007).

11. A. D. Pelligrini and P. K. Smith, "Physical Activity Play: The Nature and Function of a Neglected Aspect of Play," *Child Development* 69 (1998): 577–98.

12. J. P. Perry, *Outdoor Play*; R. Kozlovsky, "Adventure Playgrounds and Post War Reconstruction," in *Designing Modern Childhoods: History, Space, and the Material Culture of Children,* ed. M. Gutman and N. de Coninck-Smith, 171–91 (Piscataway, N.J.: Rutgers University Press, 2008).

13. L. Katz, D. Evangelou, and J. Hartman, *The Case for Mixed Age Grouping in Early Education* (Washington, D.C.: National Association for the Education of Young Children, 1990); P. Smith, "Play Training: An Overview," in *Play and intervention,* ed. J. Hellendoom, R. van der Kooij, and B. Sutton-Smith, 185–94 (Albany: SUNY Press, 1994); L. S. Vygotsky, "Play and Its Role in the Mental Development of the Child," *Soviet Psychology* 12 (1967): 62–76; L. S. Vygotsky, *Mind in Society: The Development of Higher Psychological Processes* (Cambridge, Mass.: Harvard University Press, 1978).

Elizabeth Jones and Eric M. Nelson

THE OUTDOOR CLASSROOM PROJECT

Elizabeth Jones is a member of the Human Development Faculty at Pacific Oaks College in Pasadena, California, and a consultant on the Outdoor Classroom Project. She is author of *The Play's the Thing* (Teachers College Press, 1992), *Emergent Curriculum* (NAEYC, 1994), *Playing to Get Smart* (Teachers College Press, 2006), and other books and articles.

Eric M. Nelson, M.A., is the Director of Consulting and Educational Services for the Child Educational Center, which he co-founded with his wife, Elyssa, in 1979. He currently directs the Outdoor Classroom Project, a $1M, 5-year project to train staff of child care centers in development and enhancement of their outdoor environments and programs.

No Place to Play

The vast majority of 10 million residents of Los Angeles County are packed into a coastal plain and two valleys, the archetype for urban sprawl notorious for lack of parks and open public spaces. This territory is also home to over 3,000 programs of early care and education (ECE) serving over 160,000 children—over 3,000 locations where excellent outdoor experiences could be provided to children.

By law, ECE facilities in California must provide an outdoor space equivalent to 75 square feet per child for the building's total enrollment capacity. Aside from a few other minor items, very little regulation is provided to guide the design and development of outdoor spaces. The results are found in the bleak landscape of playgrounds from East L.A. to San Fernando and South L.A. to Pasadena. As with the field of early care and education as a whole, the outdoor environment and programming are pretty much an afterthought. Predictably, this also is reflected in children's utilization of the outdoors. Despite Southern California's benign climate, even in programs with demonstrated interest in the outdoors, children are spending 75 percent of their time indoors. This emphasis on the indoor classroom ill serves the fundamental developmental needs of young children, much less addressing the current epidemics of overweight, type 2 diabetes, and imposition of behavior-modifying drugs.

A New Focus on Young Children Outdoors

In 1998, the voters of California approved a 50 cent per pack tax on cigarettes, the funds to be used exclusively on services for children 0 to five years old. The money is dispersed through specially established county commissions (called "First 5" commissions) that are also responsible for finding or developing programs to support. One such L.A. County program is the Community Developed Initiatives (CDI), which allow ECE professionals to propose programs for funding. In the fall of 2002, the Caltech/JPL Community Child Educational Center (CEC), which had a 23-year history of focusing on outdoor environments and programming, submitted a proposal for the Outdoor Classroom Project.

Beginning October 1, 2003, the project was funded for five years at $1M. Its goal: "to increase the quantity, quality, and benefit of outdoor experiences for children ages 0 to five in Los Angeles County child care centers." The project's approach is to educate teachers, administrators, and parents from child care centers in L.A. County on the value of outdoor environments and activities, and then assist them in cultivating both at their individual center sites. Other objectives include increasing public awareness of the project's importance and building alliances with other similar initiatives.

There are five primary project activities:

1. Refining and enhancing the CEC program as a model for the "Outdoor Classroom";
2. Holding semi-annual conferences for L.A. County child care providers;
3. Providing on-site consulting and training to over 120 centers county-wide;
4. Refining and strengthening the CEC observation and practicum program;
5. Developing and disseminating information and data, including project materials and evaluation results.

Spreading the Word

Perhaps the most important achievement of the project is articulation and promotion of the Outdoor Classroom concept, which creates the mechanism by which teachers who are focused on the indoors can successfully refocus on the outdoors. This articulation is important because there has been no such prior widespread dissemination. The articulation addresses the questions of What? Why? and How? and is provided in a variety of ways. Foundational to the articulation is the CEC Outdoor Classroom site and program, which provide an experienced, operational model for ECE professionals to see and learn from. For many teachers, seeing the program in operation is the turning point in shifting their focus from inside to outside. The CEC site also serves as an information source for problem-solving about both environmental and programmatic challenges that may be impeding implementation of the Outdoor Classroom in other programs.

Articulation and promotion of the concept is provided in other ways. The twice-yearly county conferences provide materials and workshops that describe the Outdoor Classroom from a variety of perspectives, including that of landscape architects, playground designers, early childhood educators, psychologists, environmentalists, and health care professionals. As interest in the concept has spread, modified presentations have been prepared and provided in venues outside the scope of the grant.

Supporting Implementation

Supporting implementation of the Outdoor Classroom concept is also a key focus of the project. Attendees of the conference are trained in implementation and organizational change strategies and techniques. Follow-up surveys indicate that centers whose staff have attended the conference almost universally make some change following the conference. A limited number of conference attendees are selected to receive a year's worth of on-site consulting and training support. This part of the project works with all types of child care centers throughout the county. Implementation support focuses on change in three areas: physical environment, curricular approach, and teacher attitudes. Individual centers vary widely in how they use the services and where they focus their energy; however, the objective is to tailor the support to most benefit the center. Centers also vary widely in how they use the services, largely depending on their unique circumstances. One new center had an undeveloped yard with nothing but open lawn. Using the Outdoor Classroom model, the center transformed both their entire indoor and outdoor program structure to double the children's daily outdoor time and created eight outdoor activity centers. Participation in the project helped another center that had a large yard at a distance from the building to obtain $10,000 from their sponsoring church, which they used to build a new, sophisticated trike path, eliminating the old one that was a safety hazard and developmentally inadequate. Their involvement in the project also generated parent participation in additional playground renovations. A third center (a parent co-op) completely renovated its small outdoor environment, throwing out broken and useless items, moving equipment around, creating totally new activities with scrounged materials, and altering its schedule to create a totally different outdoor experience for its children.

Building Sustainability, Integrating with Others

Unlike many other CDI projects, the Outdoor Classroom Project must introduce its concept and build a foundation of new awareness before it can begin educating teachers to effect change. The increase in awareness required to build sustainability comes from producing solid materials, holding successful events, and providing productive services. It also requires networking and collaboration-building. The third year of the project was identified from the beginning as a period when enough should have been accomplished that the CEC could demonstrate its track record and attract continuation funding after year five. To this point, networking has been successful in raising visibility and interest, but results are not yet conclusive. However, two unanticipated developments may have future impact. While the project was not funded to establish demonstration centers, an outgrowth of the consulting work is that it has produced some programs that could qualify. In a totally different vein, a presentation at an international ECE conference in 2005 led to formation of a partnership to establish an international collaborative on children and nature via an international conference on that topic.

The Outdoor Classroom concept lies at an intersection of a number of trends and initiatives and requires multifaceted networking. This produces unique challenges and opportunities. The international conference was designed to bring together early childhood educators, landscape architects, urban planners, environmentalists, and professionals working with the natural sciences. Locally, the Outdoor Classroom Project is beginning to work extensively with health care professionals.

Summary

As an innovative work in progress, the Outdoor Classroom Project provides a strategy for how a large urban area can bring to light the importance of outdoor play areas and programs in centers of early care and education and begin the process of refocusing ECE teachers on the outdoors.

Janie Paul

DRAWN TOGETHER

Detroit Connections

I love art because you get to make your own world and then you get to own it.

JAMYRA, FOURTH GRADER
GREENFIELD UNION ELEMENTARY SCHOOL

Janie Paul is a visual artist and Associate Professor at the School of Art and Design at the University of Michigan, where she founded Detroit Connections project, which promotes art-making with college students and children in Detroit elementary schools. She is also a member, curator, and faculty advisor of the Prison Creative Arts Project, based at the University of Michigan, which organizes and sustains arts workshops, exhibitions, and mentorships with incarcerated and formerly incarcerated adults and youth in Michigan.

In 2000, I began working with two under-served Detroit elementary schools through my Detroit Connections project at the University of Michigan School of Art and Design. Each semester, my students and I teach weekly art classes at Greenfield Union Elementary and Harms Elementary schools. Working with about twenty fourth-graders at each site, we have developed art projects that use skills shared with science, math, and writing. We celebrate the children's work, bring them to visit our school in Ann Arbor, create public art for the schools, and become attached to the entire school community. The project described here was developed in collaboration with Ceci Mendez, the first project coordinator at Harms School.

I stand before twenty fourth-graders in the multi-purpose room of one of the poorest elementary schools in Detroit. About three-fourths of the children are Black and the rest are Chaldean. All come from families living below the poverty level. Looking at their clear, bright eyes, feeling their energy bursting, I notice the care with which each is dressed: brightly colored barrettes, hair ties, and belts individualize each child's uniform. I know that at home many experience hunger, neglect, and abuse, and witness violence in their streets. And I know that these problems are a direct result of an economy that has left their parents without employment, access to good health care, and educational opportunities. Even so, many caring, attentive parents work hard at jobs, help their children with homework, and listen to their stories. But it is a daily struggle for many families to exist without the resources they need, and I see it on the faces of some of the older brothers and sisters, parents, or grandparents who come to meet the children who tumble out of the school building at dismissal time.

The stately brick school building with large vanilla-colored columns at its entrance is surrounded by both boarded-up wooden houses and homes with neatly tended front yards. We are working in the city with the highest unemployment rate in the country, in a state with a slow rate of economic growth, in the country with the highest incarceration rate in the world.[1] I know that some of the Greenfield children have parents or other family members in prison. And I know that children of incarcerated parents are five to six times more likely than their peers to end up in prison.[2]

My college students learn about a world very different from their own: Nicole draws a picture of children floating up to the sky and tells us that her cousins were killed in a fire over the weekend. She returns to these drawings throughout the semester. We find Damon hoarding the snacks that we bring, to take home to his younger brothers and sisters. And the day before Thanksgiving, David is missing from class, making sure that the local church volunteer has delivered a turkey to his home.

After an introductory name game, we have pushed the long folding tables back toward the school library, two walls lined with colorful books and posters. Boys and girls are sitting on the carpet, whispering and nudging each other with excitement. These lucky ones have been chosen from 80 fourth graders to attend a weekly art class for three months. Because of the severe budget cuts in the Detroit schools, this may be the only art class they will ever have.

"Can anyone can tell me what a shape is?" Hands fly into the air: "a heart!" "a square" "a circle!" "an octagon!" Taking turns, eager volunteers come up to the large poster board taped to the wall and draw a shape. "Now," I say, "we're going to make some shapes that nobody has seen before! Here's a game: Can someone make a shape out of two straight lines and a curved line?" Hands fly up again, all wanting to be the one in front of the class. "Destiny, come on up!" Destiny's eyes flash as she uncoils from a sitting position next to giggling friends. Proudly, she walks up to the front and takes the crayon from my hand, then realizes that she doesn't know what to do. Her legs cross, finger against her cheek. She looks at the ceiling. No one has ever asked her to make up her own shape. I draw two connected straight lines and ask her to connect them with one curved line. "Oooooh, it looks like an ice cream cone!" Can she make another shape with two straight lines and a curved line? Destiny looks at me. I nod at the poster board. She carefully draws a curvy, loopy line, then stops and wonders. Ali rushes up, takes the crayon and draws a straight line that connects to hers. She takes the crayon back, slowly touches the end of his line and very carefully ties it back to her line. A smile broadens across her face. Ali says "It looks like a pizza with a bite out of it."

We break into groups, one college student to three children. Paper, oil pastels, and scissors are distributed while boys and girls spread out on the floor and at tables to play the game and make new shapes. Some draw a tiny shape in the middle of the paper. They are coaxed to draw larger next time. Some do not understand that a shape is a bounded form enclosed by an outline. But all soak in the attention. They are used to following directions, so they get excited, one by one, like kernels of corn popping with increased frequency, excited by this simple act of creation.

As I look at the shapes proliferating, I remember stones washed up on the beach of Lake Michigan, sticks under foot in the woods, and all the leaves I've seen, each unique. Most of these children have never been to the beach, to a forest, or in a garden. So we offer them a way to create their own unique forms and drawings that in time will develop into increasingly personal images and narratives.

Activities that enable the creation of meaning are scarce in schools under pressure to meet the high-stakes testing requirements mandated by No Child Left Behind. Like many other schools, Greenfield must work very hard to make up for the disadvantages the children come to school with. Unlike my college students, who had colorful toys, blocks, and puzzles to stimulate them when they were young, most of these children have grown up in homes without money for toys, books, or paper. One principal explained that it was a bad day when grocery stores switched to plastic because for some households, brown bags provided the only paper they had.

After setting our box of supplies down on one of the tables where the children have just finished lunch, some of us organize supplies, and some collect fourth graders from their classrooms. So much is exciting! Sitting at a table with college students, getting out of class early, making a brightly colored posterboard folder to hold drawings, boxes of colored pencils and pastels, and the large, simple, pre-cut shapes that we are now handing out.

We have pre-cut these simple shapes out of colored construction paper that are the same width or height as another piece of construction paper that they now choose. For example, one child might have a piece of blue paper and may choose a yellow pre-cut shape that is triangular and whose base is as large as the blue paper. Each child has these two large pieces of paper and the shapes they made last week. College students encourage children to look at big and little shapes and to move them around into different combinations. In the same way that we might look for images in cloud formations, we look at shapes to see what they remind us of. We trace, rotate, and make patterns. We start to see birds, chickens, hats, and cars. We move shapes around the paper with the large shape underneath to see what suggests itself. A simple, large shape with a jagged edge or a curve can become a hill, a house, a corner, or a river. It is a structure to help organize the space and with it, the imagination. "This looks like a dog!" "If I put these two together it's a butterfly!" "This could be my grandma's house!" Each child makes connections, some making pictures, others exploring patterns

"Confrontation in the Hills" by fourth graders, Greenfield Union Elementary School

and designs. Some are puzzled by such freedom, not knowing where to begin. Slowly the room settles. Michael, immersed in his work, head bent close to the desk, turns his curved shapes into reptiles, elaborating them with intricate drawings of a jungle around them. Nancy makes large symmetrical designs, reaching for every color of oil pastel, bearing down hard to make the color intense.

Through a series of drawing, painting, collage, and writing activities, each child builds a collection of art and writing that he or she keeps in an individual folder. When the collection is substantial, we make photocopies of the children's drawings in a variety of sizes. When the folders are brought back and the copies emptied out onto the tables, the children are thrilled to see their work reproduced. On a large piece of brown paper, each group starts to place and combine their images, moving them around, using the stories they have written to develop a larger narrative together. Over the next few weeks, each group will solidify their work into a collaborative painting on a wood panel. In the process, excitement and joy, sulking and fight-ing, reflection and reverie, and finally much pride emerge until the paintings are celebrated in a ceremony in front of the whole fourth-grade class and mounted permanently on the walls of the school.

The school building is a site in struggle. The gym that is unused because there is no gym teacher, the lack of toilet paper, the torn auditorium curtain, and cafeteria library all manifest the indifference of people who make policies that disadvantage poor communities. But its gleaming clean floors, bustling front office, and colorful posters adorning the classrooms tell you of the daily effort by teachers, staff, and administrators to combat these forces. The fourth graders join in this struggle to make their school matter, and they find a sense of power inside themselves when they change their school environment with the art they have created. We know that some of them, now in high school, still bring their friends and family back to see their work. They come in, periodically, proud of their accomplishments, pointing to what they made, remembering how they invented their own world in a painting.

Notes

1. "More Than 1 in 100 Adults Are Now in Prison in U.S.: Inmate Population is the Highest in the World," Adam Liptak, *New York Times*, February 29, 2008, p. A14.

2. Children's Defense Fund, *The State of America's Children 2005* (Washington, D.C.: Children's Defense Fund, 2005), 149.

Rosemarie Hester

THE LOT, THE DUMPSTER, AND THE SCHOOL

Rosemarie Hester is a playwright and teacher. Her most recent one-act, *You Can't Leave That There!* (2008), was produced at the Players Theatre Loft in New York City. She teaches at a private high school in Brooklyn and is a member of both the NYC Play Coalition and the Volunteer Committee for the Philharmonic Orchestra of the Americas.

During my early years as a teacher, I would ask my students to respond to informal surveys about our class. Questions differed from year to year, but I always included a range of topics from the mundane to the self-reflective. *What are your favorite books? How do you evaluate your own level of interest in school? What subjects do you find most challenging? What three things would you change about our class if you were the teacher?*

While I became accustomed to a wide variety of responses, to one question, I regularly received the same answer: *What time of day do you enjoy the most?* "Recess."

I experienced almost visceral resentment. Didn't you appreciate the wonderful poetry boxes we made together? What about that nature music I selected to inspire your writing? All those hands-on math activities? The carefully chosen literature, the enriching homework, the field trips, the bubble projects? *The shaving cream we used to wash our desks?*

Fifteen years and four schools later, I now respond: "Recess? Yes, of course. That's my favorite time of the day, too."

Currently, I teach fourth through sixth graders with learning differences at a small private school. Our building is inadequate. Our room is either too hot or too cold. We can't get away from bells that punctuate the days of the middle and high school students with whom we share the building. We have no soccer field, nor do we have a playground with a swing, a climbing structure, or a tether ball.

Instead, our students have recess behind three graffitied dumpsters in a gravelly, partially paved parking lot where people leave their cars. Four scraggly trees edge the lot. Beyond the trees, an occasional train runs past on the railroad tracks.

In the fall of 2005, when the students, the other teacher, and I all were new to the school, we began taking walks to local parks. That worked well enough when we had enough time. But we needed a closer alternative. That's when we looked out at the dumpsters and the lot and began to see possibilities.

First, it was with chalk. We drew two four-square courts and bought a couple of mustard-colored gym balls. When we had a lot of arguing over rules, calls, fairness, what someone thought had happened and someone else thought hadn't happened, we printed rule sheets off the internet

and tried to stick to them. Each day got a little better.

We improvised obstacle courses out of orange traffic cones, hula hoops, an old tumbling mat, and a tennis footwork training ladder. We made up drills for hand-eye coordination, sequencing, endurance, speed, accuracy. Quickly, everyone improved.

Then, one of the high school students built a basketball hoop that we could wheel in and out of school. The students lined up to make shots, took turns amicably, and were delighted when some of the younger male teachers from the upper grades joined the play.

When the weather turned rainy, then cold, and then rainy and cold, water collected and froze. Students slid across their "rink" in boots, carved pictures with sticks, and invented games with stones.

When the rink thawed to a pond, they built a circular rock dam in the high part of the water and placed rocks and branches to make a walkway. The engineering and construction took team work. The sounds of play had changed. Arguments had given way to giggles, shared ideas, and the snappy hum of compliments.

The next week, the class made balsa wood boats. As they hammered and glued, some sang quietly to themselves. Recess seemed magical, with little boats floating and colliding like bumper cars across the surface of the water.

Meanwhile, another project was underway. We

had begun collaborating with a University of Michigan course called "The Poetry of Everyday Life." Pairing children with college students, we planned to read poetry, play in outdoor spaces, write, and draw.

Meeting just a few steps from the dumpsters, we agreed that our first encounter should involve a snowball fight. There wasn't enough real snow, so my students crumpled up pages from phone books. We had six large garbage bags full by the time three cars containing thirteen students and a professor parked at the school.

As the college students walked back to where the younger students waited, I had the sense of what it must have been like when armies met in battle, the ground under everyone's feet serving both as meeting and leveling place. In this case, it was big people facing off against little people. The big people were smiling, and, of course, the armies had come not to destroy, but to create. The younger students introduced themselves, shaking hands with every college student. And, then, the fight began.

Giggling. Rushing. The fear of hitting someone, the fun of hitting someone, the fear and fun of being hit. On this playing field, the ice was breaking as connections were being made.

A week later, the younger students were sailing their boats as the older students arrived for the second time. Nithya Joseph, a freshman (p.123), e-mailed afterwards. "What amazed me the most…was how the parking lot had been transformed…the flat, icy land that had been on the outskirts of the space used for our snowball fight last week had been become a natural haven, right in the middle of the cars. Watching the kids splash, drift their boats over the surface, and build the stone path that wound its way through the pond with such sincerity and determination reminded me of how natural spaces exist everywhere, and of how they can be accessed and enjoyed, with just a bit of imagination."

The next week, we explored the train tracks, searching for human footprints or evidence of animals in the mud as well as little treasures. A bracelet. A beautiful piece of glass. Someone thought she found a fossil.

When we returned to the classroom, everyone hunkered down at tables and worked intently with their partners. Engaged in animated conversations, the partnerships yielded drawings and poems that we shared at the end of the session.

One student made a connection between the grasses along the tracks and descriptions in *The Little House on the Prairie*. Although she hadn't had time to finish her poem, she read as much as she had and then spoke extemporaneously. We praised her for making a connection with literature, using historical imagination, and having the courage to present to the group.

One day in early April, my seventh-grade drama students asked if they could go out back and play for a while in the lot like the younger kids. One of the students, a drummer, picked up a ruler and struck the dumpster. Then he tapped. He picked up a stick and used it with the ruler like a set of drumsticks. He played the dumpster's side. He played the black plastic cover. He played the metal handles. He walked around and played the other side. Every place he hit produced a different sound, and he worked hard at listening to see if he was making music.

One by one, the other students heard and joined, one kicking the bottom of the dumpster with his foot, big whole notes like a bass drum, while someone else started slapping like it was a *gembe*. Soon there was a layering of clicks, slaps, thuds, taps, and beats that made everyone think of *STOMP*.

I ran to the music teacher. "Come listen."

"I'm teaching a class. I can't. But I can hear it from here *and it's great*!"

Several days later, we tried to film, but it wasn't the same. "It's a bad day. It doesn't sound good. There's too much garbage," our drummer said.

Later in the week, the twin brother of a student came to visit. We were playing outside and heard the whistle of a train in the distance. Everyone ran to look. At first, we couldn't see anything. Then, from downtown, the powerful light pierced the grey. We heard more whistling as it got closer. We waved, the engineer waved back. Over the course of the next ten minutes, we counted eighty-three cars. The students were excited, but they had seen other trains on other days. For them it wasn't a first. For our fifth-grade visitor, it was different. He kept yelling, "This has never happened to me in my whole life. A train. A *train* came by."

In one child's life, a train caused great excitement. But what had the lot provided to the other students who used it every day?

Simply, it was a space for the expression of freedom and imagination; it was a space for human joy.

Mark Powell

FORT CULTURE

The Hidden Curriculum
of Recess Play

We have speculated that in games children learn all those necessary arts of trickery, deception, harassment, divination, and foul play that their teachers won't teach them but are most important in successful human relationships in marriage, business, and war.

BRIAN SUTTON-SMITH[1]

Mark Powell has taught in Montessori schools at the elementary level for fourteen years, most recently in the San Francisco Bay area. He spent eight years with lower elementary children at Lexington Montessori School in Massachusetts. Mark is also a teacher trainer with the Center for Montessori Teacher Education in, New York. He holds a Master of Education degree with a specialty in Conflict Resolution and Peaceable Schools from Lesley University, Cambridge, Massachusetts. He grew up under wide open skies in Brisbane, Australia, accustomed to supervised access to the suburban wild spaces around him.

Is Recess Over?

Recess beckons well before it actually arrives. Its allure can be heard in children's lunchtime conversations as they discuss imaginary roles, plans, and alliances with an appetite as hungry for play and its unbounded possibility as for food. For some children, recess provides the most important reasons to come to school. In team sports, games of chase and tag, clique-bound conversations, solitary wandering and exploration, pretend and war play, recess provides reliable access to a scarce resource of immense value in the lives of children: spontaneous self-direction. Although watched over by the protective though generally unobtrusive gaze of supervising teachers, children at recess interact with their natural environment and with each other almost completely as they choose—a freedom denied them at all other times while at school, and increasingly also in their homes and neighborhoods.

In the memories of most adults, recess was a diversion from the regular rhythm of adult-directed activities, a time for children and their teachers to relax, recharge, or "blow off steam" in order to recover their composure and focused attention for the academic afternoon. But over the last couple of decades, a policy debate has emerged: In many schools, recess in its traditional form is seen either as leaving children vulnerable to aggression and anti-social behavior, or as an inconvenient interruption to the academics on which students will be tested and their teachers judged. In response, many districts across the United States have reduced recess or replaced it with structured physical education; in others, it has been modified so that only children of the same age are allowed out on the playground at the same time. As a result, in many schools, recess is no longer the festive occasion it traditionally has been with its multiplicity of elements, ages, sexes, and forms of play.

The adult preference for more organized and purposeful activity has always been at odds with children's greater tolerance for chaos and flexibility and their need to exercise their own decisionmaking powers. The rise of institutionalized, adult-dominated after-school programs, the over-scheduling of children's free time, and the increasing pressure on children to adopt the work ethic as they begin elementary school (or even before) have emerged as major social problems. Free play and "doing well at school" have become mutually exclusive in the minds of many adults, and this perception has now begun to transform one of the last vestiges of free choice in every child's day—recess.[2]

The LMS Forts

As a lower elementary teacher at Lexington Montessori School (LMS) in Lexington, Massachusetts, from September 1994 through June 2002, I witnessed for eight years the development of an extraordinary child-centered and spontaneous world of recess play. As children entered the elementary program at LMS, they were initiated into a culture of fort building by their peers. Many continued this form of play through sixth grade as their main recess activity. Even after more than a decade of evolution, fort play remained one of the most popular forms of social interaction at the school. Fort play was theirs alone, a brief window of opportunity among hours of mostly adult-inspired activities and expectations for these children to manage their own lives and interact with each other on their own terms. The forts, built entirely from sticks, leaves, and found objects from the surrounding woods, were the site of considerable experimentation with different forms and rules of social organization and various styles of construction. They were also the vehicle for much of the conflict that occurred at the school. Children negotiated and clashed over ownership of land and resources, and argued about the rules and roles of fort play and about whether the rights of those already identified with a structure outweighed the rights of outsiders to be included. In doing so, they developed and influenced each other's reasoning about such moral principles as benevolence, justice, and reciprocity. Fort play was unpredictable, immediate, exciting, and fun, in a way that classroom work only occasionally could approximate.

As important as it was to the children, fort play was tolerated by LMS teachers for the most part with a mixture of fascination, confusion, and frustration. Fort conflicts and issues requiring mediation and arbitration by teachers seemed to fill staff meetings and dominate classroom discussions. One teacher recalled a period in the mid-1990s "where recess was one long stream of crying children saying 'Someone stole my stick!'" At one point, the faculty came very close to banning forts altogether, but most understood how important fort culture was to the children who engaged in it, and so were prepared to allow it even while secretly wishing it would disappear.

The most obvious prerequisite of fort play at LMS was the opportunity offered by the upper recess field and its surrounding woods. This field was created in 1990 after the new elementary building was constructed to house 58 children—42 lower elementary students in two classrooms and 16 upper elementary students. An adjoining three-acre woodland property was leased and cleared. Grass was laid and a sprinkler system installed in anticipation of the children's need for soccer and other organized, competitive games at recess. For most supervising adults, the open field constituted the optimal play area for recess, since it allowed for large cooperative and competitive sports and games, and for easy supervision of large numbers of children.

From the very first weeks of the new field, however, most of the children were drawn away from its large open spaces and the organized games and into the woods still surrounding it on all sides. From all accounts, fort play began almost immediately with sticks piled up from the clearing process, despite the best intentions of those who had sought to plan the children's free-play activities. As in the case of other schools where fort play has flourished, this was in no way a programmed activity but rather a spontaneous one that simply wasn't stopped.[3]

As children were released for recess each day, they made their way across the small lower field and up a gently inclined path through woods to the upper field. As they reached the crest of the path, an open field roughly the size of a soccer field emerged before them through the trees. The woods surrounding the upper field were a multisensory wonderland of microhabitats, with an unlimited array of elements to touch, taste, smell, hear, and feel. They provided enclosed areas for both solitary and social play—spaces to stroll easily among fern groves or cedar and oak trees with a friend, as well as places to retreat by oneself. The woods also provided for a great diversity in interest and ability level. There were hills to climb, nooks to explore, animals, plants, and rocks to find, and innumerable loose parts for both collection and construction. For those children who on any particular day were either not interested in competitive sports or cooperative games like tag and chase, or who were unwilling or unable to navigate the rules of access to these games, the woods provided a textured canvas for their malleable and social imaginations.

What Drew LMS Children to Fort Play?

By the spring of 2000, the elementary program at LMS had grown to a population of 104 students in three lower and one upper elementary classrooms. Almost 60 percent of these children were involved in eleven forts over the period I conducted my observations, interviews, and surveys, with greater interest (68 percent) at the lower elementary level than at the upper elementary level (44 percent). Although a greater percentage of girls (57 percent) than boys (43 percent) claimed on their surveys to be participants in fort play, this difference probably had more to do with the lack of interest or exclusion many girls may have felt from organized games of soccer and football happening on the field than with any marked difference in interest in fort play between the genders. While fort play did not engage every child at each recess, almost all elementary children at the school during the spring and fall of 2000 had participated in fort play at one time or another.[4]

Despite the ambivalence of many teachers, the students I interviewed were quite clear about what fort play offered them. Their responses were diverse; children—even the same child—may participate in fort play for different reasons. I found that the interests of LMS fort players, both past and present, clustered around several main attractions.

The excitement of building. Some reported being drawn to fort play for the excitement of building and maintaining a structure they felt was their own. Carlotta and Zeke began their first fort as a structure to serve as the Warner Tower in a game based on the television cartoon *Animaniacs*, but soon discovered that they were having more fun building the fort than imitating the characters. Alfie said that he and his friends found the woods "more interesting than the barren field." He recounted how they used the fallen branches and other found forest detritus to construct their fort, "because it just seemed like the right thing to do…It was as if we built the structure itself because we had nothing better to do, but the reality is that we did: We had a whole field at our disposal with balls and Frisbees and cones, but for some reason building a fort seemed like a more productive use of our time."

The LMS forts generally were constructed either as open spaces with boundaries marked out with stones or sticks or as enclosed structures, which were limited to "teepee," "lean-to," and "pile fort" designs by the lack of binding materials. The open forts tended to be used more intensively after construction as a locus for social gatherings or for the practice of domestic skills like sweeping or making "food."[5] For enclosed huts—usually though not always constructed by boys—the act of building itself was often the important thing. Once these structures were complete, there was often little room and few sticks for further expansion, which meant that the only way to keep the excitement of construction alive was to demolish and rebuild either in the same place or in a new location.

Many of my fall 2000 interviews were spent following children around as they swept out leaves from the dirt floors of their forts or ran off to find just the right stick to fill a gap in a wall or roof. This interest in building generally had a social aspect. When asked what he liked about his fort, one boy looked thoughtfully at his structure and said, "It's strong, it's roomy, and it's a teepee shape. People in it work on it together. We have no boundaries. Everyone's allowed in it, but you can't steal from it." When I asked him if having a fort had taught him anything useful, he didn't hesitate in answering: "Cooperation, like holding big sticks [to put them in place]. You have to learn how to build a fort. You can't just make it up! You have to stand on it to see if it's strong." One girl, with a makeshift twig broom in her hand, told me as she swept, "It's a small fort; we don't have to do so much work. But we have to rake up all the twigs and put them in the fire. Long sticks are for the doorway." Many fort members wished they could make their forts more weatherproof, and one boy lamented they weren't able to keep the bugs out.

Sharing social spaces. Another attraction of forts involved the containment offered for friendships. Forts were both a way for these children to get to know others whom they might never have otherwise met and a manageable vessel for friendships they already had. Dale said he "enjoyed forts for three reasons. First, they were fun to build. Second, it was fun to be part of an 'exclusive group.' Third, I got closer to my friends in this setting." Victor's special place was more of a "hangout in the corner of the recess field" than a "real fort." "It was merely a place where me and my friend would play during recess, and eventually, it became 'ours'…I guess it might have helped me build friendships with those I played with in our fort. It also maybe gave me a sense of belonging in recess."

Others spoke or wrote of needing to have a semi-private place to go by themselves or with a close friend or two to be away from the crowd.

129

As one group put it, "We just wanted an area to ourselves. Like in childcare, we could play by ourselves. It gets out of hand with too many people. In another fort, two years ago over there in the valley, we had a bad time with too many people. [Our teacher] made us have everybody in it. We don't know why." A younger girl new to the elementary program told me she liked her new fort, which was just for first-year lower and first-year upper elementary children, because "It's small, and it fits a few people. It's our space. No one can come into it without asking." This girl started her own fort with some new friends "because no one was inviting us into their forts—we felt sort of left out."

Forts were also a way of learning how to work with and get along well with others. According to one girl, being in a fort ensures "[You're] not bored at recess just standing there. It's fun! We have invisible horses in it....It's also annoying when you get mad at your friends and they stomp off!" A group of girls in a fort known for its strong-willed leader told me that having a fort has "taught us survival maneuvers. You know, in business, how to trade, argue, and fight with other forts [over ownership of sticks]!"

Living in nature. A refuge in the natural world or enjoyment of the physical space surrounding a fort were a third set of reasons cited by LMS students for their interest in fort play. Renata, who described her fort as "a beautiful place" and "sort of a little house in nature,"

began it by herself as a timid new elementary student. She required a secret code to enter, picked ferns to "brew," ground flowers to make "food," and used Frisbees from the field to catch water and carry things. Several forts showed me little gardens they had cultivated. Another girl enjoyed the site chosen for her fort because she had found berries in the woods nearby, remarking that "I like how we can make ink with berries. I made a quill with a feather, and we also make chalk with a soft rock." The sight of a snake further off in the woods, which the group wanted to identify, heightened their experience. Another child known for his profundity was succinct about the advantages of his fort: "Nature. We know we can plant things. We can play together too. We get bored with the play structure, but there's always a challenge in the forts." Having a fort, he said, "gives us a better connection with nature, the stuff that's around us. We don't have to bring in stuff like string because what we need is all around us. We don't want to pollute." When I asked a different group whether being in a fort had taught them anything useful, one girl echoed this common double reply: "It teaches me to live in nature. And it gets me more friends."

An interest in natural or found objects and in the social relationships of fort play also coincided in another fort's reputation as a trading post. "We used to sell slate, sticks, pipes, and natural things that were cool and beautiful. And we once had a war with [another leader's] fort over a box of dry acorns!" In another interview, one boy said that working on his fort had given him a sense of how people lived "in the olden days." Several children even thought they might be better off if they ever had to survive in the wild.

Inclusiveness and competition. Some former students—mostly those who were leaders in their forts during the early years in the evolution of fort culture at LMS—mentioned another reason for their consuming interest in fort play: self-esteem. Many, and by some accounts the majority, of the early forts were in-groups with hierarchies of command based on status or age, which formed into tight units through their competitive relationships with other fort groups. Several students described being unashamedly seduced by the combativeness and intrigue of fort culture and the competition with other fort groups for sticks and other resources that heightened the camaraderie and solidarity of their own group. Some who were not at the top of their fort hierarchy mentioned feeling important through their association with a powerful fort or warlike leader. And the leaders were not all boys. Lorena wrote that having her own fort taught her to be an "uncompromising, no-nonsense, those-sticks-are-mine" leader, and expressed the opinion—gained through fort play—that people who were too nice tended to get taken advantage of.

Carlotta wrote with glee about her "wooden empire." She noted that the forts were "a way of organizing a social hierarchy—typically the fourth and fifth graders ran the show, and younger kids would 'work for them' in the hopes of one day inheriting the property. For me, forts [became] a source of power….Carrie and I were extremely strong personalities, and we wanted to command a fort that was politically active and involved. However, the strongest fort on the field was a boys-only empire built on top of the hill. So after trying to join the few 'ninny' girl-forts, we set out to create a fort of our own that would one day rival Wilbur and Geoff's….Fort playing ultimately taught me to be an effective military commander….Dale and I often drew out actual battle plans for our raids on Wilbur's fort. And these were not just dumb attacks—we chose paths, we divided ourselves into platoons, we had commanders, and we had signals. This was a complicated military system—and to us, these were real wars."

Wilbur's fort gave him "a home, a cool place to chill, a club, friends, a shelter, a federation, a barracks, a castle, a ski resort, a hotel." It provided "an opportunity to have a semi-exclusive group of friends whom you could trust more than others. You could declare war on another fort and attack them and raid their surplus, plunder their villages and steal their valuable merchandise."

Almost all of those former students surveyed reported playing in their forts every recess. Although Carlotta and her friends spent much of their third elementary year participating in team sports at recess, "as time went on, we found ourselves once again drawn to the idea of forts." In fact, for those children whose identities were heavily invested in their forts, it was difficult to do anything else at recess except play in the forts. The fort culture Carlotta helped create each day had also become her captor. "If there was a day that I did not feel like going to my fort, I was stuck. If I left my fort alone for one day, then by next recess it would be completely destroyed by Wilbur and Geoff. It was a full-time recess commitment, with no breaks and no vacations." Even children lower down on the hierarchy of their fort sometimes reported feeling pressure to participate each recess or face the threat of losing their position in the chain of command.

For those former students especially who seemed to have a strong personal investment in maintaining the hierarchical structure of the forts they were a part of, conflict and competition with other forts was the most important part of fort play. According to Carlotta, "Forts competed with each other in two ways: Which fort was physically bigger, and the other, which fort had a greater following. These two issues often resulted in 'fort wars' which were sometimes very violent. Fort competition was huge….Wilbur's and mine were the ultimate rivals—the Yankees and the Red Socks of the recess field. We had battle plans, we had recruits, we had wars—we were basically building empires. Like France and Britain, we fought for recess field domination in the greatest war of LMS. [As good sticks became scarce] our competition was fueled by the need for more supplies—and what better place to get them than your opponent's fort? The economic structure of the forts was essentially that of the mercantile system, driven by the zero-sum principal, 'a gain for my enemy is a loss by me.' Therefore, we would raid, attack, and steal from Wilbur's fort in an attempt to expand the size of our own."

Wilbur's recollections were similar: "We would loot and plunder forts during wars with materials such as distraction a very fine powder dust, which, when thrown into the air correctly, leaves you in a cloud of dust with time to get away unseen. We had 'oogabooga sticks' to use as make-believe spears, swords and knives. But before all this we would usually have a meeting similar to a Mafia meeting between two crime families. The head of each fort would meet somewhere in the woods or inside a fort to discuss things. All the members of both forts would wait outside a little ways away ready for new orders. If an agreement could not be made there would be war."

All respondents agreed that the most common cause of conflicts between forts involved either sticks ("the universal currency" in Lorena's words), or the ownership of territory surrounding a fort.[6] But other conflicts occurred within forts themselves, remembered by many former students who were not at the top of their fort's hierarchy, or who had less overtly competitive interests in fort play. Donald remembered more arguments over leadership and decisions within forts than conflicts between forts. Many, such as Victor and Eliza, referred to conflicts over who should join and what position people should occupy within their fort. In other forts, conflicts occurred over such decisions as which renovations to make, and who was doing more of the work of maintaining the fort.

The Need for Agreement over Rules

While forts functioned as containers to hold friends in, they also often functioned (either inadvertently or by design) to keep others out. On the one hand, most children didn't want to exclude others because they remembered how it felt to be left out. On the other, forts provided a safe and manageable social space precisely because they limited access. This contradiction emerged more clearly as I asked students to tell me about the rules of fort play. Leaving the environment unharmed was mandated by at least one fort.[7] Some cited rules such as "doing your fair share of the work," "sharing," and "being considerate." Interestingly, several students stressed the important principle of not excluding others, and in several cases these were the same individuals who said they enjoyed being part of an exclusive group or "club" of friends.

In the early years of fort culture at LMS rules were not discussed explicitly among students, and many former students believed that there were no commonly accepted rules of fort play, aside from the general school rules that teachers imposed. But those in leadership positions sometimes saw a benefit in the lack of common rules of fort play and the lack of direct teacher involvement. Many leaders hinted at the importance of not getting caught stealing sticks and of limiting violence so that teachers would not be called to arbitrate. For Lorena, it was important to not "get someone so mad that they'll tell a teacher." The most common rule acknowledged by former students active in the early years of fort culture was the imperative of loyalty to one's fort. Loyalty meant no joint membership or switching to another fort. For some, loyalty meant not trespassing in others' forts, as well as guarding against trespassing by others in one's own. For Alfie, as for other leaders, "there was no greater crime than treason, punishable by what is best summed up as an excommunication from the fort."

In written surveys, I asked children to describe the worst thing about playing in forts. Some answers focused on uncomfortable conditions or difficulties with construction, including collapses, being too cold to play in during winter, leaking when it rained, difficulty keeping forts clean and free of fallen leaves, or just being too small and overcrowded. However, by far the most common complaints—particularly at the upper elementary level—were related to the social dynamics of fort play. Arguments within and between forts over property or rank, stick stealing, exclusion, being "fired" or "bossed around" by leaders who expected younger or newer fort members to spend recess gathering sticks or sweeping out the fort, and fort "wars" all were cited by both girls and boys as the most unpleasant aspects of fort play.

The Crisis

Whether forts were the chicken or the egg of conflict between students at LMS in the early to mid-1990s remains unclear. But as the competitive nature of many forts escalated already existing tensions both on and off the recess field, parents and teachers were becoming increasingly concerned and frustrated. By 1994, the new interim Head of School had begun facilitating weekly lunchtime community meetings for any interested students on issues of their choosing. These voluntary meetings soon came to be dominated by fort disputes. Rules decided at community meetings were supposed to be binding on all elementary students. However, these meetings generally were avoided by those fort leaders whose competitive interests often were driving the conflicts. Several scoffed at what they saw as attempts by less powerful children to use these teacher-sanctioned meetings to challenge their authority.

In December 1995, after many long, voluntary community meetings, *The Ultimate, Absolute Fort Rules* were agreed upon by those children who attended and then presented to the rest of the community. In the hope of removing some of the ambiguity that was a source of much of the hurt feelings and intrigue in fort play, these rules governed ownership and boundary rights, stick-trading rights, and under what circumstances members could be "fired." Conditions and exceptions, however, left plenty of room for maneuver by distorting and misrepresenting the intentions of others. Although negotiated by students themselves with facilitation and sanction by the Head of School, all former students surveyed (several of whom were at those meetings) unanimously reported feeling that these rules were subtle impositions by teachers that did not help their situation.

One rule proposed by some teachers but never officially adopted was the rule "You can't say you can't play" (from the title of Vivian Paley's 1992 book). It challenged one of the central tenets of exclusivity in fort culture—the right to deny membership to anyone seeking access and the right of leaders to "fire" existing members who didn't play by "the rules"—and stood in direct contradiction to the exclusive nature of forts that many children still openly valued. Although it was never imposed by teachers, this rule was resented by many fort leaders as a teachers' attempt to control a culture that essentially belonged to children. However, several students not in leadership positions mentioned the importance of this unofficial "rule" to those with lower social standing, and the relief it brought them from the whims of their fellow students.

A New Generation Unites
to Oppose Fort Wars

Fort culture regenerated every other season. Except for those few diehards willing to dig out their forts from under the snow in winter, most elementary children at LMS participated in fort play during the autumn months before the snow set in and again in the spring months after the forts had thawed. The forts were used during the summer months by children attending the school's Summer Camp program, although many of these children did not attend LMS during the rest of the year and so did not respect the ownership, territorial boundaries, and social conventions of fort play reestablished each fall and maintained in children's memories until spring. While the larger, more elaborate forts often survived the natural and social ravages of the summer months with few alterations, many fort players complained that they had to begin again or substantially remodel old structures come September. "Somebody took my best sticks!" became a leitmotif filling the air of recess, classrooms, and staff meetings in early fall.

Other changes interrupted the continuity of the forts from one year to the next. New students entered the elementary program from the Children's House early childhood program or from other schools, and were initiated into the culture of fort play by older classmates or siblings. Memories faded over the long summer months and alliances shifted as personalities matured and children looked for new roles in a fresh social landscape that offered both stability and change. While many friendships persisted from year to year—giving some forts a persistent core of dyads or triads over time—all forts interviewed showed a substantial change in membership between spring and fall. Fort membership was also somewhat fluid throughout the year, as some children learned to cope with conflict by leaving established groups to start their own forts, and others consecrated new friendships made during the year with invitations to join each other's forts. Many fort groups also periodically sought out new sites, with favorite sites sometimes changing hands when it was agreed that they were no longer "owned."

A noticeable change took place in fort culture from the spring to the fall of 2000: Fort membership had become increasingly fluid, with larger numbers of children involved in more than one fort simultaneously. The structure of forts showed greater diversity in many respects, including race, class, gender, and inter-classroom membership. However, one of the most interesting developments was the resurgence of open war games between at least two fort groups, and the reactions of the community. These fort wars were different from the mere conflicts over ownership of sticks and boundaries that had become endemic to fort play. They were initiated by a new fort group composed of four or five six-year-old boys and one six year-old girl (the sister of one of the boys), all unfamiliar with the flavor of fort culture as it had developed to that point. Calling themselves either the "Global Radar System" or "The Army Base," this fort group was led by a determined and uncompromising Napoleonic "general" (as he often referred to himself) with a strong personal interest in proving his authority on the battlefield, an interest that harked back to some of the leading figures in the early days of fort play at LMS.

During the first weeks of school that fall, this fort group appropriated an abandoned fort structure that had been built and abandoned the previous spring by some upper elementary boys who had since lost interest. This fort was in a strategic position on top of the sledding hill overlooking the field, a stone's throw from "Wilbur's fortress." Imagining his "battle center" filled with "guns, computers, skateboards, all the best stuff," the General saw his fort's mission as guarding and protecting themselves from "the evil bad guys" whom he was convinced were trying to steal his sticks to make their own forts. To do this, he believed, he and "his men" needed to hide out, spy on others, and proactively attack those other forts who were, or might be, planning to attack them. Some of the little General's

"men" were not as sure of this plan, but were drawn into the conspiratorial drama by their leader's apparent eye-witness accounts of how older boys allegedly had taken their sticks.

When I asked some of the others what the purpose of their fort was, one member reluctantly replied, "Well, I didn't exactly want to be in it, but [the leader] asked me and he's my friend." When asked whether fort play had so far taught him anything useful, one member offered this profound observation: "If poor people came, we'd just build a fort for them and give them the materials. Life isn't just one huge thing you know, it's about friendship. Life is hard work. Doing stuff for forts is really hard work!" War play for these young boys apparently was not intended to be about violence and destruction but rather about their opposites: friendship, bravery, and protection of one's honor.

But other children took this fort group's actions to be either a hostile provocation, or perhaps even an invitation to add interest to their own recess play. While the members of this fort, and the General in particular, were alone in their single-minded immersion into the symbolism of war play and the intrigue of spying on other forts, it wasn't long before their repeated threats, accusations, and defensive aggression had pulled one or two other forts into this self-fulfilling drama. Within a month, and despite the intervention of staff members, this fort's fantasy play had become a reality, with daily raids and counterattacks, yelling, the occasional physical scrape, and lots of hurt feelings. Only recently having begun to live down its ominous reputation in the community to become a relatively peaceful activity of home-making and construction, fort play at LMS now seemed to be headed quickly back toward its roots.

Although the central conflicts that these boys' own needs for war play were engendering involved only one or perhaps two other fort groups, the reaction to this form of fort play was much broader. It is this reaction, and the vociferous unwillingness of many other children to tolerate openly aggressive war play, that suggests that some big changes may have been taking place in fort culture at LMS since the halcyon days of openly warring forts. The fort group with which the "Army Base" fort primarily engaged was composed of four older and larger boys. Feeling the disadvantage of his smaller size, the General tried to gain a strategic advantage in numbers by relentlessly demanding the support of some nearby forts in his campaign to liberate his fort from his perceived aggressors. Several of these other children, mostly girls, decided that they did not want this war play on their playground, and tried to convince the General that he was safe and that his campaign was unnecessary. Other children's attempts to interrupt his war play generally were interpreted by the General as hostility and as a threat to the survival of his fort. Complaints about the

General's behavior had begun to come to staff more and more frequently from many other children—even from many who were not involved directly in fort play.

In mid-November, I facilitated a discussion between the General and the group who were demanding an end to his war play. Each side was asked to listen to the other side's position and the interests that lay beneath. Hearing his need to protect his fort, the group offered to help him resolve his conflict without fighting by confronting his attackers peacefully. At first the General insisted that he and "his men" needed to resolve their conflict alone, and that the only way he could "win" was if his opponents were to "surrender." After much negotiation, he agreed at this meeting to ask his opponents to surrender peacefully, and that if they would not then he would accept the help of the group. Over the following weeks, fort conflicts at recess precipitated by the General's and others' war play continued, but so did the complaints and the resistance to this behavior by the community of children, staff, and parents who signaled in no uncertain terms that ongoing behavior of this kind would not be tolerated, whatever its value for the General and his fortmates. By mid-December, a truce was called and the war was declared over by the General himself, allowing his dutiful minions off the hook and his otherwise sound relationships with other children to flourish once again. While intervention by the

General's parents and teachers in searching for other ways for him to "win" and in affirming limits to aggressive play had been crucial to re-establishing peace on the playing field, so too had the limits offered by the unwillingness of many other children to accept this behavior as an inherent part of the culture of fort play.

Creating Social Contracts in Fort Play

A good portion of the disagreements and hurt feelings resulting from fort play may have stemmed from the difficulties many children had in organizing themselves into large and stable groups. In my interviews with fort groups, I asked how decisions were made, and what happened if the group could not decide something. Although some change occurred over time as children's awareness and organizational skills evolved, three styles of decisionmaking seemed to emerge. In all of the spring and fall interviews, only three forts admitted to having an autocratic or top-down style with a clear hierarchy of command. These forts gave their founders (those who started the fort by choosing the site and inviting others to join) undisputed control over all decisions related to the fort. A member of one of these forts said of her leader, "[She's] the boss, sort of like the mama. [She] has veto rights."

Some forts clearly were struggling between the simplicity of this top-down approach and their awareness that a more democratic style of organization possibly was fairer for everybody, if also more difficult to arrange and adhere to. One group of boys told me in the spring that their "owner" had the final word, "but would rather consensus on bigger issues." A few groups referred to several or all of the members as "heads," even though this had little or no impact on their organization or style of decisionmaking.

By far the greatest majority of the new generation of forts had a democratic form of leadership. This involved a founder who acted as fort leader with special rights and privileges, but who also had a clear sense of the value of including others in decisions as well as a plan of sorts for how that inclusion would be organized. The emphasis in these forts was on fairness and negotiation rather than on the arbitrary exercise of power—although the mechanics of the negotiation process were sometimes quite primitive. Democratic forts were most often mixed gender, and decisions generally were made at group meetings by voting or discussion.

A smaller group of forts had decided that no member of their fort should have any more rights or privileges than any other member. These children, most of them older, tended to have a clearer sense—perhaps born of experience—that rank and privilege were prime sources of conflict and hurt feelings in fort play. In the only all-boy leaderless fort, decisions were made by majority rule. When this group couldn't reach a decision, the founding member told me, "We leave it as it was before." Another boy added an afterthought that hinted at the difficulties inherent in this style of decision-making: "Some people who are dominant do it anyway." When decisions could not be reached and no one had a legitimate authority to make a decision for everyone else, the continuity of the fort group was left open and vulnerable. When I asked them what happens when members can't agree, those in leaderless forts showed greater awareness of the need to consider the others' points of view. Some said they tried to compromise: "We negotiate. We argue most about the fort's shape. We try to combine our ideas." Others gave wide berth for individuals to follow their own inclinations. One lower elementary boy in a mixed-gender leaderless fort replied to my question matter-of-factly: "We don't make decisions. We just ask each other 'Is this okay?'"

A final set of interview questions asked children about their relationships with other forts, and whether they would like to see some way for all children involved in forts at LMS to discuss fort problems with each other. Only three of the eleven forts in the spring and five in the fall claimed to have no conflicts with other forts, and virtually all of these were located well away from others. Overcrowding seemed to be a common cause of conflict here. Although adventure-driven "wars" sometimes transpired between forts on opposite sides of the field, most conflicts between forts appeared to be the result of accusations and arguments about boundaries and the ownership of sticks among forts in close proximity.

Despite the perception of a high level of conflict between forts, roughly equal numbers of fort players were for and against the idea of a community-wide discussion of fort-related problems, similar to those that had taken place in the mid-1990s. Some of those opposed to the idea of a meeting thought that the problems of forts were too specific to each group for a community meeting to resolve adequately. Some were skeptical of a community meeting because of their negative experience of voluntary community meetings in the past. One group of older girls told me that "Community meetings didn't work because not everyone came and no one listened. Lots of people broke the rules." Another voiced her ambivalence like this: "Maybe. No. It did help last year. Well, I don't know, maybe. It'd be good if forts started being nice to each other. But then after the meeting it might go back to the way it was." A little later, a member of another all-girl fort admitted what I felt some others had not been willing to spell out explicitly: "Well, it was kind of interesting stealing sticks!"

Apart from the problem of getting fort players to follow the decisions made at such a meeting, members of a mixed-gender fort voiced another dilemma that many children felt was left unresolved after community meetings in the past. After saying they would not want to participate in such a meeting, a boy in this fort added that he "would like it if people didn't have to say 'You can't say you can't play' because there'd be too many people." A girl in his fort added quickly as he finished, "But you feel bad to say no!" While children generally seemed willing to commit to an abstract rule that prohibited the exclusion of others, when it came down to their own control over the management of the conditions in their own fort, the principle of inclusion was not always easy to apply.

Conclusion: Let Recess Serve Children's Whole Development

Fort play at LMS has been a primarily social activity that was collectively constructed, owned, and negotiated at recess and beyond through a culture generated entirely from the spontaneous interests of children. This peer culture of fort play, with its rules and roles, had been passed down to succeeding generations of elementary students since it began at its present site in 1990. Fort play was not simply a break from the "real" learning that took place within the classroom, but has been, from the perspective of many students, a significant part of their overall learning experience at the school. The appeal of this activity for children derived in general from its free-ranging nature, from the control it gave them over their interactions with each other and with the natural environment. Although some children complained of having no alternatives to fort play, it seems clear that most children's interest in fort play has not been simply a result of having nothing else to do.

Individual forces in each child's personal development created or precluded the potential for this form of play. However, the social dynamics of the playground and classrooms confined and shaped this individual potential through the lure and language of friendship. As children created personal "special places" in the woods to which they could retreat physically, they were also creating manageable social environments for themselves from which they could escape the madding crowds that gathered around the play structures and in ball games on the open field. Various models of fort organization, involving social hierarchy and in-group differentiation, were negotiated collectively over time or imposed by powerful individual leaders. Conflicts erupted and were resolved—either with the guidance of teachers, parents, or other interested adults, or by the children independently. A new and spontaneous resolution to the problem of intergroup friction appeared to have been evolving toward the end of the study period in a tendency among many fort players to claim multiple membership of two or more forts at the same time. Unquestioning loyalty to one's fort was no longer the imperative it once had been.

It may not be possible to know conclusively how and why fort culture at LMS evolved over time because so many variables were involved.

However, one thing is clear: spontaneous, unstructured, imaginative play with minimal but watchful adult supervision provided a powerful medium for lessons children at LMS learned through interactions and negotiations with peers in the forts. A key ingredient was the freedom to choose their own responses and to see for themselves the consequences of their own and others' actions. Play is a powerful medium for children to construct their own understandings because it integrates the many and various sides of human being. When children play, their activity touches all areas of their physical, social, emotional, and cognitive development. This may be one aspect that gives play its pleasurable nature, that makes it fun. It also makes it unpredictable, and sometimes loud and chaotic. Outdoor natural environments provide the ideal container for children's play because they are more infinitely malleable and because, there, vigorous activity is the norm. As the natural and social habitat for outdoor play shrinks, it becomes more and more urgent that schools, the one institution dedicated to children, preserve theirs. [8]

Notes

1. Quoted in Andy Sluckin, *Growing Up in the Playground: The Social Development of Children* (London: Routledge & Kegan Paul, 1981), 111.

2. Curt Hinson, for instance, in his recent popular guide for schools "who despite their best efforts, continue to be plagued by fights, arguments, and unmotivated students on their playground," writes that "Recess in the elementary school should be an extension of the learning that takes place within the classroom…Children should be taught that recess is a time when they can play and learn without the constant constraints of adult supervision. However, this means they must take on a higher sense of personal responsibility and be on their best behavior. Recess should be a productive learning time where everyone has a purpose and works to fulfill that purpose. In essence it's still free time, but free time that must be used to accomplish specific outcomes." Curt Hinson, *Six Steps to a Trouble-Free Playground* (Hockessin, Del.: Play-Fit Education Inc., 49. While there are some useful ideas in his books, Hinson's conception of play leaves no room for self-discovery and free play because in his view children cannot be trusted with free choice.

3. See K. Dovey, "The Life and Death of the Arlington Huts," *Children's Environments Quarterly* 4, no. 4 (1987): 18–26; P. O. Maynard, *The Forts at the George C. Soule School,* unpublished manuscript; D. Sobel, *Children's Special Places: Exploring the Role of Forts, Dens, and Bush Houses in Middle Childhood* (Tucson: Zephyr Press, 1993; R. Brown-Lavoie, *Play Observation of "Martianland" at The Cambridge Friends School,* unpublished manuscript, 2000; and C. L. Sturges, *The True History of Martianland,* unpublished manuscript.

4. Some children who chose not to participate in fort play did so because of difficulties adjusting to the social challenges it can present. As his mother wrote in answer to the parent survey, one upper elementary boy "decided long ago that it was not worth the hassle to fit in. For a while he attempted to find jobs that did not mean joining a fort. Rather he would supply sticks, materials, etc. for whoever wanted them. Though I believe there was a part of him that wanted to be a part of this process, he was too aggravated by the hierarchies and in-fighting. He now mainly tries to walk the field and ignore the forts." Even though this boy did not participate in fort play, his recess choices were certainly influenced by his experiences of fort culture.

5. "Food" production was always an important domestic chore in open forts at LMS. Making food entailed scraping the soft decaying wood from fallen sticks with sharp shards of slate found in special sites around the woods. This food (or "tuna" as it was sometimes called) and the slate used to make it later were traded

or sold, and fresh-smelling cedar wood sticks were at one time used as currency. But economic exchange was never the central activity of LMS forts, unlike at the "Martianland" forts of the Cambridge Friends School, where fort construction has been more limited by the lack of woods, according to Rob Brown-Lavoie, a fourth-grade teacher at Cambridge Friends School, Massachusetts.

6. The atmosphere of hierarchy, enmity, and suspicion between fort groups was reflected in the content of *Fort News*, a spontaneous newspaper devoted to fort culture and published for several issues by another former student of the time.

7. The first rule of the Cobra Club fort was that "if three times you are caught purposely hurting nature you are out of the club." The second rule stressed punctuality to club meetings, and the third rule stated that all members "must show some way of helping nature at least once every two weeks." Cobra Club's leader awarded stars for planting or adopting plants, as well as

for researching nature topics and talking about them to the members.

8. The loss of safe, accessible, outdoor play spaces across the industrialized world is a trend that was borne out among the LMS parents surveyed in this study. Of the 38 respondents to the parent survey mailed out to families of elementary children at Lexington Montessori School, 74 percent of parents reported that they had enjoyed a special private place as children in their own neighborhoods where they could go to be by themselves or with other children unsupervised directly by adults. By comparison, only 43 percent of these same parents reported that their children currently have a "fort" or other special place outdoors where they can go to be by themselves or with friends. Even lower numbers of children reported having access to "forts" in their own neighborhoods: 33 percent of lower elementary and 21 percent of upper elementary children claimed on their survey returns to have forts in their neighborhoods, with virtually equal numbers for girls and boys.

NATURAL ARTISTS

Nurturing Childhood Creativity

Nature is so much richer than culture; one very quickly exhausts the range of manufactured products as compared with the fantastic diversity of the animal, vegetal and mineral worlds.

CLAUDE LÉVI-STRAUSS[1]

We teach our children well—to be little consumers, that is. In almost thirty years of teaching studio art at the college level, I have seen a distressing trend: Many students are so far removed from the natural world that if they are given a choice of what to draw, their subject matter is cell phones, lipstick tubes, sunglasses, keys, athletic shoes, and so forth. They draw that with which they are most familiar and most comfortable; they show little curiosity about a spider, no appreciation of the beauty of bleached bones picked up in a field, no interest in the uniqueness of a plant gathered along a roadside. This observation is symptomatic of a larger trend toward the indoor sequestration of children, their overexposure to television, computers, and video games, and their lack of contact with nature.

A culture's relationship with the natural world is reflected in its art, and our culture isn't

Ann Savageau, an associate professor of Design at the University of California-Davis, teaches courses in textiles and sustainable design. She does mixed-media sculpture and exhibits widely. Her latest work is an installation on the theme of global warming, exhibited at Washtenaw Community College in Ann Arbor, Michigan. Her work can be viewed on www.annsavageau.com.

doing as well as it should be, judging from the work favored by the contemporary art world that often speaks to irony, ennui, hubris, and disengagement from nature. In his thought-provoking book, *Balance: Art and Nature*, John Grande takes aim at some of the most cherished icons and assumptions of twentieth century and contemporary art, contending that we have lost sight of art's ultimate basis in nature, with a resulting aesthetic deprivation that goes hand in hand with environmental deprivation.[2] Marcel Duchamp, who grandly declared "Art has no biological source. It's addressed to a taste," exemplifies the ultimate expression of the divorce from nature.[3] Grande counters that, "seen in environmental terms, the artistic process is indivisible from nature because it involves working with materials. Our entire world—the fax machines, the stone and cement our buildings are made of, the paint and canvas an artist uses—all ultimately derive from and are materials in nature."[4]

Children who grow up deprived of frequent contact with the natural environment are handicapped in significant ways. Our society doesn't recognize this deprivation as a handicap, because we undervalue nature; but it still prevents them from being as knowledgeable, as sensitive, and as creative as they could be. I see this frequently in students who have grown up sheltered from the out of doors. They can't read the landscape and its inhabitants in any profound and meaningful way unless it is presented through an exhibit, aquarium, or zoo. They are bored or frightened by the natural world, and retreat to the world of manufactured goods and packaged entertainment for their sources of inspiration.

I feel fortunate that I grew up on a farm outside Fort Collins, Colorado, and that I spent most of my childhood out of doors. Our house was primarily a place to return to when you were hungry or when it was getting dark outside. Even in bad weather, I played out of doors or in the barn. We didn't buy a television until I was thirteen; my evenings were spent reading or doing homework. I can point to my years on the farm as the most important influence on my artistic and intellectual formation. Even today, those years enrich my professional work and my private life. Sustained and intimate observation of nature taught me valuable lessons and gave me a broad knowledge of plants and animals and natural processes. It also taught me self-reliance and enhanced my creativity. When people ask me where I get the ideas for my work, I think to myself: not from television or the mall.

As an artist and art educator, I am acutely aware of the importance of children's sustained contact with the outdoors in their formation as adults who will have a creative imagination and who will love the natural world enough to be committed to preserving it. As Baba Dioum, Senegalese conservationist and statesman, has observed, "In the end we will conserve only

limbs, dirt piles, lumber, large cardboard boxes, cast-off furniture, and the like. Children learn best by doing things on their own, but their creations aren't going to resemble what adults can create. All too often I have seen tidy little art projects brought home that resemble something that an adult would like to see. The teachers chose materials and projects to please parents, not to stimulate children's imaginations.

On our farm there were many things, natural and manmade, to collect and use in creative play. My friends and I spent countless hours fashioning forts, houses, and animal dwellings; by the stream we dug diversion channels and dams to create pools; we made hollyhock dolls and dollhouses; and we created imaginary environments and put on plays. We did all this without adult supervision, and in the process we developed self-reliance, initiative, and imagination.

Second, remember that nature is the source of originality and creativity, and everything else is secondhand and derivative; then act accordingly. Expose young children to the natural world on a regular basis and in a variety of settings. Let children draw, paint, sculpt, and write from direct observation of natural objects or natural settings. Keep spiders and insects and reptiles in the classroom for children to observe and draw. We experience nature in its particularity and uniqueness: *this* flower, *that* fish. Students who are separated from nature tend to come up with unimaginative, trite, generic images: daisies for flowers,

what we love. We will love only what we understand. We will understand only what we are taught."[5] How can we reverse the unfortunate trend toward children's separation from nature and encourage more direct engagement with it? I can suggest four strategies.

First, all children can be given special spaces in backyards and parks that are their own and can be used as *they* see fit. But to do this, we must be able to tolerate untidiness and free play. The raw materials that stimulate children's building instincts and creativity are exactly those that we tend to remove from our yards and parks: tree formulaic landscapes of no particular place, houses that are no particular house. Students who create from the *particular* gain enhanced powers of observation and fresh interpretations of objects. Frederick Franck's book, *The Zen of Seeing: Seeing/Drawing as Meditation*, provides a wonderful introduction to the intense observation and drawing of the particular. He notes that there really is no "ordinary" thing, and he quotes Walt Whitman: "A mouse is miracle enough to stagger sextillions of infidels."[6]

In our fast-paced society, most activities last a few seconds to no more than ten minutes. Our challenge as educators is stretch the length of time that students can focus their attention on a single activity. Frederick Franck describes drawing as a form of meditation that can be practiced by anyone. My drawing students spend the three-hour class session concentrating on the extraordinary details of a single object or on a still life—a weathered piece of driftwood, a bone, a pine cone, an insect, a rusted coffee pot. Initially, it is difficult for them to devote so much time to observing a single object or group of objects; but in a few weeks they are more focused for long periods of time. Their drawings have the special, fresh quality of drawing the *particular* that can't be achieved by drawing from memory. Even the most ordinary objects become extraordinary when drawn with attention. For example, I gave my students a piece of popcorn to study, then had them draw it large-scale, on a piece of

paper 18 by 24 inches. My students' popcorn drawings were some of the most extraordinary I have ever seen.

Third, keep in mind that humans have been hunters and gatherers for eons; settled urban life is a minute fraction of our history. Hunting and gathering and making things are our human heritage, and we must find ways to engage in these activities even today. Children are natural-born hunter-gatherers—it is one of their primary ways of experiencing and learning about the world. We need to encourage them to collect and to create from what they collect. Urban children can still do this if parents will let them scavenge from neighbors' cast-off items or bring home plant trimmings and stones to construct shelters. Teachers can ask children to bring in natural objects of their own choosing for art projects. The beauty of this practice is that it costs nothing: The outdoors is one huge, free "shopping mall."

When my children were young, we spent a

154

lot of time collecting natural objects such as acorns, sticks, rocks, seed pods, and shells and using them to fashion "critters." Then we composed stories about these "critters" and their adventures. I also involved my children in collecting expeditions, to gather raw materials for my art or for their own use. The three of them became expert at spotting what all of us might use, and at seeing the creative possibilities in what other people might consider "trash." My sons were insatiable builders of all sorts of projects made from found objects, and my daughter continues to help me collect art materials to this day.

Many artists are contemporary hunter-gatherers, scavenging found objects from a wide range of sources, including trash heaps and roadsides. My students at the Residential College of the University of Michigan had a unique opportunity in 1998 to gather willow saplings and build structures from them, in conjunction with artist Patrick Dougherty's campus residency. Dougherty specializes in making gigantic outdoor structures from woven branches, and he enlisted the help of campus volunteers. My students helped Dougherty gather the raw materials and construct his piece called *Bottleneck*. They also built their own woven willow structure that stood in the Residential College courtyard for three seasons.

Fourth, we should remember that we are descended from *Homo habilis*, an ancestor with the ability to make and use tools. Making things is something that humans have done for over a million years. Yet many of us are rapidly losing the ability to make anything, let alone tools. It is vital that we teach our children to be comfortable in nature and to work with natural materials to create things, instead of relying on store-bought materials. How are they to know what can be

made with natural materials unless they have grown up handling them, building with them? Does the average urban child know the origins and manufacture or cultivation of the items her family purchases in stores?[7] We are so removed from the natural origins of the things we depend on to survive, that if we had to depend on our own skill and knowledge to provide them, we could not.

There is a lot to be said for objects that carry the look of being crafted by human hands from "imperfect" natural materials. These pieces feel more personal; they touch us in ways that machine-produced articles cannot, even though the latter may look more "polished" or "perfect." They speak to us of deep human history, of our connection to the earth and all of its inhabitants, of our abilities and knowledge. Author Leonard Koren, in his book *Wabi-sabi for Artists, Designers, Poets and Philosophers*, sets forth the principles of "wabi-sabi," the traditional Japanese concept of beauty.[8] It is a philosophy, an aesthetic, and a way of life that celebrates the rustic, the natural, the hand-made, and much more. Koren's book could form one of the bases of artistic practice for children from elementary school through high school.

My students love to create things with their own hands—there is nothing more deeply satisfying. This is clearly evident as they collect their materials and spend long hours in the studio constructing, critiquing, refining, and helping each other. College term papers may be thrown away, but art projects are saved. Whether it is a coiled pot, a woven basket, a drawing, or a secret space, the magic of creating with one's own hands should be the birthright of every child.

These four strategies for fostering creativity don't make for a lively childhood; they have important implications throughout life. Many thinkers have commented on the fact that children's play, and their early experiences, lay the foundation for "the themata that characterize all great investigators."[9] The formative influence of childhood experiences has been documented brilliantly in two books that come to mind. In Robert Root-Bernstein's book *Discovering: Inventing and Solving Problems at the Frontiers of Scientific Knowledge*, he contends that "the arts provide tools of thought for the sciences."[10] Non-discipline bound skills such as pattern forming, visual thinking, and aesthetics are the cornerstones for many disciplines. And in *Inventing Kindergarten*, Norman Brosterman provides convincing evidence that the nineteenth-century European kindergarten system, founded by Friedrich Froebel, was a seminal influence for many of the twentieth century's most influential artists and architects.[11] His list of artists and architects who were kindergarten graduates includes Frank Lloyd Wright, Le Corbusier, Paul Klee, Josef Albers, Piet Mondrian, and others. Artist Patrick Dougherty told an interviewer, "I believe one's childhood shapes his or her choice of materials…. For me, it was exploring the underbrush of my hometown in North Carolina, a place where tree limbs intersect and where one can imagine in the mass of winter twigs, all kinds of shapes and speeding lines. In adulthood, the saplings, so plentiful along my driveway, become the raw materials with which to sketch out a series of large gestural forms."[12]

What I've outlined above can be summarized as follows. The natural world is the richest source of our creativity: Each stick, leaf, and shell is unique. Mass-produced goods are all alike. So if children collect and use natural objects for art, each object that is created will be unique, even if they use the same kinds of objects. This is excellent training for children's powers of observation and analytical thinking. These skills can carry over into their careers, whether they work in the trades, business, education, law, or medicine. We must never lose sight of our origins in, and ties to, the natural world, and to our hunting-gathering and tool-making heritage. We must devise ways to enable all children from a very young age to be part of that natural heritage, to fashion objects with their own hands, and to engage all of their senses in the exploration of the natural world; in short, to be children of *Homo habilis* as well as *Homo sapiens*.

Notes

1. As cited in John K. Grande, *Balance: Art and Nature* (Montreal: Black Rose Books, 2004), 58.

2. Ibid., 30.

3. Ibid., 60.

4. Ibid., 30.

5. From a paper presented by Baba Dioum in New Delhi in 1968 at the General Assembly of the International Union for the Conservation of Nature.

6. Walt Whitman, from *Leaves of Grass,* quoted in Frederick Franck, *The Zen of Seeing: Seeing/ Drawing as Meditation* (New York: Vintage Books, 1973), 6.

7. John C. Ryan and Alan Thein Durning, *Stuff: The Secret Lives of Everyday Things* (Seattle, Northwest Environment Watch, 1997).

8. Leonard Koren, *Wabi-sabi for Artists, Designers, Poets and Philosophers* (Berkeley, California: Stone Bridge Press, 1994).

9. Robert Root-Bernstein, *Discovering: Inventing and Solving Problems at the Frontiers of Scientific Knowledge* (Cambridge, Massachusetts: Harvard University Press, 1979), 314.

10. Ibid., 32.

11. Norman Brosterman, *Inventing Kindergarten* (New York: Harry N. Abrams, 1997).

12. Interview with Roberta Sokolitz, *Sculpture Magazine* 19, no. 2 (March 2000), as cited in Grande, *Balance,* 235.

IV. PLAYGROUNDS MATTER

The first thing you need for kids to be able to play is safe places. You can tell parents, "Let your kids play," but if bullets are flying or it's dangerous, responsible parents aren't going to let that happen. So we really have to protect childhood. It's not just about play. We have to think about who will lead us into the future and the answer is our children. We need them to be emotionally healthy. For that to happen, they have to have a childhood. We have to invest in the kind of places where children can play and develop and figure out who they are. Playgrounds. They matter.

Kids are victims of a changing perception of what good parenting is. Good parenting has become about signing your kid up for many, many different activities, about making sure that they get in the best college, and you're thinking about that when the kid is ten? When this happens,

> **What does it mean to be a child in a place where you can't walk outside?**

childhood changes. It becomes parent-driven and adult-driven rather than child-driven. We need parents to redefine success.

If success in this generation is defined as getting a fat envelope from a particular college, then we're going to produce kids who are scared to fail, who are highly regimented, who are doing precisely what adults tell them to. Why? To please adults. If that happens, we're going to lose the major thing that is going to lead our next generation: creativity and innovation. You want to hear my definition of success? Success is being happy, being kind, being compassionate, being generous, being creative, being innovative.

Kenneth Ginsburg, M.D., Associate Professor of Pediatrics, University of Pennsylvania School of Medicine. Quoted from film interview, *Where Do the Children Play?* (2007)

Anna Halverson, Nancy M. Wells, Donald A. Rakow, and Sonja Skelly

THE GROWTH OF CHILDREN'S GARDENS

Anna Halverson studied the emergence of children's gardens as a graduate student in the field of Public Garden Leadership at Cornell University.

Nancy M. Wells, assistant professor in Design and Environmental Analysis, is on the graduate faculty in the Horticulture Department at Cornell University.

Donald A. Rakow is Elizabeth Newman Wilds Director of Cornell Plantations, the arboretum, botanical garden, and natural areas of Cornell University, and an associate professor in the Department of Horticulture at Cornell.

Sonja Skelly, Ph.D., is director of education at Cornell Plantations and a lecturer in the Department of Horticulture at Cornell University.

A curious thing has happened since the 1993 opening of the Michigan 4-H Children's Garden. The garden, which was designed "to promote an understanding of plants and the role they play in our everyday lives; to nurture the wonder in a child's imagination and curiosity; and to provide a place of enrichment and delight for all children" (Michigan State University n.d.), has created a groundswell. An idea that began in a half-acre site on the campus of Michigan State University in East Lansing, Michigan, has spread across the country. According to the American Horticultural Society's website, "landscape architects and designers, teachers and botanic gardens consider the 'children's garden' as one of the strongest trends in gardening ...it continues to generate interest and does not appear to be slowing down" (American Horticulture Society n.d.-a). In recent years, children's gardens have been added at many major public gardens.

Maureen Heffernan, former Director of Public Programs at the Cleveland Botanical Garden, calls children's gardens a "horticultural revolution" that "has gently swept across the country since the early 1990s." In her book about the creation of the Hershey Children's Garden at the Cleveland Botanical Garden, Heffernan explains the appeal of these new gardens:

> Most children are not thrilled by regular public gardens…[they] become bored and restless just strolling past tastefully maintained beds and borders….However, if a garden is created with child-sized structures, secret spaces, interactive features, fun theme plantings, big bright flowers, and water, it will attract and hold the interest of children for hours—even have them crying when it is time to go.
>
> (Heffernan 2004, 2)

The children's gardens that have been developed at public gardens in the last fifteen years differ from traditional school or community gardens that focus primarily on gardening as an activity. They depart from traditional display gardens by emphasizing play. Yet they cannot be understood simply as playgrounds. They present a new paradigm for children's environments. We propose a comprehensive definition of children's gardens based on an analysis of their missions, descriptions, and stated goals:

An interactive outdoor environment, designed specifically for children, which provides opportunities for learning and playful exploration through hands-on experiences with plants and the natural world.

These gardens resonate with both children and adults because they address a need for meaningful first-hand experiences with nature in settings that promote wonder and delight. By providing settings where children can playfully explore, discover, and interact with the natural world, children's gardens fill a niche that frequently is missing from children's environments today (Moore 1996).

A powerful testimony to the impact of these gardens is that visitors often return home inspired with the vision of creating a children's garden in their communities. Maureen Heffernan remarked in a conversation in 2005, "I can't tell you the number of people who have gone through the Hershey Children's Garden and said 'Ah! Let's create this in our community!' People absolutely fall in love with this idea."

This chapter is intended for those people who "fall in love with the idea" and are inspired to embark on the process of starting a children's garden in their own community. We hope this chapter will be both informative and motivational.

Roots of the Children's Garden Movement

Children's gardens are the product of the confluence of three direct influences: playgrounds, children's museums, and children's gardening programs. Playground design has influenced children's gardens by emphasizing the importance of play in child development and by underscoring the value of safe, developmentally appropriate outdoor environments for children. From children's museums come the influences of interactive exhibits designed for children's active learning styles. Children's gardening programs have sought not only to educate children about gardening techniques but to strengthen the understanding of the essential links between people and plants (National Gardening Association 2005). We will consider the history of each of these three influences on contemporary children's gardens.

History of Playground Design

Historically, the first influence on children's gardens is playground design. The first organized playgrounds in the United States were the German-inspired "sand gardens" created in Boston in the late 1880s (Frost 1992). These playgrounds were funded by progressive civic organizations that were concerned about the lack of safe play space in the tenements of the increasingly over-crowded cities (Eriksen 1985). These playgrounds were expected to instill moral values in the children who used the space. According to a 1909 report of the Playground Association of America, games and social play were thought to inspire, "cleanliness, politeness,

formation of friendships, obedience to law, loyalty, justice, honesty, truthfulness, and determination" (as quoted in Frost 1992, 121).

Hundreds of playgrounds were created in the early part of the twentieth century at schools, churches, and in city parks. These playgrounds consisted of manufactured steel play equipment such as swings, see-saws, jungle gyms, and slides situated in paved and fenced lots (Frost 1992). The design of the traditional playground fostered gross motor skill development, but little or no thought was given to imaginative or creative play, and these playgrounds were often unsafe and presented hazards to children (Crowder 1997).

In the 1950s, playgrounds began to undergo a redesign when artists and architects began designing them (Crowder 1997). Playgrounds designed during this "Novelty Era" were filled with concrete "play sculptures" that had futuristic abstract shapes and were brightly colored. These aesthetic considerations were thought to inspire imaginative play in children, but more often appealed to adults than to children. According to Frost, such playgrounds failed because they were "abstract, fixed, lifeless and resistant to change, movement, or action by children" (Frost 1992, 125). Most troubling was the fact that the novelty play sculptures were often as dangerous and developmentally inappropriate as the traditional manufactured playground equipment (Crowder 1997).

In the early 1970s, designers became responsive to contemporary child-development theories. They created more complex play environments that fostered a variety of different play experiences (Frost 1992). Modular playground equipment was linked together in massive structures that contained slides, climbing apparatuses, and bridges. Moving from one apparatus or activity to the next was integral to the play experience. An influential designer of this period, Paul Friedberg, wrote that "moving from one experience to the next is an experience in itself. The choice of what to do next becomes an experience. The more complex the playground, the greater the choice and the more enriched the learning experience" (Friedberg 1970, 44). This type of modular play structure is still found on most playgrounds today (Frost 1992).

A type of playground design that failed to take root in the United States but nonetheless has influenced children's gardens is the "Adventure Playground." First developed in Denmark in 1943, this concept spread throughout Europe in the ensuing decades (Allen 1968). Playground designers had noticed that children seemed to gravitate toward junk yards and building sites. In those untidy sites, children invented games and developed their own forms of play incorporating unused or abandoned materials. Adventure Playgrounds attempted to replicate this type of environment by providing loose parts such as discarded lumber, tires, and bricks. Children were supervised by a play leader who showed the children how to use the tools and who ensured safety (Allen 1968, 56). The children who played at these Adventure Playgrounds were free to alter the environment in any way they wished: building, digging, demolishing, and painting. The National Playing Fields Association of England describes an Adventure Playground as

> a place where children of all ages, under friendly supervision, are free to do many things that they can no longer do easily in our crowded urban society; things like building—huts, walls, [and] forts…; lighting fires and cooking; tree climbing, digging, camping; perhaps gardening and keeping animals; as well as playing team and group games, painting, dressing up, modeling, reading—or doing nothing. (quoted in Eriksen 1985, 24)

The fundamental premise of the Adventure Playground, that children direct their own playful learning by interacting with rich, stimulating environments, is evident in today's children's gardens.

Currently, a movement is afoot among innovative playground designers, early childhood educators, and children's environments experts to create playgrounds that use vegetation and the natural environment as the foundation of playground design. Notable examples of "naturalized playground" initiatives include the Natural Learning Initiative, Planet Earth Playscapes, the White Hutchison Leisure and Learning Group, and the Natural Playgrounds Company. According to Randy White of White Hutchison,

…these new naturalized play environments do not depend on manufactured play equipment. Rather than being built, they are planted—they use the landscape and its vegetation and materials as both the play setting and the play materials…[They] are designed from a child's perspective as informal, even as wild, and as a place that responds to children's development tasks and their sense of place, time and need to interact with nature. They…stimulate children's natural curiosity, imagination, [and] wonder. (White 2004)

Naturalized playgrounds have much in common with children's gardens. Robin Moore, director of the Natural Learning Initiative, describes naturalized playgrounds as "stimulating places for play, learning, and environmental education—environments that recognize human dependence on the natural world" (Natural Learning n.d.). According to Moore's description, a naturalized playground might also fit the definition of a children's garden used in this chapter. The main difference is that naturalized playgrounds are play spaces connected to a school or early childhood center (Natural Learning n.d.; Planet Earth Playscapes 2001; White Hutchinson 2005). This distinction may disappear as naturalized playgrounds are created outside the context of school or early childhood center grounds.

History of Children's Museums

A second historical influence on the development of children's gardens is children's museums. The Brooklyn Children's Museum opened its doors in 1899, followed a few years later by museums for children at the Smithsonian, and in Boston, Detroit, and Indianapolis (Gibans 1999). Early children's museums focused on natural history and displayed collections of fossils and rocks, insects, American Indian artifacts, and stuffed birds and turtles (Lewin-Benham 1997).

The founders of these institutions were influenced by such late nineteenth-century educators as John Dewey and Maria Montessori, who emphasized the value of learning by exploration (Gurian 1997). The museums sought to educate children about the natural world by allowing them to examine the artifacts in their collections. The educational objective of early children's museums was to "delight and instruct the children who visit," and "stimulate their powers of observation and reflection" (Alexander 1999, 192).

After World War I, children's museums' primary focus on the natural world expanded to include the study of other cultures, including their history, geography, and art. Until the 1960s, their collections remained under glass in a traditional exhibit format. During this time, children's museums experienced modest growth. About thirty children's museums were created in the sixty years after the founding of the Brooklyn Children's Museum (Gibans 1999).

Until the 1960s, children's museums tended to serve a much older audience than is typical of a children's museum today. Most of the visitors were upper elementary school students who participated in clubs and workshops that were offered by the museums (Gurian 1997). In the 1960s, Jerome Bruner, whose research contributed to the development of the Head Start program, showed that very young children benefit from stimulating experiences and environments. A result of these findings was that parents began to seek out enriching opportunities for their youngsters, which included bringing them to children's museums. The ensuing drop in the average age of visitors prompted children's museums to design exhibits that were geared to the developmental needs of younger audiences (Maher 2001).

In 1964, Michael Spock, son of famous pediatrician Dr. Benjamin Spock, revolutionized the children's museum experience by creating an interactive exhibit called "What's Inside" at the Boston Children's Museum (Lewin-Benham 1997). Children were given the opportunity to take apart a variety of different familiar objects to find out what was inside. This innovation marked a paradigm shift in exhibit design at children's museums and led to the explosion of children's museums across the country (Lewin-Benham 1997). Another important influence on the evolution of children's museums was the approach to science exhibits developed at the Exploratorium in San Francisco in the early 1970s. Visitors were given hands-on access and guided in open-ended exploration of scientific topics (Maher 2001). The exhibits were designed to encourage children to touch, experience, and investigate the materials, components, or principles illustrated in the exhibit.

The excitement generated by the interactive exhibits at the Boston Children's Museum and the Exploratorium resulted in the creation of more than eighty new children's museums in the 1970s and 1980s (Maher 2001). Now the fastest-growing type of cultural institution, more than one hundred new children's museums opened between 1990 and 2003 (Association of Children's Museums 2005). Well over two hundred children's museums operate in the United States and approximately eighty-five are in the start-up phase. In 2003, over 25.7 million children and families visited children's museums (Association of Children's Museums 2005).

For most of their hundred-year history, children's museums have been started through grassroots organizing (Gurian 1997). The Association of Children's Museums (ACM) has published a comprehensive guide to establishing children's museums called *Collective Vision: Starting and Sustaining a Children's Museum*. This manual covers many of the start-up issues of a children's museum and is a valuable resource for organizers of new children's gardens as well. ACM also maintains an email list-serv for children's museum professionals that serves as a forum for the exchange of ideas related to operating children's museums or children's gardens. Instructions for joining the list can be found at https:mailman.rice.edu/mailman/listinfo/childmus.

History of Children's Gardening Programs

The first organized children's gardening programs in the United States were started in the early twentieth century as part of a progressive effort to provide wholesome activities for the children of poor and working-class families in cities (Crowder 1997). As with the earliest playground designs, the designers of these gardens had moral and pedagogical objectives. Advocates of gardening programs believed that they would teach children "civic virtues; private care of public property, economy, honesty, application, concentration, self government, civic pride, justice, the dignity of labor, and the love of nature by opening up to their little minds the little we know of her mysteries, more wonderful than any fairy tale" (Greene 1911, 4, quoting Mrs. Henry Parsons in Report of the First Children's School Farm in New York City, for 1902–1904). The first public children's gardening program was established in 1914 at the Brooklyn Botanic Garden. The program focused on teaching horticultural skills and related subjects, and provided garden-related art and craft projects as well (Crowder 1997).

The School Gardens Association of America was formed in 1910 to help individuals and communities establish gardens (Crowder 1997). School gardens flourished during the war-time years when planting a vegetable garden was considered an act of patriotism. These programs taught not only gardening, but also values such as hard work, perseverance, and cooperation.

Today, gardening programs at schools and in community gardens increasingly are focused on integrating gardening and plants into other areas of the formal curriculum such as math, science, language arts, history, and social studies. The American Horticultural Society (AHS) is a founding member of the Partnership for Plant-Based Learning, a coalition of organizations devoted to promoting the use of plants in formal educational programs (American Horticultural Society n.d.-b). AHS and the National Gardening Association (NGA) strongly emphasize the philosophy that plants can be used in many areas of the curriculum, not just in science or ecology.

The NGA focuses on gardening, not on the garden, as a unique environment for children's development. The NGA youth gardening website, www.kidsgardening.com, has a great deal of information about gardening project ideas, activities, and educational programs. It is also a good resource for teachers, parents, and others who are gardening with children, and contains information about small grants and awards for youth gardens.

AHS developed a demonstration children's garden at their headquarters at River Farm in Alexandria, Virginia. Since 1993, AHS has organized the annual Children and Youth Garden Symposium. This meeting originally focused on children's gardens, or "reconnecting children with nature through …landscapes designed specifically for children and the way they play, explore, and interact" (American Horticulture Society n.d.-a). Recently, the focus of the symposium has expanded to include a school gardening component reflecting the popularity of such programs among teachers and parents. The annual meeting continues to serve as the leading forum for the exchange of ideas related to children's gardens.

The AHS youth gardening webpage, www.ahs.org/youth_gardening/index.htm, contains many links and references that are useful for organizers of children's gardens. The AHS has commissioned several white papers on the importance of gardens and plants in the school curriculum. Also on the website are a link to their "National Registry of Children's Gardens," information about the annual national children and youth garden symposium, and their resource list for children's gardening.

Two particularly notable gardening programs are "The Life Lab" and "The Edible Schoolyard." The Life Lab is a nonprofit organization devoted to "environmental stewardship by promoting science and garden-based education for all learners" (Life Lab n.d.). The Life Lab has developed curriculum manuals, educational programs, and training for teachers who want to incorporate garden-based learning. The Life Lab organization has also created a two-acre Garden Classroom at the Center for Agroecology and Sustainable Food Systems at the University of California, Santa Cruz, to serve as a model school garden.

The Edible Schoolyard at the Martin Luther King Middle School in Berkeley, California, is an organic gardening program developed by chef and author Alice Waters. At the Edible Schoolyard, middle-school children actively participate in all aspects of food production from planting to harvesting to preparing recipes using the produce grown in the garden. The program relates the food kids eat to the land where it is grown in order to teach ecology and environmental stewardship, provide nutrition education, and develop more healthful eating habits. The Edible Schoolyard's website, www.edibleschoolyard.org/homepage.html, also has resources about starting a school garden.

The history of playgrounds, the development of children's museums, and the evolution of the children's garden movement all have left their mark on the contemporary children's garden. These three historical influences have affected both the designs and the missions of children's gardens. In particular, the contribution of current trends in playground design is seen in the deliberate use of vegetation and natural materials in the design of a place for children to play. The influence of children's museums is manifested in the use of engaging, interactive designs and is also reflected in the custom of garden spaces being called "exhibits" or "galleries." The children's garden movement contributed the notion of using plants to teach about culture, science, art, history, and nutrition. Children's gardens are the happy result of the confluence of these three elements.

Design of Children's Environments

A successfully designed children's garden reflects unique aspects of the physical and cultural setting in which it is located. No standard formula exists for designing a children's garden, but research in the area of children's environments provides insight that can be incorporated in the design process. According to Moore (1997), children prefer naturalistic, somewhat "wild" environments over manicured and highly ordered environments. Many researchers have looked into the specific elements of a naturalistic environment that are salient to children (see Eberbach 1988; Francis 1995; Harvey 1989; Heffernan 1994; Heft 1988; Raymund 1995; Whiren 1995). Among the most frequently cited components are water, tall grasses, bushes that afford refuge, flowering plants, plants of extreme size (large or small), and habitats for other creatures such as birds, butterflies, bats, or beneficial insects.

Kirkby (1989) suggests that an important characteristic of naturalistic environments is the presence of semi-enclosed, small spaces where one can see but not be seen. She found that children overwhelmingly prefer to play in such "refuges" and that in these refuges they tend to engage in developmentally significant play behaviors such as role playing, cause-effect actions, and constructive play. According to Appleton's (1975) evolutionary-based habitat theory, human beings are predisposed to seek out refuges because they provide cover from predators. Kirkby suggests that because the refuges afford a feeling of safety, children are more likely to engage in dramatic, creative, or imaginative forms of play that are fundamental to cognitive development. Kirkby found that the richest play experiences occurred in enclosures that were primarily vegetative where twigs, leaves, grass, and blossoms served as props for dramatic and constructive play. Moore (1997) notes that an outdoor environment made up of a number of different spaces of varying sizes encourages socialization in various size groups. This in turn promotes friendships and positive social interaction.

Randy White (2004), advocate and builder of naturalized playgrounds, integrates much of this research in his recommendations for the basic components of a naturalized play environment. According to White, these components include water; plentiful indigenous vegetation, including trees, bushes, flowers, and long grasses with which children can interact; animals such as creatures in ponds, butterflies, and bugs; sand; diversity of color, textures, and materials; ways to experience the changing seasons, wind, light, sounds, and weather; natural places to sit in, on, under, lean against, climb, and that provide shelter and shade; different levels and "nooks and crannies," places that offer socialization, privacy, and views; and structures, equipment, and materials that can be changed, actually or in children' imaginations, including plentiful loose parts.

These recommendations and research of children's environments experts can serve as a starting point for designing a garden that engages children's imaginations, stimulates playful learning and an appreciation for the natural world.

Conclusion

As cultural institutions and as built environments for children, children's gardens occupy new territory in the landscape of childhood. They are the product of the combined influences of the children's gardening programs, children's museums, and playground design. They fill a niche by affording interactive experiences with plants and nature at a time in our cultural history when children's access to the natural environment is becoming increasingly rare. Children's gardens are designed to nourish children's active and playful learning styles, creating spaces that encourage exploration and engage children's unique perception of the environment. Understanding what children's gardens are, the cultural factors surrounding their emergence, and the benefits they provide for children help define their place in the geographic and cultural landscape of childhood.

References

Alexander, E. P. 1999. "Anna Billings Gallup Popularizes the First Children's Museum." In *Bridges to Understanding Children's Museums*, ed. N. F. Gibans, 191–200. Cleveland: Mandel Center for Nonprofit Organizations, Case Western Reserve University.

Allen, M. 1968. *Planning for Play*. Cambridge, Mass.: MIT Press.

American Horticulture Society. n.d.-a. Youth Gardening Homepage. Retrieved August 1, 2006, from http://www.ahs.org/youth _gardening/index.htm.

American Horticulture Society. n.d.- b. Youth Gardening—Partnership for Plant-Based Education. Retrieved 6/16/05, from http:// www.ahs.org/youth_gardening/plant_based _education.htm.

Appleton, J. 1975. *The Experience of Landscape*.

New York: John Wiley.

Association of Children's Museums. 2005. Frequently Asked Questions. Retrieved June 16, 2005, from http://www.childrensmuseums.org/about/fax.htm.

Crowder, L. E. 1997. *Islands of Enchantment and Enlightenment: Designing Children's Gardens as Developmentally Appropriate Playspaces and Outdoor Learning Environments*. Unpublished MLA thesis, Georgia State University, Athens, Georgia.

Eberbach, C. 1988. *Garden Design for Children*. Unpublished MS thesis. University of Delaware, Newark, Delaware.

Eriksen, A. 1985. *Playground Design: Outdoor Environments for Learning and Development*. New York: Van Nostrand Reinhold Company.

Francis, M. 1995. "Childhood's Garden: Memory and Meaning of Gardens." *Children's Environments* 12, no. 2: 183–91.

Friedberg, M. P. 1970. *Play and Interplay*. New York: Macmillan.

Frost, J. L. 1992. *Play and Playscapes*. Albany: Delmar Publishers.

Garden Conservancy. 2001. *Taking a Garden Public*, vols. 1 and 2. Cold Spring Harbor, N.Y.: Garden Conservancy.

Gibans, N. F. 1999. *Bridges to Understanding Children's Museums*. Cleveland: Mandel Center for Nonprofit Organizations, Case Western Reserve University.

Greene, M. L. 1911. *Among School Gardens*.

New York: The Russell Sage Foundation.

Gurian, E. H. 1997. "The Changing Paradigm." In *Collective Vision: Starting and Sustaining a Children's Museum*, ed. M. Maher, 20–21. Washington, D.C.: Association of Children's Museums.

Harvey, M. R. 1989. "Children's Experiences with Vegetation." *Children's Environments Quarterly* 6, no. 1: 36–43.

Heffernan, M. 1994. "The Children's Garden Project at River Farm." *Children's Environments* 11, no. 1: 221–31.

———. 2004. *Hershey Children's Garden at Cleveland Botanic Garden: A Place to Grow*. Athens: Ohio University Press.

Heft, H. 1988. "Affordances of Children's Environments: A Functional Approach to Environmental Description." *Children's Environment's Quarterly* 5, no. 3: 29–37.

Ithaca Children's Garden. n.d. Ithaca Children's Garden. Retrieved August 21, 2006, from http://counties.cce.cornell.edu/tompkins/ithacachildrensgarden/design/index.html.

Kirkby, M. 1989. "Nature as Refuge in Children's Environments." *Children's Environments Quarterly* 6, no. 1: 7–12.

Lewin-Benham, A. 1997. "Children's Museums: A Stucture for Family Learning." In *Collective Vision: Starting and Sustaining a Children's Museum*, ed. M. Maher, 8–13. Washington, D.C.: Association of Children's Museums.

Life Lab. n.d. Life Lab Science Program Welcome! Retrieved June 16, 2005, from http://www.lifelab.org/index.html.

Maher, M. 2001. *Capturing the Vision: A Companion Volume to Collective Vision: Starting and Sustaining a Children's Museum*. Washington, D.C.: Association of Children's Museums.

Michigan State University. n.d. 4H Garden at Michigan State University, Frequently Asked Questions. Retrieved 8/01/06, from http://4hgarden.msu.edu/tour/faq.html#mission.

Moore, R. C. 1996. "Urban Vegetation and Child Development: What Can Be Done to Restore the Natural Habitat of Urban Childhood?" In *People-Plant Interactions in Urban Areas: A Research and Education Symposium*, ed. P. Williams and J. Zajicek, 81–87. College Station: Texas A&M Press.

———. 1997. *Natural Learning: Creating Environments for Rediscovering Nature's Way of Teaching, The Life History of an Environmental Schoolyard*. Berkeley: MIG Communications.

National Gardening Association. 2005. About NGA. Retrieved June 16, 2005 from http://assoc.garden.org/about.

Natural Learning. n.d. Natural Learning Initiative—About Us. Retrieved June 16, 2005, from http://www.naturalearning.org/aboutUs.html.

Planet Earth Playscapes. 2001. Play Environments for the Soul-Earth Play Home. Retrieved June 16, 2005, from www.planetearthplayscapes.com.

Raymund, J. F. 1995. "From Backyards to Barnyards: An Exploration through Adult Memories and Children's Narratives in Search of an Ideal Playscape." *Children's Environments* 12, no. 3: 362–80.

Whiren, A. P. 1995. "Planning a Garden from a Child's Perspective." *Children's Environments* 12, no. 2: 250–55.

White Hutchinson. 2005. Children's Play and Learning Environments. Retrieved June 16, 2005, from http://www.whitehutchinson.com/children.

White, R. 2004. *Young Children's Relationship with Nature: Its Importance to Children's Development and the Earth's Future*. White Hutchinson Leisure & Learning Group. Retrieved June 16, 2005 from http://www.whitehutchinson.com/children/articles/childrennature.shtml.

Susan G. Solomon

LET'S RETHINK RISK

Susan G. Solomon, author of *American Playgrounds: Revitalizing Community Space* (University Press of New England, 2005), is a consultant for the Rockwell Group's "Imaginary Playground." She received a Ph.D. from the University of Pennsylvania in 1997 and is president of Curatorial Resources & Research.

Americans have difficulty assessing risk. They shun raw milk cheese—a product from which there is no chance of infection—but spend millions of dollars on unregulated, possibly harmful dietary supplements; they purchase tons of antibacterial cleansers without considering how those products destroy necessary (and healthful) microorganisms.[1] Analogous concerns, echoed on playgrounds in the United States, are additional indicators of misplaced fears that have altered our daily lives and shaped our physical environment. Today's playground—an enclosed space dominated by a single piece of manufactured equipment—has become a risk-free zone. It is so safe that it is doing a disservice to kids.

Psychologists, biologists, social workers, educators, and designers argue that overly safe playgrounds cheat kids. A gap presently exists between what constitutes worthwhile activity

175

and where kids play. Playgrounds should supply opportunities for individual exploration, socialization, negotiation, fantasy, and gentle unexpected consequences.[2] Psychologists Kathy Hirsh-Pasek and Roberta Michnick Golinkoff have underscored the significance of uninhibited play, concluding that it "is the very fuel of every intellectual activity that our children engage in. Researchers are in universal agreement that play provides a strong foundation for intellectual growth, creativity, and problem solving…emotional development, and for the development of essential social skills."[3]

A glance at contemporary playgrounds yields a different picture. Children can climb up, run across, and slide down standardized equipment; sometimes they can scamper on a low wall or put their fingers into sand on an elevated, antiseptic table. They have few opportunities to do much else. Kids encounter a directional, isolating, unchallenging sector. There is no room for experimentation. Children rarely interact with each other, thereby limiting their chances for fantasy and social maturation. A *New York Times* feature piece in 2000 investigated kid's recreation and titled the report: "When Child's Play Is Too Simple: Experts Criticize Safety-Conscious Recreation as Boring." Citing landscape architect Paul Friedberg's notion of "safety fundamentalism," author Janny Scott referred to the frequent demise of movable parts, swings, or sand. Scott observed that safety and easy maintenance had become the major determinants of playground design, resulting in a "deadening sameness."[4] The situation has not improved in the six years since Scott's assessment. Kids are smart enough to recognize the dullness of what they are offered; they either find new (often extreme) ways in which to use playgrounds or they don't show up at all.

Our culture needs to rethink this sad condition. The playground should be transformed into a place for education, a venue that is not predictable. It should be a location for ongoing discovery, and perhaps, a site for the thrill of doing something a bit dangerous. We have to develop settings where kids can try something new, *not* succeed, then keep plugging away until they overcome obstacles. Kids with that playground experience will gain a sense of achievement; they will learn that taking a chance has its own rewards. Jennie Lindon, a child psychologist, has noted that children "need opportunities to take acceptable risks in an environment that encourages them to push against the boundaries of their current abilities, to stretch their skills and confidence."[5] Hara Marano, editor at *Psychology Today*, warns that if we eliminate "error and experimentation," then "kids are unable to forge their creative adaptations to the normal vicissitudes of life." Marano concludes that "we're on our way to creating a 'Nation of Wimps,'" filled with citizens who are indecisive, anxious, and unprepared for adulthood.[6]

Kids who engage in freer play become risk takers. That doesn't mean that they become the irresponsible folks who jump off roofs for the fun of it or set fire to homes to see what happens. They embrace a different sort of risk, the kind that Gregory Stock of the UCLA School of Public Health advocates as necessary for technological and societal change.[7] Professor Stock believes that children who take risks grow up to become scientists who reach startling conclusions by employing unproven techniques or quirky hypotheses; they become business entrepreneurs who acquire underperforming companies because they are willing to invest in the potential for positive outcomes; they become artists who know that composing or painting in unorthodox manners will allow them to have creative breakthroughs.

The American playground needs an overhaul in spite of exterior forces that stall its transformation. A safety industry argues that we can never be secure enough. Evaluators, including the Consumer Protection Safety Commission and American Society for Testing and Materials, set safety standards that are excessive. Well-meaning but misguided organizations, such as Public Interest Research Group, make surveys of playgrounds and then announce that most do not meet their stringent requirements. Parents understandably are seduced by the rhetoric of fear. In this atmosphere, what self-respecting parent would be willing to abandon the presumably safest playgrounds for their own offspring? Only those who see a bigger picture; parents who want children to acquire life skills through experiential learning. The medical community endorses such parental decisions because they have not seen the dire circumstances that the "safety lobby" proclaims. Emergency room physicians and orthopedic surgeons recurrently note that playground injuries rarely occur because of equipment or its inherent design.[8]

Americans need to recognize what British play proponents have long advocated: Distinguish between minor and major threats. Tim Gill, past director of the Children's Play Council in Britain, has argued for making a differentiation between the possibility of slight injury, which is acceptable, and the threat of serious injury, which is not.[9] Psychologist Lindon has asked if kids are "Too Safe for Their Own Good?" For Americans, even very limited risk can be a hard sell. Architect Mark Horton learned that when he designed a Montessori School in San Francisco. Horton drew a roof "slope that would send rainwater spilling down into a cistern; children would then use a hand pump to retrieve the water for gardening or play."[10] Parents nixed that innovative proposal by citing safety fears that included the breeding of mosquitoes!

Adults—recalling times when their own play focused on crawling through sand, climbing trees, digging into mounds, and building forts—need to take a look around. Kids no longer get dirty (detergent sales appear to be slowing!) and that should be a warning that something is wrong. In the past, children scraped their knees and sometimes broke an arm or leg. It just happened. A simplistic view of responsibility has supplanted earlier acceptance of injuries. The prevailing consensus is that even the most trivial accident has three components: a cause, someone to blame, and a financial payout. Lack of universal health care does make the situation a complex one.

It is up to parents to know what local schools and parks are installing for outdoor recreation. They must demand that their kids be given a chance for real play that is messy, interactive, and unpredictable. Architects can lend a hand. The Rockwell Group, a multidiscipline design firm, has been working with the New York City Department of Parks and Recreation, to create a new model that could be adapted throughout America. It might just provide inspiration for other municipalities, all of whom are free to adapt this "open source" plan. In addition to an abstract space that will allow climbing as well as hiding, Rockwell has reinstated sand and water to the primary roles they should occupy in children's play. They are also bringing back "loose parts," with which kids can manipulate their surroundings, and play workers who will allow kids to experiment but prevent any truly dangerous interactions.

Playgrounds will change when parents, educators, administrators, and designers accept the fact that risk (in small and tolerable doses) is essential if we are to have generations of competent adults. Adults who insist on risk care deeply and passionately about young people; they want kids to thrive now and have a rewarding, fulfilling future that will be packed with memories of an invigorating past.

Notes

1. Jeffrey Steingarten, *It Must've Been Something I Ate* (New York: Vintage Books, 2003), 110–12; Michael Specter, "Miracle in a Bottle," *The New Yorker* (February 2, 2004).

2. Jane P. Perry, *Outdoor Play: Teaching Strategies with Young Children* (New York and London: Teachers College Press, 2001); and Jim Greenman, *Caring Spaces, Learning Places: Children's Environments That Work* (Redmond, Wash.: Exchange Press, 1988).

3. Kathy Hirsh-Pasek and Roberta Michnick Golinkoff, *Einstein Never Used Flash Cards: How Our Children REALLY Learn and Why They Need to Play More and Memorize Less* (New York: Rodale, 2003).

4. Janny Scott, "When Child's Play is Too Simple," *New York Times,* July 15, 2000.

5. Jennie Lindon, *Too Safe for Their Own Good: Helping Children Learn about Risk and Lifestyles* (London: National Early Years Network, 1999).

6. Hara Estroff Marano, "A Nation of Wimps," *Psychology Today* (November/December 2004).

7. Gregory Stock, telephone conversation with author, July 21, 2003.

8. Dr. Nafi Khan (emergency room physician at Mt. Sinai Hospital, New York City), quoted in Michael Needham, "Scuffle Erupts on Playground Safety," *New York Sun,* June 21, 2002; Dr. O. Alton Barron (Assistant Clinical Professor of Orthopedic Surgery, Columbia University College of Physicians and Surgeons), conversation with author, June 8, 2004, New York City; Stacey Suecoff, J. Avner, K. Chou, and E. Crain, "A Comparison of New York City Playground Hazards in High- and Low-Income Areas," *Archives of Pediatric and Adolescent Medicine* 154 (April 1999): 363–66.

9. Chris Young, "Play: Equipment and Surfacing," *Landscape Design Extra* 63 (February 1996).

10. John King, "On A Mission to Put 'Play' Back in the Country's Playgrounds," *San Francisco Chronicle*, December 1, 2005.

David Hawkins

LOVING LIFE

Wild Zones and the Edible Schoolyard

David Hawkins has worked with young people in schools, colleges, adventure playgrounds, arts centers, their homes, and the street. For ten years, he worked in Inner London with boys who had been suspended from school for violent or racist behavior. He was the founding Project Manager of the Edible Schoolyard at Martin Luther King Middle School, a diverse school in Berkeley, California. dhawkins@wild-zone.net.

There is a question I return to again and again when seeking a hopeful way forward in my work with young people: How do we raise a generation of young people who love the earth and love their own lives? Given the priorities of the economy and its over-determining relationship on the education system, such a question can seem far too idealistic. After all, how many people of any age love their lives?

A quote from the great civil rights activist Howard Thurman has always given me inspiration in thinking about this. He said, "Don't ask yourself what the world needs. Ask yourself what makes you come alive and go do that, because what the world needs is people who have come alive."

In asking these questions, my wife, Karen Payne, and I have developed the idea of Wild Zones as an attempt to create a new form of social space where adults, children, and teenagers can come alive through working and playing together.

The Edible Schoolyard

The seeds of the idea of Wild Zones were planted when I was the founding Project Manager of the Edible Schoolyard at a very diverse public middle school in Berkeley, California. The Edible Schoolyard was the idea of Alice Waters of Chez Panisse and it became well-known through press and television coverage. The vision was to improve the children's nutrition and understanding of ecology by creating a garden, a teaching kitchen, and gradually developing a school-lunch program serving fresh, locally grown produce. The story, as told many times in the media, tends to focus on Alice as a celebrity with a rare and very laudable commitment to public education, nutrition, and sustainability. But how the garden was actually built by the 11- to 13-year olds, with the help of their teachers and community volunteers, is hardly known at all. This is a pity, because some things emerged there that were not foreseeable, and were more complex and harder to describe than the stories told in the media.

Although I came to love gardening as an adult, I hadn't enjoyed gardening as a child or as a teenager when doing garden work was a chore and a source of conflict with my parents. When I told an African-American neighbor about get-

ting the job at the Edible Schoolyard, he told me his great grandmother had been a slave and it concerned him that children were being expected to do compulsory garden work as part of their school day. A teacher at the school told me she was concerned that many Latino parents would be uncomfortable with their children doing the dirty, low-status work that gardening involves—just the things they hoped their children would avoid by going to school.

The weedy, trash-littered asphalt acre was a daunting prospect and some students expressed amazement that they were expected to build a garden during their school day without pay. But I think many of them were intrigued that we had so much faith in their potential. Most school gardens are created by skilled adults and sometimes by landscape architects. I knew that the garden experience had to be fun and playful if it was to capture the hearts of a majority of the kids. I also have tremendous faith in the value of free play.

Free play develops our capacity to feel at home in our own bodies and the world about us. It enlivens children's connection with the world, and with each other. It is important for their social development, in fostering their ability to negotiate, to converse, to empathize, to imagine, to organize, and to understand. Play is also important in familiarizing young people with the nature of the material world that we inhabit and the tools that we use to deal with it.

When we began creating the garden, we had a huge mound of municipal compost delivered—around 24 tons of it. I showed the team who volunteered how to wheelbarrow the compost to the beds, how best to shovel it from the edge, allowing the compost to tumble loosely down onto the shovel. When I returned fifteen minutes later to see how they were getting on, they had their wheelbarrows in a joyful throng around the crater of a smoldering volcano. The mound was being trampled and compacted in just the way I had warned them to avoid. Their joy in delving and tunneling in the warm compost disarmed me. I knew it had to be playful; it had to be fun if it was going to work.

Over the next several years, the Edible Schoolyard became the location of a great deal of energetic and high-spirited work and play for the hundreds of 11- and 12-year-old students who built the garden. My favorite part of the garden was the Middle River, which the students began to dig quite spontaneously to drain a waterlogged part of the garden where they wanted to plant apple trees during our first relentlessly soggy El Niño winter. Never have I seen such a splendid playful application of youthful energy by so many young people over such a long time. The combination of water, mud, dams, floods, jokes, and earnest hard work was a rich brew our children experience too rarely.

The students also reclaimed a particularly overgrown part of the site, cutting back and uprooting the invasive cotoneaster, terracing and replanting the bank with hazelnuts they had grown from cuttings. The huge acacia tree that was crowding the California live-oaks was harvested gradually and provided the material for building the Ramada, a circular shade structure the students built as their meeting place for the beginning and end of the garden class. Students figured out how to demolish the heavy steel railings that marked the upper edge of the bank. They planted, made pathways, bridges, and walls, and wove a huge bird's nest large enough for four or five students to nest in. Students were trusted to use axes, pickaxes, sledgehammers, and crowbars to go about their jobs, and never once did a serious accident occur in all the thousands of child hours they worked in the garden.

The Edible Schoolyard fostered a very special sort of collective activity. It is rare in our culture for young people to be given the chance to create something tangible, to care for the earth, to choose the task they would like to do, and to learn to work together in a team. Of course, there were some students who were not very interested, who hung out and watched or who had conversations, some who hindered or just got in the way. But the learning was incredible. It was not the kind of learning you could test anyone on. Sometimes it was a chance to learn what you could do, what resources and intelligence you could muster, whether your friends would be supportive, whether you could work with someone you didn't like; to learn what kinds of interaction were constructive, and how things could fall apart. It was also a chance to find out about some of the elements we depend on to live on this planet—dirt, rocks, water, and plants.

An incident from the Edible Schoolyard that always stands out in my mind is the day a reporter from National Public Radio came to the garden and interviewed some of the students. It was after school hours and she had to catch whoever came by. The garden was unfenced and always open to the public. Patrick, who had been on the first summer project when we began building the garden, happened to be in the garden. He had moved and gone to a school in another city, but he came by the garden quite often when he was visiting relatives who lived in town.

She asked him about working in the garden and then whether he liked vegetables. He screwed his face up. "Not much."

Do you like any greens?

"Not really"

"No vegetables at all?"

"Well, I don't mind carrots. We planted some carrots and after I left I came back and harvested some."

"What's your favorite food?" she asked

"Burger King."

She evidently was not getting the answers she hoped for and in a tone that was just slightly exasperated, she asked,

"Well what did you like about the garden?"

Patrick thought quite carefully for a while.

"It was the way the adults treated us."

She switched the tape recorder off and put it in her bag. She didn't ask what it was about the way the adults treated him that was important to him.

I could hazard a guess that at least one thing Patrick enjoyed about the way adults treated him was our readiness to encourage play in the garden. I have memorable photograph of him jumping in abandon over the huge compost pile. Every lunchtime, he participated in the "Royal Rumble" that took place on the big sand pile. Despite being slight and the only white boy on the summer project, Patrick held his own in joyful tussles that were never vicious or humiliating. He cooperated with two other boys in making a raised bed with branches woven together and covered with a mix of clay and straw. They called it Fort Adobe and they grew a rich mixture of corn, summer squash, carrots, lettuce, and flowers in it. It was, to my eyes, a beautiful creation that no adult could have conceived.

Wild Zones

The Edible Schoolyard served as model and an inspiration for the concept of Wild Zones. Wild Zones are ecologically rich environments that offer open-ended possibilities for self-designed play, creativity, socializing, and solitude. They differ from parks and nature reserves in that they afford the opportunity to do practical and adventurous things, such as building shelters, making trails, climbing trees, damming creeks, creating sculptures from natural objects and other types of exploration and free play. They are places for people of all ages to form bonds of caring and connection with the beauty and riches of the natural world. They will be co-created in a process that evolves as children, teens, and adults interact with a piece of land in ways that express their interests and aspirations. Wild Zones will be a resource for mobilizing both youths' and adults' sense of initiative, adventure, cooperation, spiritual healing, and enjoyment.

On one level, Wild Zones may sound like a new version of a community park or a nature reserve. The crucial difference is that in a Wild Zone, teenagers, children, and adults take the leading role in developing a place that is to be used by the whole community. People will work in intergenerational teams, as families, individually, and with friends to develop the site, allowing their vision to evolve as they gain skills, develop a better understanding of the natural world, and form interests related to the specific possibilities of their site. This context could be the beginning of a movement toward a rethinking of both how we raise and educate children and how we relate to the natural world.

Depending on the interests of the youth and adults involved, a Wild Zone will provide places to play and work with water, mud, sand, plants, and trees. They could include such elements as tree-houses, shelters, dens, forts, and other structures using natural and recycled materials; imaginative and challenging pathways and trails; planting and caring for trees, a community orchard, hedges, and wildlife habitat; earthworks, stonewalls, megaliths; sculpture and assemblage with natural materials and found objects; earth-based construction of a meeting place, camp kitchen, and other facilities for the site; water features, ponds, dams, bridges, boardwalks, and waterslides; mountain bike trails; adventure courses with imaginative play structures that include built and natural features designed to stimulate physically, mentally, and emotionally challenging activities.

The process of developing Wild Zones can contribute in many ways to community life—beyond recreation and open space—because a Wild Zone will:

- use an asset-based approach that builds on people's strengths and interests rather than focusing on their problems;
- nurture relationships of respect and trust between the generations;
- provide a context for enjoyable and challenging exercise that will combat obesity and improve overall physical and mental health;
- address environmental justice issues by inviting youth and adults of all ethnicities, classes, and abilities to engage in activities

that appeal to them and encourage them to bond with the natural world;

- be a living laboratory of conflict resolution, since every collaborative endeavor involves differences of opinion—even among like-minded and well-meaning individuals;

- encourage learning and literacy by offering an appreciation of cognitive diversity and collaborative learning, the development of practical and emotional intelligence, and pathways for stimulating children's curiosity about the world. Informal and embodied learning will give a sense of achievement to youth who are not succeeding in academic subjects;

- develop communication skills in young people through the excitement of having something to say and adults eager to listen and engage in conversation.

Skilled and playful adults will be required to facilitate the activities of a Wild Zone. In some cases, these adults might come with their families or work in youth programs. Wild Zones will be an opportunity for people in the community who are not parents to be involved. They may be artists or people who love nature or adults who want to build a treehouse or muck around with branches and rocks to make a sculpture or dam a stream or make a nest.

The experience of the Edible Schoolyard, which involved hundreds of community volunteers, showed that many adults find joy and meaning in their lives through working with two or three kids on something they enjoy. It's nothing like having the pressures and responsibilities of parenting or trying to control and teach a class of twenty or more kids who are mostly complying under duress.

In such seed relationships, community is reborn and so may be the possibility of loving one's life. We generally do not love life because of the things we buy, the places we escape to, or the status we manage to attain. It's my experience that I love life when I am able to be myself and be in authentic relationship with other people. I also find it nourishing to be aware of the beauty and complexity of the life of this planet. I imagine this is true for a great many people.

A Nut

by Caitlyn Fisher, age 9

Nut, a nut,
I have half a nut
Nut, a nut,
it was eaten by a squirrel
Nut, a nut,
I have half a nut

Nels Christensen

BABE FLY LIKE BIRD

Nels Christensen is an assistant professor of environmental writing and environmental studies at Albion College in Albion, Michigan. He has taught at the University of Michigan's New England Literature Program (NELP) since 2001. He currently is writing a critical history of NELP that posits the necessity for and efficacy of environmental education in traditional classrooms.

Depending on the season, my walk to work looks dramatically different. In the winter and fall, when I teach at Albion College in Albion, Michigan, I leave the comfort of the house I share with my wife and daughter and head east into Victory Park, an expanse of manicured sports fields, concrete pathways, and discrete play areas. Once inside the park, I cross over the south branch of the Kalamazoo River, which spills over a small dam before finding itself shunted into separate decorative chutes until, at last, joining up with the east branch at a confluence known locally as the Forks. From here, I pass the site of the city's historical spring that once bubbled up through rock and loam but now passes through concrete footings and metal pipes. A sign warns: "This Water Unsafe for Drinking." And there, to the right, I move past the town's largest and most elaborate playground: an enclosed, multilevel village of ladders, swings, tubes, and slides, where my daughter plays almost daily.

In the spring, when I teach at the University of Michigan's New England Literature Program (NELP) in Raymond, Maine, it seems that my walk to work couldn't look more different. A place-centered experiential literature and writing program, NELP builds a community of forty students and twelve teachers who cook, hike, read, write, and in all ways live together for six weeks in the woods of Maine. There I wake early in a rough-cut cabin without heat or electricity, greeted by the heavy shadows of hemlocks, the blue pattern of Lake Sebago, and, more often than not, the sight of my own breath in the cold morning air. I leave the cabin and head up a steep, rocky slope, stumbling over slick tree roots and moss-covered rocks, past other cold and quiet cabins pegged along the boulder-cut edge of the lakeshore until, at last, arriving at the dining hall, where my day of work begins by helping three students make breakfast for the other forty-eight people living and learning there together.

In many ways, these two landscapes—one deliberately engineered to shape natural open spaces into areas safe and inviting for play of all sorts, and the other relatively untouched by human intervention, its rough, natural edges intact—appear to have little in common. But, having recently returned to Michigan and my walk through Victory Park after two months of walking that other path in Maine, I'm struck now by what these two seemingly different landscapes have to tell us about how and where we learn.

This thought first began to move in my mind many months ago as I packed my gear in preparation for my time teaching in Maine. I found myself reading an unpublished research project on outdoor play spaces in Albion by Lesley Jurasek, an Albion native and undergraduate at the University of Michigan. Insightful and sensitive, Lesley's project investigates the relationships among race, class, and the availability of safe outdoor playing environments for the children of Albion; it is both an economic history of Albion and a cultural documentary of its children. Lesley's pages drew my attention to the exceptional quality of Victory Park—exceptional, that is, in contrast to the dilapidated or nonexistent parks near Albion's housing projects, the unfortunate legacy of changes in Michigan's automotive industry. A once-thriving industrial town that drew African-American migrants from the south to work in its booming metal foundries, Albion has left many of those same workers unemployed and in severe economic need as a result of a shifting economy.

Lesley's work got me thinking about the important link between where children play and how they learn later in life. That is, she reminded me that the educational attitudes and strategies of the college students in my classes, at both Albion College and the University of Michigan, were stimulated and shaped in outdoor spaces much like Victory Park or, as it may be, in the vacant lots and run-down basketball courts found in the neighborhoods of housing projects across the river and, in fact, across the country.

Take, for example, Natalie Corbin, a student in an interdisciplinary environmental literature and education course I taught last semester at Albion College. This class was an educational experiment, for I tried in it to transfer some of the important pedagogical ideas and methods that shape my teaching at NELP in the woods to a traditional classroom in Albion—namely, the deliberate and self-conscious examination of our relationship to places through many different forms of writing. Much of our work found voice in reflective journals, as it does at NELP, and half of our class time was spent outside in Albion College's Whitehouse Nature Center observing and writing about the natural world and our place in it. Natalie—a remarkable creative writer, sophisticated thinker, and current recipient of a Fulbright grant to teach English language in Germany—seemed instinctively to take up the experiential modes of learning I encouraged, so much so that the ideas we were pursuing in class about the relationship between individuals and their environments found their way into her life outside of class.

One day, Natalie found herself back in her hometown, Kalamazoo, a farming and industrial town about an hour west of Albion. There, she witnessed an event that, judging by the depth and specificity of her rendering of it, struck a chord in the sound track of her past and present: "Today, a bulldozer tore out the playground at Winchell Elementary. I suppose it was too old fashioned …I mean, it was older than I am, at least. I'd played there for nearly 22 years." As if conjured by the sight of the uprooted metal swings, memory after memory rose up in Natalie—of measuring her height against that of the monkey bars, of being followed up ladders and down slides by her family dog, of being chased out of the playground at night by the Kalamazoo police. "I can't help the tangents," she writes, "it's all tied up in this playground."

I take the "it" in that last sentence to signify something important about who Natalie was as a child when she entertained herself in that playground, fashioning imaginary worlds, discovering the strengths and limitations of her mind and body as she interacted with that physical playscape. I also understand "it" to say something equally important about the thinker and writer Natalie grew to be—one who approaches learning with the open inquisitiveness of a child at play. Of course, I can't say with certainty that Natalie became the remarkable student she is today because of the multiple ways she began to learn about herself and her world in that playground. But I can say beyond doubt that I saw her climb, swing, and slide with language and ideas in new and exceptional ways. I can say that I saw her mind concurrently at work and at play.

These thoughts of Lesley's research, of Natalie's experiences as a child and an adult, and of my own daughter playing in Victory Park accompanied me on my journey north and east to the wooded shores of Lake Sebago. As April became May and the flatlands of Michigan and Ohio gave way to the hills and then mountains of New York and New Hampshire, the towers of Victory Park playground, the deracinated swings of Winchell Elementary, and the physical and intellectual landscape of NELP began to speak to one another. As I made my way through the White Mountains, I began to understand what Lesley's research about Albion's outdoor play spaces and Natalie's educational experiences in the past and present have to do with the place I was heading for and the learning that happens there. The connection lies, I believe, in how the natural setting at NELP disorients its students in safe and generative ways that revive the instincts of childhood in which playing, learning, and living are one.

Started in 1975, NELP has evolved from a pastoral possibility in the minds of its founders Walter Clark and Allan Howes into a 32-year-long educational experiment. At its most basic, it transplants forty University of Michigan undergraduates to a physically alien world of rocks and roots where they deliberately give up many normal aspects of their daily lives—recorded music, cell phones, computers, temperature-controlled living spaces—in order to think about the daily acts of living and learning. For six weeks, they live in what seems a different world, a world that asks them—indeed, requires them—to live differently. The students come to NELP knowing, at least intellectually, that they will live in cabins that lack heat, water, and electricity, that the food they eat they will make for one another, that the work of their minds will be matched by the work of their bodies. Nonetheless, the process of stripping away these comforts is powerfully disorienting. Cold, wet, and dirty, NELP students find, many of them for the first time, that the work of living is just that—work.

At the same time, though, the work of living and learning at NELP comes to resemble something akin to what we might rightly call play. That is, on the pitched shores of Lake Sebago, stripped of the familiar tools they use to make their way through the world intellectually and physically, NELP students must experiment, must do what they don't know. At NELP, they begin to see and imagine differently, to think and create, to witness and interact with the world around them in exciting and unforeseen ways. If that is not play, what is? Their classrooms—the swamps and rivers, the rocks and trees—look like no classrooms they have ever known, but the learning that happens there resonates with that rich, generative testing and transforming of the world they experienced as children. The powerfully defamiliarizing affect the physical world has on their minds and bodies turns their new place of living and learning into a playground: a place to scale, to leap, to dare, a place that offers them the opportunity to know by creation, to learn by discovery, to lay hands on the world.

I witness this first-hand everyday at NELP, be it in class settings when students engage critically and intellectually with a Dickinson poem by writing poems of their own, or when they find—by playful experimentation—that the best way to remove seventy frozen sausage links locked tight in a box is with their bare hands and a hammer. As in the playgrounds of their youth, the learning at NELP is hands-on. It comes about when students use both their minds and their bodies to play through the challenges of words, ideas, and the necessities of life.

Since my return from Maine, I am aware of a similar imaginative, intellectual, and physical engagement in my two-year old daughter Emmylou. As the light of summer moves on the surface of the Kalamazoo River flowing past Victory Park, I watch as Emmylou creates a place for herself in that playground. She observes first, using her mind and voice to name the objects that make up her environment—swing, tunnel, slide.

Then, volition joins cognition, and she begins to climb. The towers and tubes, once merely shapes in her mind, become part of her bodily experience; they come alive to her and through her as her mind and body create an interactive relationship with her environment. It may be coincidence that she uttered her first simile on the swings of Victory Park: "Dad, babe fly like bird." But it may also be that a bird's flight and her own and the possibilities of language all took on life and meaning there, at play in that moment, in that place, as she moved through the sky near the banks of the Kalamazoo.

Gary Rieveschl

GROUNDINGS

Over the years, Gary Rieveschl has been planting what he calls Lifeform Projects in an effort to help people forge a closer relationship with the earth and to come to a better understanding of what "growth" really means. Among many other kinds of planted forms, he has often planted his figure and the figures of others at varying scales with diverse materials in numerous places and contexts. Contact Gary Rieveschl at Box 26, Cedar Grove, IN 47016 or grieveschl@earthlink.net.

Remarkable things happen when you lie down on the ground and plant your outline with flower bulbs.

First, you lie on the ground on your back. You look straight up into the universe. At the same time you can feel the weight of your body spread out on the ground. You are perfectly positioned between sky and earth. You sense this connection from an effortless perspective. It's easy to pause right here for a while.

Next you mark your outline with magic powder, like sprinkled bone meal, or have it marked by a friend who is planting their outline with yours. You can also mark your outline with thin sticks stuck in the ground along your contour. If there are two of you, maybe your outlines are touching. Maybe there are lots of you. Maybe you all form a circle or a long line of connected outlines stretching through a meadow or a park.

Or maybe it's just you.

Then you get up and look down at your outline on the ground and are amazed by how small you appear—so much smaller than you thought.

Now, do you plant just your outline or do you plant your whole figure?

What kind of flower bulb are you?

When do you want to bloom in the spring? Dwarf tulips bloom later than crocus.

And are you tight to the ground or tall to the sky? Snowdrops are short and daffodils are tall.

And what color are your flowers? Yellow, white, purple, red, orange, pink, speckled, striped, solid, bi-color….

Maybe you are more than just one kind of flower. Maybe your outline blooms first in white and your body blooms later in red.

Whatever you choose, to plant you must dig. You can plant your outline by digging individual holes along it and setting a flower bulb in each hole. Or you can plant your whole figure by preparing the ground inside your outline like a flower bed and planting it full of flower bulbs.

Daffodilman Daffodils outline a friend lying in his front yard.

Either way it's a good idea to dig a test hole in the area you plan to plant to see how well the soil in that location will drain. Bulbs like to grow where there is good drainage and they don't like soggy locations. Fill the test hole with water. If it does not drain out overnight, you should dig out your entire outline or figure and replace the soil with a mixture of humus, peat, and sand in roughly equal portions, and then plant the bulbs. While you are at it, add some more bone meal to the soil mix for fertilizer.

If you are planting your outline by digging holes with a bulb spade, sprinkle some loose soil in the bottom of the hole before setting the bulb and filling the hole. If you are digging the holes through sod, save the grass caps to put back on top of each hole.

If you are planting your whole figure, cut your outline in the sod with a spade and peel up the sod in big pieces. Put the sod aside the way it came out of the ground so that you can put it back the same way after you have set all the bulbs and covered them with loose earth.

Grassman A two-sided tapestry of my figure made from soil and grass seed quilted between two layers of burlap. When sprayed with water, the seeds sprout and grow out through the burlap mesh as a living portrait of the artist.

Make sure you know where the top of the bulb is. Most bulbs have a flat bottom and a pointy top. The top needs to point to the sky. The bottom of the bulb below the surface of the ground needs to be about two to three times the height of the bulb. Leave at least two bulb diameters between neighboring bulbs.

Cover the tops of the bulbs with earth and replace any sod. Gently press the sod into place or sow grass seed on top of the planted areas.

Since everything about the landscape changes throughout the winter, you might want to mark the location where you planted yourself.

You're done, for now. Everything just disappears for a couple of months. That is a long time, almost a whole school year. But you must wait and be patient, in order to take part in nature's pace.

You also need to remember to search for yourself in late winter or early spring as the bulbs you planted last fall start to poke their way out of the ground.

And finally, glorious blooming flowers bring with them the excitement of accomplishment and a profound sense of fruition.

After the bulbs have bloomed, make sure that leaves are left standing and not mowed for at least a month. That way the bulbs can gather the nourishment they need for blooming the following year. Some bulbs will bloom year after year for a decade or more, providing an earthbound way for children to measure their growth.

The photographs within this essay and following are examples of strategies that use living materials and human figures. Many of them can be done with your kids, who will also have their own ideas about what, where and who to plant.

"Children's Circle." An elementary school class joins hands, forms a circle on the ground, has their outlines marked and plants their own figures with crocus bulbs that bloom the following spring. (194)

"Neighbors." I roam an urban neighborhood with a shovel and a bag of flower bulbs offering to plant people's figures anywhere and everywhere—in yards, in front of stores, next to sidewalks, in traffic medians, in parks, wherever they wish. (199)

"Path of Life." Numerous classes of schoolchildren plant their outlines in a long chain of figures meandering through a public park. Each child in turn chooses how his or her figure joins the preceding figure and which direction the chain is continued. (200–201)

"Man Mound." A life-size mound of my own figure lying on the ground planted over with grass. (202)

"Father Trash." A proposal to the City of Bremen, Germany, for a new solid waste disposal site. Pile up your millions of tons of trash in the form of a giant human figure. Eventually you can cover the half-mile-long pile with earth and plant it with grass, flowers, and trees. That way, people might be reminded of their complicity in creating such a huge pile of trash, even after it is transformed into a public park, and see themselves reflected in the form and the content of the mountain. (203, top)

"Trace Mound." A proposal for a park-size footprint mound along the Ohio River in Cincinnati, Ohio, signifying the trace of human presence, from the mound-building cultures that originally inhabited the area to Cincinnati's later role as a stepping-off point for the westward expansion of the United States. (203, bottom)

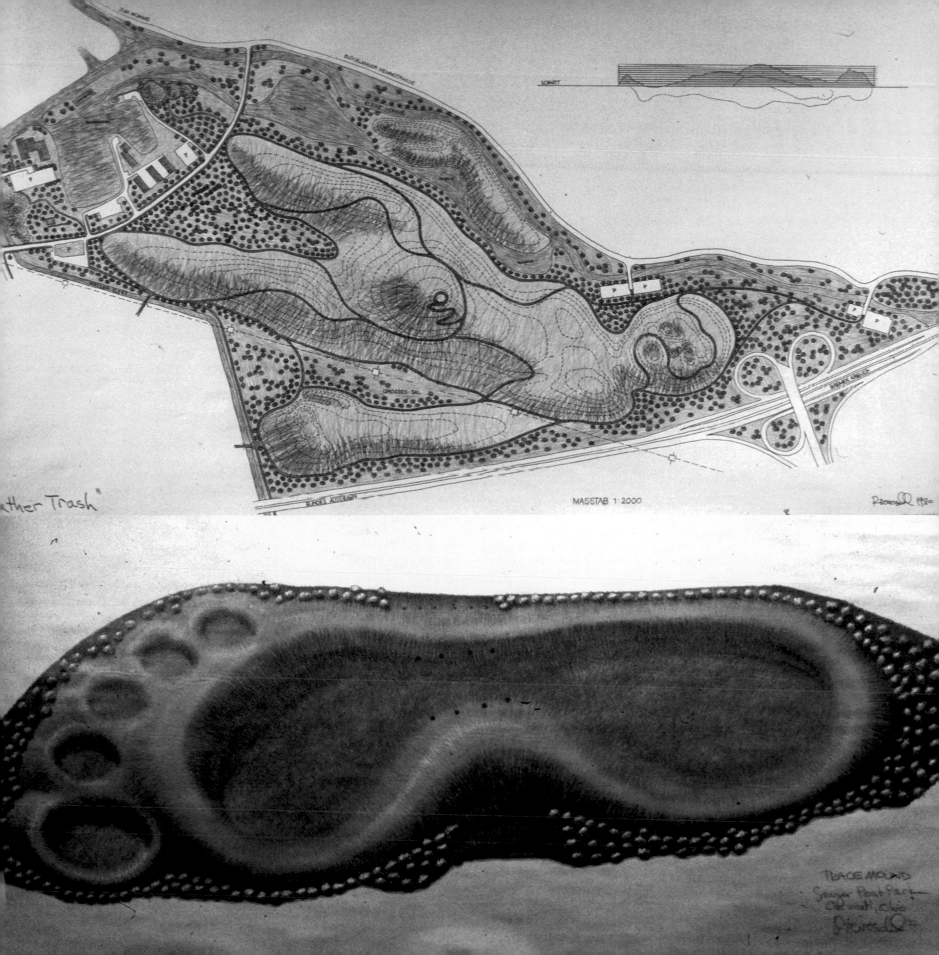

V. CHILD-CENTERED CITIES

Right after *Last Child in the Woods* came out, I got an email from a developer, the COO and co-founder of the largest privately owned residential development company in the world. He said he was profoundly disturbed by the book.

But he went on to say that he now wanted to do something about the issue, so he invited me to an envisioning session with about eighty developers and real estate marketers. He asked me to give my sermon, and I did.

Then he did something remarkable. He said, "I want you all to go into small groups and I want you to solve the problem. How are going to build residential developments in the future that actually connect kids to nature?" They went off into small groups; the room filled with noise and excitement, and they came back with some interesting ideas like leave some land in

> It's not just going to Yosemite; it's what we do every day and how our cities are designed...

the first place, a good place to start, but also ideas about a little nature center around these developments, about nature paths through woods or to schools.

It didn't matter about the quality of these ideas as much it mattered that these were developers thinking of them who were excited to think. If that can happen in a group of developers, there's still hope that we can rethink urban design, rethink how we live in a way that connects all of us to nature on a daily basis. It's not just going to Yosemite; it's what we do every day and how our cities are designed, how our houses are designed, and we can do this. We can change this environment. It is, after all, a built environment. We can rebuild it.

Richard Louv, Chairman, Children & Nature Network. Quoted from film interview, *Where Do the Children Play?* (2007)

Suzanne H. Crowhurst Lennard

THE CITY AS PLAYGROUND

Suzanne H. Crowhurst Lennard, Ph.D. (Arch.) is the co-founder and director of the International Making Cities Livable Council and director of the *Guidelines for Child-Friendly Neighborhoods & Cities* program. Dr. Crowhurst Lennard has taught at the University of California, Berkeley and Brookes University, Oxford. She writes books and articles and consults on designing livable and child-friendly cities. See IMCL website: www.LivableCities.org. Contact: Suzanne.Lennard@LivableCities.org.

The ideal environment for children's play, for their intellectual, social, cultural, and physical development, is a city that is safe, compact, human scale, accessible, beautiful, interesting, and intricate, with streets and squares populated by familiar adults.[1]

In such a city, children are free to explore on their own from an early age, developing autonomy and self assurance. Their safety and well-being are assured by the presence of familiar adults in the public realm. They observe architectural details, the diversity of shops, services, workshops, civic buildings, and cultural facilities that make up the city. They encounter a variety of business people, laborers, clerks, professionals, and service providers from varied ethnic backgrounds and socio-economic strata, learning from each a new vocabulary, a different set of values, and a different way of being in the world.

They meet their friends in the market place, play in the fountains, climb the public art, sit on a flight of steps to comment on people in the crowd, and run to greet a parent or friend.

In the city-as-playground, children redefine street furniture—steps, walls, posts, and rails—as elements in their play, as home base or goal post, and sections of public urban places come to be identified with particular games. All of these activities occur within sight of adults carrying on their daily lives and the children are free to move back and forth between play and playful interaction with adults.

This is no utopian dream, nor is it a romantic vision of how cities were in the past. It is a conscious goal for cities around the world in which it is understood that if you create a city that is good for children, it will be livable for all.[2]

In North America, most children grow up in sprawling suburbs. They are taken everywhere by bus or car because the streets are not safe and the distances are too great for them to walk or bike. The downtowns are neither accessible nor hospitable to children, having been abandoned or zoned for commercial purposes. Children are forced to play at home alone or in supervised groups. It is now clear that sprawling suburbs are very damaging. Obesity is just the tip of the iceberg. By making it impossible for children to socialize and play spontaneously in safe and lively streets and squares, sprawl stunts children's social development and contributes to antisocial behavior, social anxiety, youth violence, self-destructive behavior, and even teen suicide.[3] It is time to plan our cities with children in mind.

Social skills are essential for success in adulthood. Forming friendships, coping with problems, developing one's own potential, furthering one's career, maintaining a business, and raising a family are all dependent on social engagement with a wide variety of people. How well a child develops socially and emotionally depends on the richness of opportunities for positive social contact, relationships, and models of behavior. Since children learn through observation, imitation, and participation, a well-functioning public realm is especially valuable in teaching social skills and attitudes.

Social competence involves relating appropriately to different kinds of people—older or younger, handicapped or from different socio-economic and ethnic backgrounds—and responding to different points of view. Social competence enables the individual to initiate and maintain a conversation, to express feelings appropriately, to interpret correctly the intentions of others, to be sociable, to collaborate, to discuss differences of opinion, and to establish consensus and decide on a course of action without resorting to violence.[4]

Sociability Equals Playful Interaction

It is through sociability, a playful form of interaction, that social skills are perfected. Like play, sociability is spontaneous, creative, serious or nonsensical, witty or intriguing. One minute it is tender compassion, the next ribald humor.

Sociability has no purpose other than the delight and entertainment of all participating; it is not instrumental—to buy or sell, obtain information, or influence others. There is no hidden agenda, no wish for personal gain or aggrandizement. Since it is playful, innocent mistakes, malapropisms, errors in judgment, and faux pas do not have such permanent consequences. But it is also an art in which subtlety and sensitivity to others are appreciated. In sociable interactions, one's family background, wealth, and social or ethnic status count for nothing; what is valued is one's ability to contribute to others' sense of well-being.

As they begin to recognize social, ethnic, political, and economic differences within the adult community, it is important that children see that these differences are not exclusive. Through sociable interaction, people with very different values, lifestyles, and cultural backgrounds can get along. Because of their natural playfulness, the presence of children within varied social groups often helps adults to be more sociable.

Where Does Sociability Flourish?

Sociability occurs when our paths intersect with others, on hospitable urban squares, at public social events, when we are not too harried for a little playful, verbal give-and-take. It flourishes in cities where people commute short distances by foot or bike, encountering people they know.

Places that generate sociability have distinct characteristics. They are visually enclosed, at the heart of the city or neighborhood, surrounded by human-scale, mixed-use buildings with shops and restaurants at street level and apartments and offices above. They are at the crossing point of pedestrian routes, but they contain some of the most important shops and civic buildings. They are traffic-free or traffic-calmed, and constructed for the pleasure of the pedestrian. They contain fountains and works of art that act as focal points and support play. Formal and informal seating, shade, and protection from the elements are available. All the major cultural and festive events take place there, and they are the site of a weekly or daily farmers' market. Most importantly, they are set like a jewel within a fine-textured, mixed-use, human-scale urban fabric that surrounds them for several blocks.

How Can Ordinary Citizens Help to Make Their City More Child-Friendly?

The characteristics of a sociable, accessible city for children—the city-as-playground—are fundamental to the "Guidelines for Child-Friendly Neighborhoods, Towns and Cities" currently being developed. You can help to make your city more child-friendly by encouraging your city government to help adopt these guidelines.

Notes

1. Henry L. Lennard and Suzanne H. Crowhurst Lennard, *The Forgotten Child: Cities for the Well-Being of Children* (Carmel, Calif.: Gondolier Press, 2000).

2. "Guidelines for Child-Friendly Neighborhoods, Towns and Cities" and a "Child-Friendly Certification Program" are currently being developed by the International Making Cities Livable Council (IMCL) and the National Town Builders Association (NTBA), working with advisory boards representing Healthy Children, Children in Nature, Cities and Neighborhood Developers. The goal is to create a program that will help cities to restore their neighborhoods, and help developers to design new neighborhoods in such a way that children have independent access to nature and community on a daily basis. Italian, Dutch, German and Scandinavian cities have been working in this direction for some years.

3. Douglas E. Morris, *It's a Sprawl World After All* (Gabriola Island, B.C.: New Society Publishers, 2005); Arno Gruen, "Livable Cities: Children and Their Needs," in *Making Cities Livable,* ed. Suzanne H. Crowhurst Lennard, Sven Von Ungern-Sternberg, and Henry L. Lennard (Carmel, Calif.: Gondolier Press, 1997).

4. "If a child has social deficits the effects continue to be crippling long after graduation and in just about every area of life...Many aspects of contemporary life can stunt the growth of key neurodevelopmental functions." Melvin Levine, *A Mind at a Time* (New York: Simon & Schuster, 2002), 43. See also T. Berry. Brazelton, *The Irreducible Needs of Children: What Every Child Must Have to Grow, Learn and Flourish* (Cambridge, Mass.: Perseus Publishing, 2000).

Bibliography

Appleyard, Donald. 1981. *The Street as a Place for Play and Learning in Livable Streets*. Berkeley: University of California Press.

Baruzzi, Walter. 1996. "La Città in Tasca." Paper given at the 1996 International Making Cities Livable Conference, Venice.

Baum, Howell S. 2004. "Smart Growth and School Reform: What If We Talked about Race and Took Community Seriously?" *Journal of the American Planning Association* 70, no. 1: 14–26.

Brazelton, T. Berry. 2000. *The Irreducible Needs of Children: What Every Child Must Have to Grow, Learn and Flourish*. Cambridge, Mass.: Perseus Publishing.

Corsi, Marco. 2002. "The Child Friendly Cities Initiative in Italy." *Environment & Urbanization* 14, no. 2 (October): 169–79.

Crowhurst Lennard, Suzanne. 1978. "The Child's Conception of Built Space." *Education* (Winter).

———. 1987. "Making Cities Better for Children." *Urban Land* (March).

———. 1988. "The City for Children." *Making Cities Livable Newsletter* (December).

———. 2000. "Why Young People Need Squares." *Planning* (August).

Crowhurst Lennard, Suzanne, and Henry L. Lennard. 1984. *Public Life in Urban Places*. New York: Gondolier Press.

———. 1990. "Usable Public Spaces for Children and the Elderly." *Making Cities Livable Newsletter* (March/September).

———. 1995. *Livable Cities Observed: A Source Book of Images and Ideas*. Carmel, Calif.: Gondolier Press.

———. 2008. *Genius of the European Square*. Carmel, Calif.: Gondolier Press

Gaster, Sanford. 1992. "Historical Changes in Children's Access to U.S. Cities: A Critical Review." *Children's Environments* 9, no. 2: 34–55.

Gestrich, Andreas. 1992. "Kinder in der Stadt. Ein Editorial." *Die Alte Stadt* 19: 93.

Görlitz, Dietmar, et al. 1992 "The City as a Frame of Development for Children: The Herten Conference." *Children's Environments* 9, no. 2: 97–00.

Gruen, Arno. 1997. "Livable Cities: Children and Their Needs." In *Making Cities Livable*, ed. Suzanne H. Crowhurst Lennard, Sven Von Ungern-Sternberg, and Henry L. Lennard. Carmel, Calif.: Gondolier Press.

Jacobs, Jane. 1961. *The Death and Life of Great American Cities*. New York: Random House.

Lennard, Henry L. 1997. "The Good City for Children." In *Making Cities Livable*, ed. Suzanne H. Crowhurst Lennard, Sven Von Ungern-Sternberg, Henry L. Lennard. Carmel, Calif.: Gondolier Press.

Lennard, Henry L., and Suzanne Crowhurst Lennard. 2000 *The Forgotten Child: Cities for the Well-Being of Children*. Carmel, Calif.: Gondolier Press.

Lynch, Kevin. 1977. *Growing Up in Cities*. Cambridge, Mass.: MIT Press.

Morris, Douglas E. 2005. *It's a Sprawl World After All*. Gabriola Island, B.C.: New Society Publishers.

Ward, Colin. 1978. *The Child in the City*. London: Architectural Press.

Susan Turner Meiklejohn

SUNNYSIDE GARDENS TODAY

What the houses lacked in imaginative design, the community as a whole made up for it in open spaces, carefully reserved for public use, in playgrounds and gardens.

LEWIS MUMFORD[1]

Susan Turner Meiklejohn is an associate professor of Urban Planning at Hunter College of the City of New York. She is a resident of Sunnyside Gardens, and currently is funded by the Russell Sage Foundation to write a book on the effect of growing up in this highly multi-ethnic neighborhood on perceptions of race and tolerance. She has so far interviewed over 80 young people and their parents for this project.

As a teaching assistant in urban design, I viewed a black and white slide: a middle-aged woman reclined on a canvas lawn chair; head tilted back, eyes closed. She sat in the middle of a well tended lawn surrounded by English-looking attached brick cottages. The slide was labeled "Sunnyside Gardens"; it was the experimental garden community founded in 1924 in the borough of Queens in New York City.

Unlike others who created garden developments in the United States, the developers of Sunnyside Gardens were not attempting to meet the aspirations of well-heeled urban workers who wished to live in settings that were at once more beautiful and further removed from the increasingly congested and largely immigrant neighborhoods of New York City. They believed that the provision of low-density housing grouped around open, communal areas would

215

encourage enlightened social and political interaction among an economically and ethnically diverse group of residents. In other words, the extensive open spaces provided by designers were the physical manifestation of egalitarian social goals.[2]

I remembered the image of the woman in the slide: I moved to Sunnyside Gardens in 1998. It is visually charming, my courtyard is green and calming, and I can take the subway and be in my yard 20 minutes after I leave my Manhattan office. In its appealing and efficient architectural design, ample public space, and relation to commercial areas and public transit, this "old urbanist" neighborhood is the equal of the best "New Urbanist" experiments. However, contemporary New Urbanists, prey to the constraints of the private market, rightly have been criticized for creating communities that are economically and socially homogeneous and impermeable to all but affluent residents. Not one can come close to achieving the economic and ethnic diversity that long has been the hallmark of Sunnyside Gardens.[3]

Queens is now the most ethnically diverse area in the world, and the larger area of Sunnyside (where Sunnyside Gardens is located) is one of the most multiethnic neighborhoods in the borough. In 2000, 61 percent of its total population of 53,736 was foreign-born, and most immigrants had arrived within the decade from over 80 countries of origin. Sunnyside Gardens itself has achieved ethnic and class integration at a level that would be unimaginable to its founders in 1924. In 2000, nearly half of its 8,234 residents were newly arrived immigrants from over 60 source countries; by 2000, the non-Latino white population became a minority for the first time (47 percent of residents were white).[4]

Although tiny single-family homes are now selling for $625,000 (a 300 percent increase in the eight years I've lived here), Sunnyside and Sunnyside Gardens remain solidly working-class neighborhoods of renters (80 percent of residents in Sunnyside and 73 percent in the Gardens). Although there are clear signs of gentrification, it is far from rampant. In 2000, very few households reported incomes exceeding $100,000 in the larger area of Sunnyside; even in the relatively affluent Gardens, 60 percent of households had incomes below $50,000 per year, and the poverty rate was 11 percent. The poverty rates of the two census tracts adjacent to Sunnyside Gardens were 18 and 20 percent respectively and child poverty rates topped 25 percent in most census tracts in Sunnyside.

Old, young, rich, poor. Black, white, brown. What a wonderful world for a child! What an opportunity to learn tolerance and consideration, and what a chance for community action and activities. However, it is more precise to say that few opportunities for interethnic and interclass interaction exist in Sunnyside Gardens. Most of the open courtyards have been fenced into private yards, and residents routinely chase children (including those who live there) out of the few that remain open. The private park, one of two in New York City (the other is Gramercy Park) is lovely. The parents I know who use it very much appreciate it, but membership fees have risen to levels unaffordable to most members of the immigrant community. If you walk around this park, you do not hear the Spanish, Urdu, Korean, and Romanian of Sunnyside's streets. The children who play there are overwhelmingly white; those in the few public parks in Sunnyside are not. Few instances of outright hostilities occur between neighbors in Sunnyside, but residents of different racial and ethnic backgrounds rarely interact.

Here, I describe Sunnyside Gardens as a "suburb" of the larger community of Sunnyside. The notion of privately owned, inviolate space as separate from the surrounding neighborhood typifies many residents' attitudes of the larger community of Sunnyside: Even when such areas originally were deemed "public." A social-psychological divide between immigrants (who now comprise the majority of residents) and the native born is palpable and nurtured through the careful control of physical space, even within the boundaries of Sunnyside Gardens.

This drive for privatization and control, to the point where neighborhood history is ignored or reinvented, is particularly ironic in a neighborhood self-consciously designed to break down class and cultural barriers. It deeply undermines an unprecedented opportunity for children to live among and learn about others who are very different from themselves. The evolution of Sunnyside Gardens, designed to create interaction among a diverse group of residents, as well as to offset the isolated anomie of Manhattan and the awkward individualization and exclusivity of outlying suburbs, provides a valuable lesson to those, such as the New Urbanists, who wish to create inclusive community-building primarily through better design.

The History of Sunnyside Gardens

> What made this neighborhood unit uniquely good...was it was a mixed community...the variety of houses provided for people with a variety of occupations and incomes....This gave the place exceptional educational opportunities, for people who live in one-class neighborhoods all too easily lose their sense of social realities.[5]

Sunnyside Gardens was implemented in 1924 by members of the Regional Planning Association of America (RPAA); its members included the urban scholar and theorist Lewis Mumford, the environmentalist Benton MacKaye, and architects Charles Harris Whitaker, Henry Wright, and Clarence Stein.[6] The development reflected the principles of the Garden City movement as originally envisioned in Ebenezer Howard's

1902 book, *Garden Cities of Tomorrow: A Peaceful Path to Reform*, including goals of class integration, housing affordability, and cooperative action and ownership.[7]

Lewis Mumford was a resident of Sunnyside Gardens from 1927 until 1936. It was through his (and fellow RPAA members') philosophy of community-building from the "bottom-up"—including mechanisms to increase purposeful daily informal interaction among neighbors from very different class and cultural backgrounds—that set it apart from the other "jewels on the necklace" of elite garden communities built in the United States from 1890 to 1930.[8] RPAA members were outspoken critics of what they considered rampant real estate speculation of the pre-Depression 1920s, when housing sales prices and rents were considered to be at crisis proportions.[9] They were seeking to create not only a well-designed community in Queens, but one that through its innovative funding plan and integrative social goals could serve as a prototype for a series of low-cost developments.[10]

Sunnyside Gardens was built on 77 acres of land (spanning eight city blocks) purchased from the Pennsylvania Railroad. Like most housing in Sunnyside, it consists of one-, two-, and three-family homes and six-story apartment buildings. However, to keep them affordable, Sunnyside Gardens' houses and apartments were much smaller than those offered in similar developments in Queens, and buildings cover only 28 percent of the tract. The rest is devoted to green space.

Each block of buildings once looked on a central court originally planned with a playground, lawn, and gardens designed to encourage interaction among families. There was also the provision of the 3-acre private park for the whole community, as well as cooperative spaces within apartment buildings for educational and community activities. Through building construction cost-saving measures, careful planning of open space, and innovative funding mechanisms, project designers sought and achieved much ethnic and income diversity.[11]

By 1926, 650 families lived in Sunnyside Gardens. Its financial success allowed the RPAA to dream of creating a full-scale Garden City, attempted in Radburn, New Jersey, in 1929.[12] Unfortunately, the Depression devastated both developments. The CHC was unable to maintain cooperative apartments, and could not help either homeowners who had defaulted on their mortgages or renters unable to meet rents. Interestingly, the cooperative political and community spirit fostered by the plans of the RPAA was fully realized when residents worked together against the CHC to create rent strikes, barricades, and other impediments to bank officials trying to seize homes.[13] In spite of these divisive events, class and cultural diversity continued to be a defining feature of Sunnyside Gardens.[14]

The 1930s protests were the last organized

progressive political activities to take place in Sunnyside Gardens. Its open spaces were protected by easements for only 40 years, and when these ended in 1966, disputes arose about the use of common spaces; most people responded by fencing "their" land (each resident has a formal private garden, and owns a share of the open courtyards corresponding to lot lines specified in deeds). Much of the once-open courtyards has been destroyed by partitioning. According to neighborhood old-timers, the issue of shared versus privatized urban space has remained an object of contention for the past forty years.[15]

> Buildings are vehicles of the spirit only so long as the spirit that produced them remains alive and at intervals renews itself. After the spirit departs, there is something derisive and ironical in the structure left behind. [16]

From the 1970s to the present time, neighborhood activism in Sunnyside Gardens has centered primarily on sporadic efforts for neighborhood preservation and policing. Work by community leaders resulted in the designation of Sunnyside Gardens as a "Special Local Planned Community District" (a zoning designation) in 1974 and a listing on the National Register of Historic Places in 1984 that halted fencing of courtyards. However, a current grassroots movement is devoted to the declaration of the neighborhood as a New York City "Local Historic District," under the auspices of the city's Landmarks Commission. The focus of this effort is on the relatively undistinguished architecture of Sunnyside Gardens. This change would further restrict modifications to buildings, while it could undermine current protections for open spaces.[17]

"A Safe Place for Children to Play"

As the building of Sunnyside went forward over the course of the next five years, the gardens and greens flourished....Sunnyside was not designed to satisfy our private fancies but our common purposes: particularly in the provision of space and activities for the young.[18]

The designers of Sunnyside Gardens realized their most important goal—to facilitate planned and casual interaction among residents from different backgrounds—could result more easily from the play of children in shared spaces. However, if you walk among the courtyards today (there are a few that are open, unfenced, and do not have locked gates), it is rare to see a child. Many residents seem to believe that the function of courtyards is to provide a picturesque, untouchable setting for their rapidly appreciating homes.

The writings of Louis Mumford oppose this idea. The RPAA conceptualized each block with its open courtyard, to be "a miniature neighborhood especially designed for families with children," to the extent that they provided playground equipment in each one.[19] Lewis Mumford described his life with his son Geddes on a courtyard in Sunnyside Gardens:

In the spring of 1927 we moved to a little row house, built on a terrace at right angles to the street...our house was fortunate enough to have a full view of the wide green common, beautiful and serene at every time of the year, but never more lovely than when children scampered over the grass in the spring twilight.[20]

The courtyard directly outside of Mumford's window was Geddes' world; he had no desire to go to the private park. "During his younger years he rarely had need for the swings and other activities of the bigger playground a quarter of a mile away; this was a self-sufficient world."[21] Mumford's commitment to the provision of magical places for children in urban settings is reiterated in his introduction to Clarence Stein's book, *Towards New Towns for America*. He writes that children must be welcomed in planned, public open spaces and compares Stein's and Wright's courtyards to the sterile, unused environments that surrounded "modern" housing developments in the 1950s:

Like Olmsted, Stein and Wright dared put beauty as one of the imperative needs of a planned environment: the beauty of ordered buildings, measured to human scale, of trees and flowering plants, of open spaces surrounded by buildings of low density, so that children may scamper over them to add to both their use and their aesthetic loveliness: a freedom not possible, on land occupied at a density of over a hundred persons to the acre, where green exists only to be looked at, not used. [22]

However, history is now being rewritten by local historic preservationists: A strong effort is being made to ban children (and adults) from courtyards, in order to "preserve" them as untouchable landscapes existing solely to be gazed upon. The leader of the Sunnyside Gardens Preservation Alliance (SAVE), the organization now pushing for further historic preservation controls, believes the courtyards were designed only for "quiet contemplation: to edify the working class by contemplation of natural beauty."[23] He emphasized, "kids are not permitted to play because it would disturb the people on the block plus there is a park to play in."[24]

Another preservationist complained about a neighbor who "sees the courtyard as a private playground. I tell them it is only for gardening...your dog cannot go out there and your kids cannot go out there."[25] She might have been referring to a young father who recently called me for advice. He felt driven to call the police because another resident was following his children and photographing them as they played. When questioned, the photographer explained that he was documenting "trespassing on private property." "What can I tell you?" I replied, "my neighbor tried to chase my honors students off my courtyard, where they were quietly sitting on blankets, discussing, of all things, the social history of Sunnyside Gardens!"

The Courtyards Are Closed,
So Where Do the Children Play?

Sunnyside has less recreational space per person than just about anywhere in New York City. Just 1.9 percent of land is dedicated to park space and recreational uses, and little more than half of it is comprised of the private Sunnyside Park. Only 5.75 acres are designated for recreational

Fig. 13—An inner court built in 1926. Photo taken in August 1949
Gottscho-Schleisner, New York

activities for the neighborhood's 53,000 residents: the George Tornsey Playground located north of Queens Boulevard at Skillman Avenue and 43rd Street, adjacent to the western edge of Sunnyside Gardens, and the Thomas Noonan Playground located south of Queens Boulevard at Greenpoint Avenue and 43rd Street. These parks are completely paved over and very overcrowded.

Sunnyside residents (particularly those who do not live in the Gardens) are very aware of the lack of public play spaces for children (and adults, for that matter). When a father of two small children was asked about open space in Sunnyside, he replied:

> What's that? I have seen children waiting on line to use a swing. Queens thought they could build one big park called "Flushing Meadows Park" for everyone. Wrong. Mothers can only go a few blocks with their kids to a playground. We have nowhere for kids to be kids. I lived on 19th Street between 1st and 2nd Avenues in Manhattan. I lived next to Union Square Park, Gramercy Park, East River Park. Here, I'll show you a nice park on Greenpoint and 43rd (Noonan Park). That's about it. Oh yes, get there early because the swings go fast.[25]

It's not just children who desire truly green, open space. A young professional noted that he thought the lack of park areas was "the biggest problem in Sunnyside; do you know where I go when I want to be outside? The cemetery!"

Sunnyside Gardens as a Suburb of Sunnyside

> In new communities that have been planned as social units…as in Sunnyside Gardens….a robust political life, with effective collective action and a sense of renewed public responsibility, has swiftly grown up.[26]

Most interviewed residents could articulate how they thought physical barriers in Sunnyside further divided people who might be different from each other. A major thoroughfare, Queens Boulevard (the "boulevard of death" as it is called in local tabloids), together with the elevated tracks of the number 7 subway line that runs over it, cut Sunnyside in half. Many people believe that the train tracks define the "good" and "bad" sides of Sunnyside. However, the neighborhood is much more integrated than this landmark suggests; census data indicate most areas on either side of the train tracks are equally ethnically and economically heterogeneous.

Perceptions of Sunnyside Gardens as somehow superior to and different from the rest of Sunnyside also persist. When my students and I presented our demographic findings to Sunnyside's Community Board (which is nearly all white and middle-class), we stated how the larger area of Sunnyside was now minority white. Not a peep from the audience. But when we mentioned that the non-Latino white population was now a minority in the Gardens, and the population was

50 percent foreign-born, we heard cries of: "No it's not!" When I said it was, they questioned my sources. "Well, you know how the census undercounts" one said. (The census might undercount immigrants, but not native-born whites.)

In reality, people's perceptions drive divides, and perceptions must be taken seriously even in physically "integrated" areas; social stigmas have social and economic effects. A public school official at IS 125, located south of Queens Boulevard, noted that stereotypes about Sunnyside's south side had repercussions: "Everything that is south of Queens Boulevard has a negative stigma. I spend a lot of my time convincing immigrant parents who heard bad things about the school that the opposite, in fact, is true." A Community Board member who lives in Sunnyside Gardens noted that because there were perceived divisions within the Gardens, "of course" some of her neighbors negatively viewed the area south of Queens Boulevard: "It's interesting, even people in the Gardens

orient themselves differently: whether they live on one side or the other of 46th street." So the gap between Sunnyside and the other side of the neighborhood, the metaphorical "other side of the tracks," is there.

An older resident of Sunnyside Gardens decidedly thought the "other side of the tracks" was his. He had no use for more public space:

> The neighborhood used to be upper class, there has been a lower-class influx—used to be all Jewish, Italian, and Irish, now that has all changed, now it's mostly Spanish. The neighborhood has really gone downhill since so many Spanish people moved in, in the 1970s....There is litter, graffiti, crime, and disrespectful youth—it's because of their culture. There are drunks and drug addicts and 43rd Avenue is too dangerous to walk down at night. I don't think more parks should be built until young people and drunks and immigrants learn to respect the ones we already have.

Another Community Board member, who had lived on the south side for all of his life, summed up the perceived differences between the north and south sides: "When I was a kid, I thought the area north of Queens Boulevard was a rich suburb."

What is not clear to many people, whether they inhabit Sunnyside Gardens or the larger planning and design community, is that perceptions of difference and a motivation to stay separate from those perceived as "others" can and often will override the best attempts to bring people together physically. The founders of Sunnyside Gardens, much like the New Urbanists today, thought that the mere provision of shared space would create shared values. This has been the case, but not in the way that Lewis Mumford and his colleagues thought. The values in Sunnyside Gardens are what many think are typically suburban: Exclusionary rather than inclusive, they celebrate social conformity and physical uniformity, and value private domains far more than public space.

In this vein, the political life in Sunnyside Gardens is not robust, but reactive. Formal and informal politics at the neighborhood level are dominated by native-born whites, and at this time "public responsibility" is expressed by those seeking preservation restrictions that will make it even more expensive to live here, and by intense efforts to eradicate graffiti. "Effective collective action" might imply that residents who are native-born might work with those who are more recently arrived to address issues that affect us all: astronomical housing costs, the social repercussions of child poverty, and a lack of play and recreational and areas for children and youth (which surely contributes to graffiti problems). However, these issues are not on the table.

Yet, many Sunnyside Gardens' residents are thoughtful. One acknowledged that most people in Sunnyside have the same goals, even if their incomes were disparate, and that neighborhood poverty should be a concern: "We all want to live in a nice place, it shouldn't be about class boundaries, whether you are poor, working class, you should live in nice places too." He spoke about the proliferation of anti-graffiti groups in the neighborhood (he is a member of one): "I don't think graffiti is the defining issue of our time. (The issue of) poverty is more substantial. There are pockets of poverty in Sunnyside—you don't see it because people suffer poverty in silence; it's there because I know it's there."

Many parents interviewed in Sunnyside Gardens stated that they valued its ethnic diversity, especially in terms of raising their children to be more tolerant and to have tolerance expressed toward them. One mother moved to Sunnyside Gardens from Manhattan when her teenagers were infants: "I liked the diversity in Sunnyside—one of my sons was adopted from Korea and I wanted the Korean influence that is here," while another of Irish descent described how his kids were more tolerant than his peers:

> I like the diversity, it's a major plus for my kids. They don't have the old prejudices because they have been surrounded by all kinds of people, especially in school. I left Manhattan when my son (who is 20 now) was three or four and ready for school. Manhattan was great, but I didn't want to spend 15K for him to have a few hours with snobs. Sunnyside is a real community with real people. My kids did

not grow up with prejudices because they are used to seeing all kinds of people. So that's a real strength.

However, in spite of the fact that Sunnyside Gardens' preservationists named a street after Louis Mumford and recently placed a plaque on the house in the courtyard where Geddes played, they and many other residents still don't seem aware of what is most historically significant about this neighborhood: It is a planned community specifically designed to positively address issues of class and cultural difference through the provision of public spaces. The fact this history is so obtuse is a testament to the shortcomings of its design.

"Private fancies," for status, for even higher housing values, for a neighborhood that is inhabited only by "wine-sipping connoisseurs" (as my neighbor described the goal of a preservationist quoted here), for now seem to have trumped the "common purpose" that Mumford envisioned: to raise children in a physically open, immediate world where economic and cultural differences are well-understood and tolerated. However, it may be that this will change as Sunnyside's children find ways (as they often do) to circumvent the physical and social barriers put in place by their parents.

Notes

1. Lewis Mumford, *Green Memories: The Story of Geddes* (New York: Harcourt Brace, 1947), 27.

2. This is a very different motive than the rationale for prior Garden City–inspired developments in Queens. For example, Forest Hills Gardens, a 1912 residential development sponsored by the Russell Sage Foundation, was planned to house lower-income Manhattan workers. It responded to the same goals as Howard's: improved housing at lower cost through the availability of inexpensive land. However, "cost-saving" building and infrastructural innovations implemented by Forest Hills Gardens' designers, Frederick Law Olmsted II and Grosvenor Attenbury, resulted in vast over-expenditures. The resulting development, although beautiful, was marketed to the affluent upon its completion and its residents have remained so since. The RPAA self-consciously planned Sunnyside Gardens as a response to what they considered to be the shortcomings of Forest Hills Gardens by keeping units small; using standardized, inexpensive materials; and ensuring that financing plans would attract and retain residents of low and moderate incomes.

3. Books advocating the tenets of the "New Urbanism" include Peter Katz, *The New Urbanism: Toward Architecture of Community* (New York: MacGraw Hill, 1994) and Andres Duany, Elizabeth Plater-Zyberk, and Jeff Speck, *Suburban Nation: The Rise of Sprawl and the Decline of the American Dream* (New York: North Point Press, 2000). A good critique is included in Chapter 8, "The Spaces of Utopia," in David Harvey, *Spaces of Hope* (Berkeley: University of California Press, 2000).

4. Demographic data are derived from the 2000 census. However, I also analyzed demographic data for Sunnyside Gardens from a variety of governmental sources to understand population trends over the past 80 years. The foreign-born population was over 34 percent in 1930 and did not dip below 25 percent until 1950 (its nadir at 21.8 percent in 1960). It bounced up to 25 percent in 1970 and to 32 percent in 1980. However, the population that was almost 100 percent white until 1980, when that proportion dropped by 14 percent with the rise of immigration. From 1980 to 1990, the poverty rate also rose in Sunnyside Gardens from 3 to 13 percent.

5. Lewis Mumford, *Sketches from Life: The Autobiography of Lewis Mumford* (New York: Dial, 1982), 411.

6. Other very interesting and influential individuals who were a part of this rather loosely organized group included the architects Frederick L. Ackerman, housing specialists and scholars Edith Elmer Wood and Catherine Bauer, and the economist Stuart Chase. Both Wright and Mumford lived in Sunnyside Gardens. For

more information about the RPAA, see Edward Spann, *Designing Modern America: the RPAA and its Members* (Columbus: Ohio State University Press, 1996). Roy Lubove, *The Progressives and the Slums* (Westport, Conn.: Greenwood Press, 1962), addresses the birth of the city planning and housing movements generally; while his *Community Planning in the 1920s: The Contribution of the Regional Planning Association of America* (Pittsburgh: University of Pittsburgh Press, 1963), specifically addresses the history and philosophy of the RPAA. Lubove, *The Urban Community* (Englewood Cliffs, N.J.: Prentice-Hall, 1967), presents the writings of these thinkers in an analytic context. Carl Sussman, ed., *Planning the Fourth Migration: The Neglected Vision of the Regional Planning Association of America* (Cambridge, Mass.: MIT Press, 1976), also examines the import of selected reproduced writings of this group.

7. Ebenezer Howard, *Garden Cities of Tomorrow* (London: S. Sonnenschein & Co., 1902). The 1965 MIT Press edition has an excellent introduction by Lewis Mumford.

8. Frederick Law Olmsted really brought the notion of the romantic English country estate to America in the 1860s. He was a populist at heart (along with Calvert Vaux, he designed Central Park specifically to integrate working people and the upper classes in a public setting) but he primarily made his living designing bucolic enclaves for the upper classes. His work per-

haps was more influential to practitioners who embraced "garden developments" in Queens than the work of Howard (for example, his son, Frederick Law Olmsted II, provided the landscape design for Forest Hills Gardens). Elizabeth Stevenson, *Park Maker: A Life of Frederick Law Olmsted* (New York: Macmillan, 1977), is a good beginning text for those who wish to know more about this man and his mission.

9. When Governor Al Smith formed a state Housing and Regional Plan Commission, Clarence Stein was its head (see Spann, *Designing Modern America*).

10. The financial plan of Sunnyside Gardens was modeled on the English Letchworth and Welwyn Garden Cities. It included a 6 percent cap on developer investment, and the offering of many financing options to residents, including apartment and house rentals, cooperative apartments, and home purchases. The financing and construction of Sunnyside Gardens was undertaken by the City Housing Corporation (CHC), a limited-dividend company formed by members of the RPAA, with the financial backing of its members and other investors.

11. See Spann, *Designing Modern America*.

12. The City Housing Corporation took the considerable profits from Sunnyside and invested them in Radburn, which they hoped would be more of a true regional "garden city." Factories and institutions were to be part of its design, and development was not restricted to an urban

grid. Homes fronted on beautifully designed large public parks, while automobile traffic was relegated to the backs of homes and vehicular drives under park and walkways (an idea pioneered by Olmsted in Central Park). Because the City Housing Corporation was dissolved as a result of the Depression, only a small percentage of homes and parks in Radburn were built and related development was never completed.

13. This rent strike is described in detail in a 1936 article by Louisa D. Lasker, "Sunnyside Up and Down," in the planning journal *Survey Graphic*. Lasker contends that Stein's resolve to create affordable housing within confines of the private market doomed it to failure when the Depression struck. As noted below, owners attempted to sue the City Housing Corporation because they felt it should have protected their investment better. They lost the suit because they owned their homes individually and were deemed to be no more deserving of protections than other homeowners during the Depression. Lasker concludes that the RPAA should have supported more radical financing schemes, such as those used by the worker-owned cooperatives in the Bronx (which were also adversely affected by the Depression, but to a lesser degree than in Sunnyside Gardens) if they wished to make this development less vulnerable to the wiles of market forces.

14. Sixty percent of Sunnyside Gardens' residents lost their homes during the Depression; many more solvent but progressive residents also moved because they felt the social promises of the developers had not been fulfilled.

15. As part of my research and planning efforts in Sunnyside, my students and I have interviewed about 150 residents, workers, agency representatives, and governmental officials in Sunnyside. Findings from these interviews appear in this essay (participants were granted anonymity, so their names do not appear). The key product of this effort was a master plan for the neighborhood, "Creating Community in Sunnyside: A Comprehensive Plan for a Highly Multi-Ethnic Neighborhood," available on line at maxweber.hunter.cuny.edu/urban/ under "projects."

16. Mumford, *Sketches from Life*, 414.

17. The Landmarks Commission wishes to rescind "Special District" status, a zoning designation that prohibits building into and fencing off courtyards; however, they do not have the legal authority to control privately owned open space. Their focus traditionally has been on modifications to building up and out (now controlled under zoning) and changes to decorative elements (roof materials, windows, doors, and the like that currently are excluded by the zoning ordinance.

18. Mumford, *Green Memories*, 28.

19. This observation comes directly from the minutes of RPAA meetings (Spann, *Designing Modern America*).

20. Mumford, *Green Memories*," 29.

21. Ibid., 30.

22. Clarence Stein, *Towards New Towns for America* (Cambridge, Massachusetts: MIT Press, 1957), 7.

23. The notion of providing green space for the "edification" of inhabitants was a rationale for the early urban renewal efforts of the "City Beautiful" movement in Chicago in 1893, an idea that was skeptically considered by reformers at the time. Real estate interests, controlled by the newly rich merchants and manufacturers in Chicago, sought to enhance the value of their urban holdings by demolishing poor neighborhoods and replacing them with gracious homes, parkways, and parks. The poor, they said, would benefit from these actions because they now could gaze upon verdant scenery and aspire to a better life. Lewis Mumford, a founder of Sunnyside Gardens, was a staunch critic of the City Beautiful movement. See his chapter "The Imperial Façade," in *Sticks and Stones: A Study of American Architecture and Civilization* (New York: Boni and Liveright, 1924; reprint, New York: Dover Publications, 1955); and James Gilbert, *Perfect Cities: Chicago's Utopias of 1893* (Chicago: University of Chicago Press, 1993).

24. Interview with leader of the Sunnyside Gardens Preservation Alliance (SAVE), April 29, 2004.

25. Interview with SAVE member, March 27, 2004.

26. Lewis Mumford, *The Culture of Cities* (New York: Harcourt Brace, 1938), 484.

William Crain

BATTLING ARTIFICIAL TURF IN A NEW YORK CITY PARK

William Crain is professor of psychology at the City College of New York and president of Citizens for a Green Riverside Park. He is the author of *Reclaiming Childhood: Letting Children Be Children in Our Achievement-Oriented Society* (Holt 2003).

In April 2004, our local New York City community board discussed a proposal to install synthetic turf in Riverside Park on Manhattan's Upper West Side. The new plastic grass would replace four acres of natural-grass playing fields.

Prior to the board's vote, New York City Parks Department officials and the public were given a chance to speak. The officials pointed out that the natural grass fields were in poor condition and stressed the positive qualities of the new synthetic turf. It drains well after a rain and would permit more Little League and soccer league games to be played. Although it would cost $3 million to install, it would require little maintenance and prove cost-effective in the long run, the officials said.

I was the only member of the public to speak, and I spoke against the plastic grass. I said that while the natural fields weren't models

of biological diversity, they were part of the Hudson River's ecosystem and hosted subtle varieties of vegetation, birds, and other life forms. We have an obligation, I said, to protect nature in our care.

I also emphasized the fields' value to children. Because today's children increasingly grow up in artificial, indoor environments, they need as much contact with nature as possible. They need more opportunities to experience the sensations of soil, grass, and breezes while they play and rest. They need a chance to observe the birds and wildlife that share nature with them. Increasing research, I added, indicates that natural settings give children feelings of peace and calm, reducing attention problems. This is especially true when they have a chance to play in the settings in a leisurely way. Natural settings also give children the feeling of being part of the larger web of life.

To everyone's surprise, the community board voted against the plastic grass. A local reporter, who had been covering the meetings for several years, told me he'd never before seen the board turn down a city recommendation. For a day, I felt good about the world. A solitary effort to protect nature had succeeded!

But my optimism was short-lived. The board received numerous phone calls (many, I suspect, from city officials), and it quickly scheduled a re-vote. It then approved the synthetic turf.

There was still time to stop the installation. I called neighbors and met with local organizations, and together we formed a group called "Citizens for a Green Riverside Park." We wrote letters to politicians, held press conferences, handed out literature on the sidewalks, and gathered 600 signatures on a petition. We picketed the office of a local politician who vigorously supported the fake grass. On our behalf, the Alliance for Childhood, a national child advocacy group, wrote a letter to the Parks Department commissioner. The local Green Party also came to our aid. We spent over a year trying to get the department to reverse its decision, but in the end it installed the fake grass.

The synthetic turf in Riverside Park is part of the Parks Department's larger plan. It is replacing numerous natural fields with plastic grass in all five city boroughs. The more we fought the effort in Riverside Park, the more we learned how deeply the department is invested in its plan. When we went to its commissioner to submit our petition, we were met by a large contingent of police officers. And when a few of us were permitted to go upstairs to the commissioner's outer office, we were

amazed to see what can only be described as a shrine to synthetic turf. On a mantle sat a large sample of the plastic grass and photos of plastic grass fields—all thrown into sharp relief by floodlights shining from below.

Although we lost the battle to preserve natural fields in Riverside Park, we have joined other community activists who are trying to stop the installation of fake grass in their own neighborhood parks. We hope a broader coalition can do what our local group could not: Preserve the little nature that still exists in our city.

Clare Cooper Marcus

SHARED OUTDOOR SPACE
AND CHILDREN'S PLAY

Clare Cooper Marcus is professor emerita in the Departments of Architecture and Landscape Architecture, University of California, Berkeley. She is the author of numerous professional and academic articles, as well as five books including *House as a Mirror of Self: Exploring the Deeper Meaning of Home; Housing as if People Mattered: Site Design Guidelines for Medium-Density Family Housing* (with Wendy Sarkissian); *People Places: Design Guidelines for Urban Open Space* (with Carolyn Francis); *and Healing Gardens: Therapeutic Benefits and Design Recommendations* (with Marni Barnes).

From the mid-1970s to the mid-1990s, I asked my students in the College of Environmental Design at the University of California, Berkeley, to write what I called an "environmental autobiography." An important component of this exercise was to draw and describe their most fondly remembered childhood place. After reading hundreds of these papers over many years, it became clear that places most often remembered were predominantly outdoors and nearly always in semi-wild or overgrown areas such as woods, ravines, creeks, ditches, mudflats, trees, vacant lots, leftover urban spaces, and spaces between buildings in public housing of apartment complexes. From among hundreds of students completing this assignment, almost no one remembered a place specifically *designed* for children. Only one remembered a schoolyard as a favorite place, and none remembered a park.

These remembered places offered qualities supportive of children's self-directed play: they were relatively close to home, sometimes frequented by a small group of close friends, not particularly valued or visible to adults, and incorporated an abundance of manipulable "loose parts." Remembered activities ranged from girls outlining "houses" with fallen leaves; boys "damming" a creek with stones and mud; friends creating a secret den under bushes in a housing project; a boy seeking solace from family problems on a platform he built in a tall tree.

One could reasonably speculate that the number of children growing up in the 1990s and the first decade of the twenty-first century who have free access to such spaces has diminished markedly. We can point to a number of reasons for this decline: (1) the erosion of "leftover spaces" where children in middle childhood (about eight to twelve years old) can find places for absorbing self-directed play; (2) the compulsion many contemporary parents feel to over-schedule their children's lives and a seeming ignorance of the developmental value of self-directed play; (3) a focus on competitive sports as an unconscious "training" or "rehearsal" for life in an increasingly competitive society; (4) the fears many parents harbor over letting their children engage in unsupervised play, out of sight of home; and (5) the increasing absorption many children have in technological connections—cell phones, text messaging, video games, DVDs, and TV.

While there is clearly not one solution to encouraging more self-directed play in contemporary urban neighborhoods, a suggestion offered here is worth considering since it counteracts some of the impediments described above.

When dwellings are clustered around an area of shared outdoor space to which only a specific group of residents has access, an environment is created where children have ready access to the outdoors without having to be driven to soccer practice or walked to a neighborhood park. Parents can see and monitor their children from the home, alleviating their fears of traffic and stranger-danger. Since the outdoors is so close to home and neighbor-children have equal access, children who might be watching TV or playing video games out of boredom or loneliness are more likely to run out to join friends for spontaneous play—no play dates necessary here. Also, since the area is so close to home, children are likely to use it for play in the odd half-hour before they are called in to dinner or during the time between homework and bed. These are precious fragments of time in perhaps an over-scheduled day, periods when tired, over-worked parents are not likely to walk their children to a nearby park, even if such a park provided an environment for self-directed play, which it usually does not.

The idea of a core of shared outdoor space enclosed by buildings is not a new one. The monastic cloister garden, Oxford colleges, 1920s bungalow courts, and 1960s Planned Unit Developments are all examples. Plenty of contemporary examples can be found both in urban and suburban settings. A study of five such clustered housing communities—all in northern California—was published by this author in 2003. These case studies indicate the following: that 80 percent of the use of shared green outdoor space is by children; given the experience of such an environment, most families want to stay there, and friends who visit want to "move in" (or get on the waiting list); children spend more time outdoors, and in one case study (that of Cherry Hill affordable housing in Petaluma), 50 percent of parents reported their children watched less TV since moving to the neighborhood. A significant indication of how much parents value clustered housing with shared outdoor space is the fact that every one of more than a hundred U.S. co-housing communities for families with children, created with design input from future residents, chose this form of housing site plan.

It is important to make clear that shared outdoor space lies on a continuum between private outdoor space (the yard, balcony, patio) and public outdoor space (the sidewalk, street, park). In most traditional neighborhoods of grid-pattern streets, with the interior of the block divided into fenced yards, shared outdoor space such as that described here is not possible. (An exception is described in Cooper Marcus 2003, where the backyard fences at the core of a Berkeley, California, residential block were removed to form a large, highly valued shared outdoor space.) Most contemporary examples of clustered housing occur where urban redevelopment has occurred and garden apartments or row houses have been built facing into a landscaped interior of the block, or in new suburban developments where a public agency or private developer has seen the value of creating a clustered housing scheme of single-family houses to fulfill the needs of families for a safe environment for their children, and one that has the possibility of facilitating a sense of community. (All the residents sampled in the case studies described in Cooper Marcus 2003 did in fact report a strong sense of community.)

For shared outdoor space in clustered housing to be successful in meeting the needs for children's self-directed play, it must meet a number of planning and design criteria. Traffic and parking (in the form of garages or grouped parking) is kept to the periphery and living spaces face into the green heart of the block. Private outdoor spaces in the form of patios or backyards form a buffer between private and shared outdoor space, a gate or break in a fence or hedge permitting easy access from one to the other. The shared outdoor space needs considerable care in its design so that it is appealing to children (who will be by far the majority of users). This means it should include open grassy areas for ball play; paths wide and smooth enough for roller-blading, tricycles, and wheeled toys; a sand box play area for small children; challenging play equipment for older children; a shaded seating area or gazebo for adult or teen gathering; small garden plots, where possible; and most importantly (recalling the environmental autobiography favorite places), an area of shrubbery, unmown grass, and mature trees where children can explore, hide, and make dens. Also important is a maintenance staff that understands that twigs, fallen leaves, pine cones, seeds, and a fallen tree are not "litter" but are precious play-props for children engaged in creative play.

So why do we not see more clustered housing with shared outdoor space? First, housing developers and designers are concerned with the bottom line and continue to build what buyers "expect": single-family houses facing grid-pattern urban streets or curvilinear suburban avenues, with neighborhood parks placed at intervals as designated in local plans. The needs of children are not uppermost in the minds of these decision makers, nor do parents know of, or demand, any other options.

Second, designers with a nod to recent urban history may point to examples of shared open space in public housing projects of the 1950s and 1960s where such space sometimes became the setting for littering, vandalism, and crime. So they assume such space never works, and "throw the baby out with the bathwater," not realizing that such social problems often resulted from ineffective site planning, poor detailing, and almost nonexistent maintenance.

Finally, resistance to the provision of shared outdoor space has come largely from the proponents of New Urbanism (NU), who emphasize the overriding importance of *public* space (streets, sidewalks, plazas, parks), who argue for the elimination of cul-de-sacs and the strict adherence to the grid, and who champion the elimination of driveways and garage entries off the street in favor of parking in back-of-the-house alleys. All of these render the provision of inner-block green space virtually impossible. One NU medium-density, urban housing scheme in San Francisco, for example, while presenting an attractive street frontage, fills the whole of the block interior with cars, a space that, sadly, is labeled "Parking-Play Space." In the NU literature, the most frequent reference to space shared by a group (that is not fully public) is the alley. In many NU communities, the presence of alleys allows houses to be sited closer together and ensures that curb cuts and garages do not "mar" the streetscape. While these may be laudable aesthetic goals, a disturbing assertion by some NU proponents and developers maintains that alleys are suitable places for children to play. It doesn't take much imagination to suggest that the experience (and possibly the subsequent environmental values) of children offered play space that doubles as a setting for cars, trash cans, recycling bins, and power lines will be vastly different from that of children in clustered housing with shared green space, such as at Village Homes in Davis, California, for example, where children can play safely amid creeks, fruit trees, wildlife, and gardens. NU-inspired building codes are increasingly being adopted. While many of their goals and principles are undoubtedly positive, in terms of the aesthetics of the streetscape and an attempt to foster walkability via mixed land uses and higher densities, the needs of children are largely overlooked. The belief that neighborhood parks will meet their needs displays a poor understanding of how, where, and why children play, and of the child-rearing demands placed on today's working parents.

The types of clustered housing site plans described in this chapter are, in places, being legislated out of existence. For example, the original site plan for an affordable housing scheme in Windsor, California, incorporated shared outdoor space and was welcomed by its client, who previously had noted the success of clustered housing for families at Cherry Hill, Petaluma, California. However, the City Planning Commission, citing NU principles, insisted that the site must have a through street, that shared outdoor space "doesn't work," and that clustered housing around such a space creates "a ghetto." Such misunderstandings of the social implications of site planning are extremely unfortunate, particularly in a lower-income setting where residents may not be able to sustain wider social networks or take their children to areas of public recreation and where access to safe, shared outdoor space away from traffic and close to home would be warmly appreciated.

Finally, it is important to emphasize that the arguments presented here for shared (as opposed to public) green open space to support creative, self-directed play close to home are not meant in any way to deny the importance of other kinds of outdoor spaces that facilitate other forms of play, such as neighborhood parks and playgrounds, schoolyards and playing fields, children's zoos and nature reserves. With more thought given to the needs of children and their parents in neighborhood design, with more attention given to the merits of clustered housing, tomorrow's children can have access to the kinds of natural spaces close to home enjoyed by their parents and grandparents in their youth. It is the least we can offer them.

This essay was published in slightly different form as "Shared Outdoor Spaces and Community Life," in *Places: A Quarterly Journal of Environmental Design* 15, no. 2 (2003).

Alex S. MacLean

IT'S HUMAN NATURE TO PLAY

Alex S. MacLean is a pilot and photographer who has spent the past thirty years documenting the landscape from the air. He has portrayed the history and evolution of the land, from vast desert regions to agricultural patterns to city grids. His work records the country's development in addition to the gradual evolution and changes brought about by human intervention. He is the author of several books, including most recently *The Playbook* (Thames & Hudson, 2006) and *Visualizing Density* (Lincoln Institute of Land Policy, 2007). He maintains a studio in Cambridge, Massachusetts.

My father studied the brain, specializing in brain evolution and behavior. He pointed out that one of many differences between mammals and reptiles is that mammals, unlike reptiles, have a natural instinct and ability to play. He wrote that play starts at infancy with interactions between mother and child, and is of evolutionary importance for survival, learning, and socialization.[1] My father's teachings made me aware of the prominence of play in my life and the lives of those around me, and I have always been sympathetic to the need to play. Playing has inspired many of my photographs, some of which I have compiled for this book.

I fly alone in my Cessna, traveling on long cross-country flights or working on aerial photographic projects that deal with environmental issues and urban planning. I often have deviated from my intended flight path to find relief, to circle and wander, amusing myself by photographing for personal interests, making my own art. I have come to realize that this type of flying is my way of playing in the air. In doing this, I have discovered interesting landscapes, many relating to play. In photographing these scenes, I feel a sense of joy and often smile to myself as I see patterns and spaces on the ground that have been devoted, built, adapted, or temporarily used for play. As illogical as some of these patterns may be, they are ultimately positive expressions of human nature that have been documented clearly on the ground.

As people begin to have more time for leisure, they make greater demands for spaces devoted to play, recreation, and amusement. Working against the demand for this type of space is suburban sprawl. Through this suburban sprawl, we are losing ready access to open lands and the freedom for children to roam. As a result, children are now driven to more organized and artificial places to play. These play spaces read as new, sterile, and unnatural, and are a product of our time.

From the air, signs of play are everywhere. We see these signs clearly in backyards with swing sets, gardens, and swimming pools. We observe community parks and their ever-present baseball diamonds and basketball courts. Schools are recognized not so much by their buildings, but by their adjacent playgrounds and athletic fields. University and college campuses have major in-door and outdoor play facilities. Prison yards are used for exercise and games such as handball. In metropolitan areas, play takes on a bigger scale, with professional league stadiums and arenas, race tracks, major parks (including amusement parks), and often zoos.

Within these built landscapes, the competitive action of play involves control of territory and the possession of an object. There are offensive and defensive positions, drives and momentum, fakes and deception, steals and turnovers; all of which fall within the rules of the game. If not within the rules, an action is deemed out of bounds, out of play, or a foul, worthy of a penalty. The rules require spaces marked and measured as territories, delineated in numerous ways with boundaries, borders, fields, courts, zones, goals, and penalty boxes.

Play usually incorporates the fourth dimension of time, which compresses an action within a set beginning and end. Unlike real-life situations, with play you can stop the clock. The dimension of time is apparent when the object of play is about acts of speed, acceleration, and endurance that take place across a given distance where landscapes are shaped into pathways, tracks, and obstacle courses. And, within all these arenas of play, we see clear division between participants and spectators.

Perhaps the most satisfying thing about play is how it can adapt to different environments, responding to climate, soils, and topography.

The desire to play despite these natural obstacles is so strong that we have used great ingenuity, inventing equipment and protective gear to expand the opportunities, places, and times where we can play. We strap special equipment to our bodies so we can climb cliffs, ski, ice skate, and snorkel, and we do this wearing special clothing, helmets, and lifejackets, allowing us to go to greater extremes. Some types of play, such as pond hockey, fishing, or surfing, can depend on the season as well as on a region's character, thus making play an important link to environmental awareness.

One does not need to look far to find evidence of people at play. It keeps us in touch with our minds, bodies, and spirits. My father always spoke of play's "civilizing influence in human evolution" and it is in play that we leave some of our better marks and traces on the earth's surface.

Note

1. Paul D. MacLean, *The Triune Brain in Evolution: Role in Paleocerebral Functions* (New York: Plenum Press, 1990), 396–97.

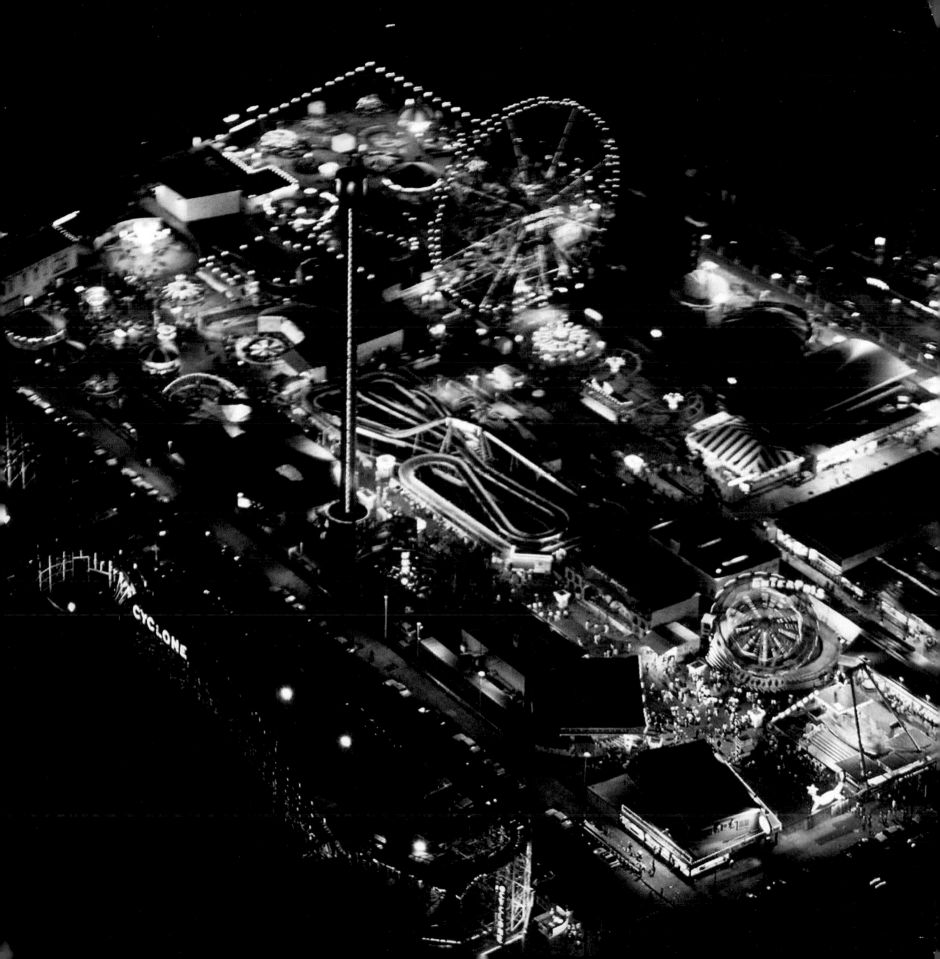

Photos for "It's Human Nature to Play"

Rows of suburban homes offer only private play space and have no pedestrian cut-throughs to contiguous blocks, limiting movement, independence, and social connections of children. Phoenix, Arizona (2005) (p. 240)

A rail bridge crossing the Susquehanna River has been converted into a caged-in pedestrian bridge to reduce risk. Reading, Pennsylvania (2005) (p. 244)

A residential construction company builds play spaces and pedestrian access routes first, a way to showcase selling points to prospective homebuyers. Phoenix, Arizona (2005) (p. 245)

Low-density suburban housing built out in rich New Jersey farm land leaves both children and the elderly dependent on drivers to transport them to more concentrated social and play environments. Edinburg, New Jersey (2000) (p. 246)

Early development of a Chicago suburb (no mature vegetation) offers little on the public street front in the way of social and play spaces. Chicago, Illinois (1998) (p. 247)

Denver's South Platte River and the newly associated recreation areas with a kayak run are leading inducements for downtown infill and urban renewal. Denver, Colorado (2004) (p. 248)

Amish children play baseball in a county schoolyard. Lancaster County, Pennsylvania (1984) (p. 249)

Play park with a plastic center and all-weather surfaces disconnect visitors from a natural environment. Las Vegas, Nevada (2005) (p. 250)

Private playground for new housing subdivision. Las Vegas, Nevada (2003) (p. 251)

A synthetic fantasy environment is created by Universal Studios. Orlando, Florida (1999) (p. 252)

Coney Island is transformed from day to night. Brooklyn, New York (1989) (p. 253)

Private fences limit backyard play. Kansas City, Missouri (2003) (p. 254)

Parts of this photo essay were originally published in *The Playbook* (Thames & Hudson, 2006).

About the Players

Film Production Team

Jennifer White, Executive Producer

A native of Detroit and graduate of the University of Michigan, Jennifer White has worked at Michigan Public Media since 1999, serving in several capacities including Director of Individual Giving and Major Gifts Officer. Jennifer has managed Michigan Television as its station manager since 2005, where she has guided the development of EMMY award-winning collaborative projects focused on the arts and humanities. These include the MATRIX series, a partnership with the Michigan Council for Arts and Cultural Affairs and the Michigan Humanities Council; and PLAY, a collaboration between the station and the School of Art and Design at the University of Michigan.

Christopher M. Cook, Producer-Director-Writer

Since 1997, Cook has written and produced more than 14 hours of documentary programming, most of which has appeared on regional PBS stations, for which he has received eleven EMMYs, three of them for work from 1999 to 2007 on Michigan Public Television's *Michigan at Risk* series. His *Sprawling of America* was nominated for best limited series in the International Documentary Association Awards in 2002 and won three EMMYs regionally. For twenty years, Cook was a reporter and held various editing positions at newspapers across the country, including the *Detroit Free Press* and *Newsday* in New York, where he was part of a team that won a Pulitzer Prize for investigative journalism.

Mark J. Harris, Consulting Producer

Harris is a journalist, novelist, and documentary filmmaker whose work has won three Academy Awards. His first Oscar was for *The Redwoods* (1968), a short documentary he wrote and produced. He also won Oscars for *The Long Way Home* (1997) and *Into The Arms of Strangers: Stories of the Kindertransport* (2001). In addition, he has published five novels for children, two books, and dozens of essays, articles, and short stories in publications ranging from *American Heritage* to the *New York Times*. He has taught film at the School of Cinema-Television of the University of Southern California for 20 years.

Elizabeth Goodenough, Film Consultant and Outreach Director

Elizabeth Goodenough is a scholar, author, and activist in the emerging field of children's studies. She earned an M.A.T. and Ph.D. from Harvard University and has taught English literature at Harvard College and Claremont McKenna College and is currently at the University of Michigan Residential College. She has co-edited *Infant Tongues: The Voice of the Child in Literature* (1994); *Violence and Children's Literature* (2000); and *Under Fire: Childhood in the Shadow of War* (2008). Her other books include S*ecret Spaces of Childhood* (University of Michigan Press 2003) and *Where Do the Children Play? A Study Guide to the Film* (2007) available from Wayne State University Press.

Matthew Zacharias, Editor

Zacharias has been a filmmaker and editor for 13 years. His work has won three regional EMMYs for PBS projects. Zacharias' films have been featured at national film festivals such as Slamdance, South by Southwest, and ResFest. His multimedia projects are exhibited in leading contemporary art galleries. Zacharias is at work on a feature-length film, which he is producing, directing, writing, and editing. Zacharias' short films include *Kim* (AWOL; 1990), *Max* (AWOL; 1997), *AWOL After School Special* (AWOL; 1998), *Ace's High* (AWOL; 2002), and *Good, Brother* (AWOL; 2002). He is a graduate of the Film Studies department at the University of Michigan.

Barbara Lucas, Associate Producer

Lucas has worked on institutional video projects and Michigan public television documentaries such as *Ticket To Ride* and *Emerald Ash Borer: Path of Death* for the Michigan PBS series *Michigan at Risk*, and *The Great Experiment: MSU, The Pioneer Land Grant University*. She helps produce the weekly public radio show *Issues of the Environment* for WEMU-FM and produces environmental education videos for nonprofits and municipal governments. Lucas holds a B.A. and an M.A. from the University of Michigan.

Mark Berg, Director of Photography

Mark Berg is a highly experienced camera operator who has worked on news and long-form programs for 12 years, including stints at four television stations in the Midwest. Berg's work has appeared on ABC News, NBC News, 20/20, World News Tonight, Good Morning America, Dateline, Today Show, Nightly News, CNN, A&E, Fox Sports, and other broadcast and cable outlets. He also shoots for the National Hockey League, Ford Motor Co., and others. He has been nominated for EMMY awards four times and has won top honors from the Michigan Association of Broadcasters in 1987 and 1990. Berg is the president and co-owner of Great Lakes Television Productions.

Gordy Marcotte, Sound Technician

Gordy Marcotte is a sound technician who earned his B.A. in communications from Western Michigan University in 1988. He began his career with Filmcraft Video, a producer of corporate and network video, and also worked for ENG Detroit before striking out on his own in 1995. As a freelance sound technician, he has worked on news stories for each of the major broadcast television networks, including stories for NBC's Dateline, ABC's 20/20, and CBS's 60 Minutes. His other clients have included Fox, PBS, CNN, NBA Entertainment, NHL Productions, GM, Ford, Chrysler, and Volkswagen.

Experts Quoted from Film Transcripts

Joan Almon co-founded the Alliance for Childhood in 1999 as a partnership of educators, health professionals, and others concerned about the decline in children's health and well-being and the growing stress in children's lives. She serves as director of the U.S. Alliance. Prior to taking up this work, Joan was a Waldorf kindergarten teacher and educator of teachers in the U.S. and abroad.

Stuart Brown, physician-psychiatrist by training and practice, has more recently engaged in independent scholarship, education film production, and popular writing. He is the founder and president of the National Institute for Play, whose mission is to bring the unrealized knowledge, practices, and benefits of play into public life. Brown was the instigator and executive producer of the three-part PBS series, *The Promise of Play*.

Kenneth Ginsburg is a nationally recognized pediatrician specializing in adolescent medicine at the Children's Hospital of Philadelphia and an associate professor of pediatrics at the University of Pennsylvania School of Medicine. He also serves as director of health services at Covenant House of Philadelphia, a shelter for homeless and disenfranchised youth. In the past seven years, Dr. Ginsburg has been named one of Philadelphia magazine's "Top Docs" five times.

Richard Louv is the author of seven books, including, most recently, *Last Child in the Woods: Saving Our Children From Nature-Deficit Disorder* (Algonquin). He has written for the *New York Times*, *The Washington Post*, *The Christian Science Monitor* and other newspapers and magazines. In addition to his writing, Louv is chairman of the Children & Nature Network, a nonprofit organization helping build a movement to reconnect children and nature. He is a member of the Citistates Group, an association of urban observers, and serves as a member of the board of directors of ecoAmerica.

Penny Wilson has been a playworker since the mid-1980s. For a large part of that time she worked at Chelsea Adventure Playground, an inclusive site where disabled children and their peers could play together. She is now employed as the inclusion worker at the Play Association Tower Hamlets (PATH), in the east end of London where she lives. She also writes about play and provides playwork training: www.theinternationale.net/playstories.

Photographers and Designers

Wendy Banning, educator and photographer, has thirty years of experience as a school director, educational consultant, and teacher. She was the founding director of a small private school in North Carolina committed to outdoor curricula and experiences for children. Her website is www.learn-outside.com. (Photos on pp. ix, 18, 34, 40, 57, 58, 82, 95, 98, 106, 150, 160, 173, 180, 188, 258, 260, 264, 267)

Jan Ziegelman Cohen is an Ann Arbor photographer, graphic designer, and mother of twin teenage boys. Her sons, Ethan and Jeremy, have been one of her favorite photographic subjects since birth. (p. 12)

Jody Fisher, a freelance graphic designer for over twenty years, is the founding director of Summer Kampers, an educational and recreational enrichment organization in Ann Arbor, Michigan (www.summerkampers.org). She has twelve years of experience in gifted education as teacher and administrator. She earned her B.A. in early childhood education and fine arts from the University of Michigan. (Photo on p. 26 by Jody's son, Nick)

Nan Knighton received a Tony Nomination for Best Book of a Musical for the *Scarlet Pimpernel*, for which she also wrote the lyrics. *Pimpernel* ran on Broadway for three seasons. She wrote book and lyrics to *Camille Claudel*, which premiered at The Goodspeed Opera House. She also wrote the stage adaptation for Broadway's *Saturday Night Fever*. Her poetry has been published in the *Michigan Quarterly Review*, and she has just completed her first book of photography: *Moody*. (pp. 17, 56, 206, 210, 212, 213, 229, 234)

David Lamb is a graduate of the University of Michigan Residential College where he focused in the sciences. He currently works as the Outreach Coordinator at the Ann Arbor Hands-On Museum. (pp. xiv, 118, 123)

Eric Lindbloom is an independent photographer based in the Hudson Valley. His photographs included in *A Place for Play* are from a series, *Pinewoods,* which he recently completed in the Cape Cod pine barrens. His study of Florence, *Angels at the Arno,* was published by David R. Godine. (pp. 8, 10, 38, 96, 158, 204, 256, 257)

Hugh McDiarmid Jr. and Brad Garmon work for the Michigan Environmental Council, a coalition of 70 environmental, public health, and faith-based groups dedicated to preserving and protecting the state's natural resources and the economic and health benefits that flow from them. (Hugh McDiarmid p. 64, Brad Garmon p. 111)

Matthew Perry lives in San Francisco with his wife and four cats. He does his best to live by the motto, "Do interesting things with interesting people." He takes many photos of the beautiful Bay Area, teaches at every opportunity, and designs games. His website is www.kidcando.com. (pp. v, vii, viii)

Robert S. Solomon, an attorney in Morristown, New Jersey, has been an avid photographer since he received a Brownie camera when he was seven years old. (p. 174)

Rockwell Group Imagination Playground was conceived and designed by Rockwell Group for Burling Slip in downtown Manhattan. Built in collaboration with the New York City Department of Parks and Recreation, this model breaks ground in summer 2008. A rich environment of diverse materials encouraging unstructured, child-directed "free play," Imagination Playground demonstrates a new paradigm for New York City as well as playgrounds across the country. (pp. 32, 33)

Polly Devlin

CODA

Collecting Ovoids

Faced with hens, we all become children. That is their magic. Nothing brings you closer to the reality of things than a hen and an egg in a nest (including the ugly peck she may give when you slip a greedy hand under that warm body to get at the treasure). It is one of the joys of my life that even the most sophisticated street-wise child—who often has absolutely no idea that eggs come from a living creature—beams with a kind of angelic pleasure when he or she finds an egg in the nest; and any adult watching is suffused with pleasure too. Something vivid and immediate has happened, some fundamental yearning has been stilled. It harks back to some atavistic urge, to the egg as a token of mythology. You don't have to explain why a child loves to find it, or why we like to look at it. That ovoid, so shapely, so contained, so secretly full of life, is dreamed about the world over, was dreamed about thousands of years ago, and I hope will be dreamed about thousands of years hence.

Polly Devlin, writer, broadcaster, filmmaker, art critic, and conservationist, wrote *All of Us There,* **now a Virago Modern Classic. In 1993 she received an OBE for services to literature.** *A Year in the Life of an English Meadow* **was published in 2007. She currently teaches at Barnard College.**